Zero Trust Networks with VMware NSX

Build Highly Secure Network Architectures for Your Data Centers

Sreejith Keeriyattil

Apress®

Zero Trust Networks with VMware NSX

Sreejith Keeriyattil
Bengaluru, Karnataka, India

ISBN-13 (pbk): 978-1-4842-5430-1   ISBN-13 (electronic): 978-1-4842-5431-8
https://doi.org/10.1007/978-1-4842-5431-8

Copyright © 2019 by Sreejith Keeriyattil

Managing Director, Apress Media LLC: Welmoed Spahr
Acquisitions Editor: Nikhil Karkal
Development Editor: Laura Berendson
Coordinating Editor: Divya Modi

Cover designed by eStudioCalamar

Cover image designed by Pixabay

Distributed to the book trade worldwide by Springer Science+Business Media New York, 233 Spring Street, 6th Floor, New York, NY 10013. Phone 1-800-SPRINGER, fax (201) 348-4505, e-mail orders-ny@springer-sbm.com, or visit www.springeronline.com. Apress Media, LLC is a California LLC and the sole member (owner) is Springer Science + Business Media Finance Inc (SSBM Finance Inc). SSBM Finance Inc is a **Delaware** corporation.

For information on translations, please e-mail rights@apress.com, or visit http://www.apress.com/rights-permissions.

Apress titles may be purchased in bulk for academic, corporate, or promotional use. eBook versions and licenses are also available for most titles. For more information, reference our Print and eBook Bulk Sales web page at http://www.apress.com/bulk-sales.

Any source code or other supplementary material referenced by the author in this book is available to readers on GitHub via the book's product page, located at www.apress.com/978-1-4842-5430-1. For more detailed information, please visit http://www.apress.com/source-code.

Printed on acid-free paper

Dedicated to my father, who introduced me to the magical world of books, and my mother, who always believes in me. And my wife, without her support none of this would have been possible. Lastly, to my one-year old son, who wonders why I am always typing on my laptop.

Table of Contents

About the Author

Sreejith Keeriyattil is VMware NSX certified professional and VMware vExpert with more than 10 years of experience with VMware technologies. He specializes in network/storage in the cloud and data center and is an expert in implementing software-defined networks with VMware NSX. Sreejith is presently working with Ericsson, India as a senior solutions integrator, where he overlooks the design, configuration, and deployment of the OpenStack-based cloud. He also documents his experience with the VMware stack through his blog, stackguy.com.

About the Technical Reviewer

 **Abhishek Kunal** has 10 years of experience in the networking industry. He currently works as a data center security architect for Dubai EXPO2020, and is responsible for designing the best security solutions for on premises and in the Amazon cloud.

Abishek holds the following certifications: CCIE No. 48639, VCIX-NV, and VCIX-DCV. He has worked with VMware as an escalation engineer for NSX and on VMware for AWS projects. He also worked for CISCO as a technical advisor for planning design and implementation on projects for Cisco partners, and worked on ACI SDN solutions. He has worked as a TAC engineer for VCE (VBlock and VXRack) and as a technical instructor. His areas of interest include routing and switching, security, data center, and public cloud. He has a degree in electronics and communication engineering.

Acknowledgments

I would like to thank my wonderful colleagues who have worked alongside me over the years. I would like to thank my friend and colleague Pugalarasan Paramasivam for his overwhelming support throughout the journey. Thanks also to the VMware community. Without them this would not have been possible.

Introduction

Zero Trust Networks with VMware NSX aims to help you understand this latest security architecture that's gaining traction. It teaches you the concepts required to implement an enterprise-grade security architecture based on production setup scenarios.

This book introduces automation- and software-defined networking solutions based on VMware NSX. It slowly guides you through the NSX distributed firewall features. This book also provides an overview of tools like the VMware Log Insight and VMware Network Insight. You'll learn how these tools can help you analyze and plan for Zero Trust networks.

Who Should Read This Book?

This book primarily focuses on VMware for security administrators and architects. But it also provides an initial understanding of the requirements and modeling of micro-segmented networks. In that sense, this book is for anyone with beginner-level VMware experience who wants to expand their knowledgebase to software-defined data center features.

Readers are expected to have some basic understanding of virtualization and infrastructure technologies, like running basic commands in Linux and understanding VMware, vCenter, etc.

About the Book

Chapters 1 and 2 cover the basics of why people are transitioning into this model. This will give you an initial perception of the topic and sound reasons for updating your current security model.

Chapters 3 and 4 cover the concepts of distributed firewall and deployment methods. These chapters will give you an idea of how to deploy and configure basic NSX distributed firewall setups and the prerequisites for the same. These chapters also cover the automation features embedded in NSX.

Chapter 5 demonstrates and explains how to implement the Zero Trust security model in a fictional e-commerce company. This will give you a decent understanding of the task and design considerations you need to make when planning a Zero Trust model.

Chapter 6 explains the automation aspects of the solution and how REST API calls and power NSX can be an added advantage when they're used correctly. This chapter gives you an overview of the automation options available in NSX.

Chapters 7 and 8 cover various tools that can aid in developing and monitoring NSX solutions. As with any networking solution, a powerful and easy-to-use toolset is required for analyzing and troubleshooting network issues. These chapters explain how a log centralization solution can be beneficial in an NSX setup and how you can use Network Insight to gain an in-depth understanding of the network topology.

CHAPTER 1

Network Defense Architecture

You've probably heard the saying, "security is the next big thing." Security has been an important industry buzzword for many years now. What most analysts fail to convey is that security is not optional. Network and application security have to be built into the design; security shouldn't be an afterthought.

This chapter covers important incidents that shook various industries because of the loopholes they revealed in the network architecture.

Malware that Shocked the World

The world's largest shipping conglomerate, Maersk, was in for a shock on the morning of June 27, 2017 (see Figure 1-1). The shipping industry is a 24/7 business. With innovations in IT, complex software applications and business logic have helped make the world's biggest and oldest business efficient and agile.

© Sreejith Keeriyattil 2019
S. Keeriyattil, *Zero Trust Networks with VMware NSX*,
https://doi.org/10.1007/978-1-4842-5431-8_1

Figure 1-1. *Notification that Maersk's IT systems were down*

Every 15 minutes of every day, a dock somewhere around the world is unloading between 10,000 and 20,000 containers. Maersk has more than 600 sites in 130 countries. You can imagine the complex logic Maersk's software system must use to make this process run smoothly across the world. Given the reliability of this kind of business, there needs to be a considerable number of engineers looking into their IT systems and ensuring that they run smoothly around the clock.

Considering the sheer amount of data that's generated and the updates that happen every day, the infrastructure that is required to attain such a feat is enormous. Along those lines, you can imagine that the attack vector also increases in these kinds of enterprise setups. They run multiple applications with different requirements in multiple data centers across the world. To keep everything in sync and to make sure only trusted clients can visit and enter these systems is a complex task. It requires months of fine-tuning and, more importantly, conducting monthly drills and security auditing.

As I don't have in-depth information on the specific IT systems used at Maersk, I can assume that they followed standard processes and architectures commonly used in IT operations.

If that is true, what went wrong? One by one, Maersk's systems were affected across the globe by the *NotPetya* ransomware (there are some discussions that consider the attack cyberwarfare, but that's up to the investigation).

NotPetya is a comparatively complex piece of code that uses multiple ways to spread its chaos. One of the ways it spreads is to use a Microsoft vulnerability called EternalBlue. The chain of attack can be in general listed as follows. (Note that NotPetya is complex and is used in multiple ways to attack and spread. What follows is the most common way it's used.)

1) Through email or by any other means whereby the user is tempted to click on a link.

2) Windows user access control requests permission to run the program.

3) If the user makes the ill-fated decision to give permission, this allows the backdoor to be installed. The remaining code required to start the targeted attack is then downloaded.

4) From this launchpad system, NotPetya starts scanning the network for any vulnerable open ports, specifically for the SMB 1 (139/445) vulnerability known as EternalBlue/EternalRomance.

5) Once it identifies the vulnerable systems, it starts spreading and infecting all the vulnerable computers in the network.

6) It then encrypts the files and the MBR and asks the users to reboot. Once users reboot, they will be greeted with a boot screen asking for a ransom.

This particular method of attack is too hard to stop. In a big corporation like Maersk, which has thousands of servers and desktops, stopping such attacks requires a well-patched system and a wide variety of access rules and restrictions. But it is very unlikely that this restriction can help once you are affected.

Maersk suffered close to 50,000 affected endpoints, with more than 4,000 servers affected. This resulted in a $300 million loss.

SamSam Ransomware

The Colorado Department of Transportation administers the state's 9,144-mile highway system and its 3,429 bridges. This amounts to millions of vehicles passing through every year. Their system was affected by the ransomware called SamSam. Its modus operandi is similar to NotPetya's— find a vulnerable port/application and use the affected system as a launchpad to affect other systems.

This specific incident caused millions of dollars in damages to several organizations. There was another reported incident of ransomware-affected hospital networks, whereby critical IT systems were affected and the employees had to resort to manual recordkeeping to continue working.

Here the target was RDP ports, which are open to the public. A third-party research institute identified that over 10 million computers face the Internet with their RDP port 3389 exposed. Attackers simply scan for any vulnerable systems online (there are multiple free tools available online for this). Once they find a vulnerable system, they use a brute force password attack tool like John the Ripper or Cain and Abel. Once they are in and have privileges to install software, they can install malicious software on the system. They can install ransomware or they can use the system as a part of the bot network for a DDoS attack elsewhere.

The point is that you don't need high-level knowledge to do these kinds of attacks; one of the most common ways to attack is through open ports and vulnerabilities. Most common vulnerabilities can be found at this site: https://www.shodan.io/.

Common Themes of Attack

Figure 1-2 shows a new attack. Note that there is a pattern emerging in these types of coordinated attacks. The attacker specifically targets the vulnerabilities in the software or operating system. Figure 1-2 shows only one specific type of cybersecurity attack among the plethora of attacks that are happening in the current IT space.

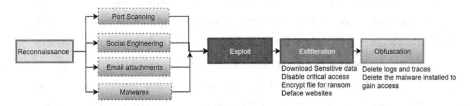

Figure 1-2. *Common attack process*

For a large organization like Maersk, the infrastructure application and server will have hundreds of open ports and external connectivity links. Blocking all ports with external access is not an option. The fine-grained access policies and firewall rules, with IPS and IDS, do the task of filtering the unwanted traffic out of the desirable traffic.

This is one of the most used and well-known attack methods. The following sections cover other types of attacks.

Reconnaissance

The primary objective of reconnaissance is to identify the attack target. This can be an entire corporation or a specific company. This is the point of entry to the system.

Port Scanning and Access

Once the target is identified, the attacker needs to enter the network. This can be done through multiple toolsets available on the public domain. There are multiple port scanners that will perform port scanning to check for vulnerable ports.

Before that, attackers need to make the victim install the payload, which contains the necessary code to do the port scanning. This can be done in multiple ways. It can be through social engineering or via email, where the victims are tricked into clicking on a link that, in turn, installs the malware. An organization with a culture of "security first" will have multiple threat detection tools and processes to prevent all these issues. Given that these types of attacks still happen around the world, it is very difficult to educate all employees of security threats.

Once the software is inside the system, it can download other feature sets required to perform further attacks. All it needs to do is attack the vulnerable ports, gain root access to the system, and do the intended task. An intelligent hacker will also make it difficult to trace his steps, by deleting the logs and software he uses. There are cases where attackers have used the same process, again and again, to gain access and then delete the trail log.

The Castle Wall Analogy

A castle wall can be a helpful analogy to explain one network defense method. As humans tend to reuse time-tested systems in new ways, the castle wall example can be used in the digital space as well.

A castle wall, as you know, is a tall wall built around a large city or castle to defend the inhabitants and their precious resources. The purpose of a castle wall is to block external threats. During medieval times, cities were under constant threat of raids and attacks. The first line of defense were the city gates, and most cities were surrounded by well built castle walls as well.

If you are a *Game of Thrones* fan, you have seen this multiple times. Consider the scene of Daenerys' army surrounding the capital, Kings Landing. The wall was surrounded by an open area, which made it easier for the bowman to detect threats looming miles away. The castle wall stopped their march, and they were easily detected as a threat. This can be further extended to the Trojan Horse story, where intruders hid inside a large horse, which was presented as a gift and therefore rolled into the city without concern.

The hidden paths in the tunnels leading into the city can be regarded as one vulnerability. The point is to make you understand how this scenario matches the perimeter-based firewall approach.

In some castle models, there is a moat surrounding the castle, filled with deadly alligators. This makes it even tougher for invading armies. In those, cases, there must be a drawbridge (a movable bridge) that leads to the castle gate. This drawbridge is like the ports you open in the firewall to enable application connectivity.

The Perimeter Model Defense Architecture

The perimeter model network security defense architecture has been in production a long time. The concept is straightforward and is based on the castle wall approach.

You make a line of defense using firewall appliances. Each packet entering the data center has to go through the firewall first. The firewall has security rules—firewall rules—that filter the packets. These rules can be based on layer 4 filtering or more in-depth layer 7 filtering. Both have their advantages and disadvantages.

Zone Defense

In a traditional security system, devices are separated into multiple security zones (see Figure 1-3). This isolates the spread of the attack yet requires more fine-grained control over the system, which in turn needs more security.

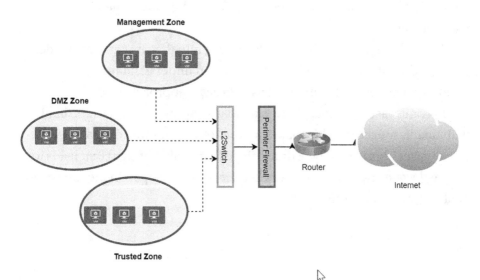

Figure 1-3. *Security zones*

Multiple security zones are created based on the threat level and the sensitivity of the content.

Centralized Security Control

You need to have a bird's-eye view of your entire IT security landscape to make better decisions, as well as to learn, analyze, and quickly respond to live threats. With the current methodology, the time it takes to isolate and respond to the attack is much more important.

The perimeter firewall method, in most common scenarios, will be a hardware-based appliance firewall. There are some virtual implementations on x86 commodity servers, but on a larger scale, it will be a Palo Alto/Checkpoint or Cisco-based firewall deployed with firewall policies. Most of these appliances can be controlled with a proprietary CLI command, and some newer firewall designs integrate IDS/IPS into the firewall, thereby providing a unified threat-management system.

In this case, blocking a vulnerable port for an entire infrastructure is as easy as blocking a bridge. In the castle wall analogy, it is similar to bringing the drawbridge up so there is no way to enter the castle directly.

IP-Based Traffic Filtering

The basic filtering mechanism in the perimeter firewall system is based on the IP address. This is a fast, simple approach, as you don't need to inspect the packets too deeply. However, for the latest threats, you need to have L4-L7-based firewall filtering for deeper packet inspection. This has been done by an IDS/IPS system. (An IDS is a detection system and an IPS is a control system.) There are different policies and rules that are applied based on the threat level. Overall, the IP-based filtering mechanism gets the job done without too much hassle.

This advantage is something you might not realize too often. Most of the time, you won't see the positives aspects. You can change policies/ rules independent of the underlying applications. You decide everything at the perimeter level—which packet to enter and what is filtered out. Considering the complexity of an application residing in a standard enterprise data center, the filtering mechanism you deploy has to be simple and efficient. The perimeter firewall does both—it stands right in the data path and filters packets based on some easy-to-use firewall rules. You therefore don't need to make any changes inside the applications.

Centralized Source for All Traffic Flow Logs

Logs are one of the most crucial parts of any security system. You need logs to trace the attack chain back and identify how the attack happened. You'll also use logs for audit purposes, to track the changes made in the system. Without a centralized logging mechanism, it would be a daunting task to identify and make sense of all the security logs. Perimeter firewall logs can be the first place to look in order to trace suspected attacks. Given that most new advanced firewall systems and architectures have very sophisticated logging mechanisms, these firewall logs remain very crucial in today's world.

IDS/IPS Use Cases

As mentioned, IDS/IPS in earlier days were used as separate appliances. Now most firewalls try to integrate both into the firewall appliance. That means that enabling IPS/IDS is as easy as checking a box in the firewall configuration software. The advantage here is you can always scan the traffic flow against an updated database of known attack types and vulnerabilities. This will help you identify a particular traffic pattern and match it against a known attack chain. Then you can quarantine the traffic before it becomes a full-fledged attack on the servers.

Problems with the Perimeter Model

Just to be clear, there are some clear advantages to this model. As it turns out, like any other system, a real advanced threat-management system has to identify and freeze all forms of attack, even ones that emerge daily.

This section discusses some problems that the perimeter-based defense system faces. To note, most of these disadvantages were not issues until recently. IT infrastructure changes exponentially. New software architecture, and along with that new vulnerabilities, have made it hard for the current system to keep up.

Single Point of Attack/Failure

Going back to the castle wall analogy, it is clear that once the wall is broken, the city defense mechanism will collapse. There is not much defense inside the city/castle to prevent the attackers from creating mayhem. All the residents' resources were gathered and used to defend the fort and to weaponize the wall. This is the first and last line of defense in almost all traditional models.

Using the same logic here, what happens when the perimeter firewall is somehow compromised? Say an intruder was able to successfully take control of the perimeter firewall appliance. Now he can change any firewall rules and even create new rules to allow and deny certain types of traffic. In the wrong hands, this will result in widespread destruction.

Even though you might use a host-based firewall mechanism and antivirus software scanners inside the application infrastructure, the main idea is that all these are built on top of the perimeter firewall. For example, when the SMB port is blocked/opened in the firewall, all the additional security tools that were added to aide the security system will take this action for granted. These tools won't go back and ask that firewall if this port is really blocked in your ruleset or not.

11

Multiple audits and specialized care have been provided on securing the security infrastructure. Yet the facts remains that this can act as a single point of failure (SPOF).

Protects North-South Traffic

The North-South traffic is the traffic flow going outside the data center. As with any defense mechanism, there are different security zones in a perimeter-based firewall. Utmost importance is given to the North-South traffic, as it is the critical traffic coming from unknown sources. This was fine, at least until recently.

There are some studies and surveys that indicate that around 77% of traffic stays inside the data center. Since the invention of the microservices architecture and CI/CD design flows, you must ask if you are doing enough to track these traffic inside the data centers. A perimeter-based security system does very little to control this. This means an insider or anyone who has access inside your network can easily navigate through various systems without encountering filters or blocks.

In the current scenario, the East-West traffic should get equal importance to any North-South traffic.

Firewall Rule Management Is Not Automated

If you have been involved in setting up a greenfield deployment for a firewall system, you might have realized how time-consuming this task is. More than that, consider the case of brownfield additions. Say a company decides to migrate from one firewall vendor to another. There are very few tools available that can successfully export and import the firewall policies. Standardization in creating firewall logs is very minimal, which can mean the vendor is locked in forever.

Gradually creating automated policies as you add virtual machines to the data center is the need of the hour.

Expensive and Appliance Based

The appliance model may have its own merits, but on a larger scale in a data center with multiple vendor hardware systems, it can end up being an isolated island. The firmware needs to be updated and all ROM settings have to be intact per the best practice of the vendor. In addition, any security vulnerabilities regarding that particular firmware and vendor software have to be frequently tracked and constantly updated. This may seem easy at first, but as the infrastructure grows and more and more hardware is used to meet capacity and demand, this will likely end up a full-time job, which most engineers hate to do.

Why Now and What Has Changed?

This section discusses what happened.

The increase in East-West traffic can be mainly attributed to the architecture changes that happened in the latest software development models. Companies are taking a more aggressive approach toward releasing software and features. Given the current competitive market, web-based applications have to roll out useful and innovative features to their customers constantly. This was not the case before, as most web applications incorporated fewer changes and features were just added yearly. This gave the IT department enough time to change the security architecture accordingly.

New features and software versions mean additional servers and new applications. All these changes have to be reflected in the security systems as well. If you are aggressively adding new features and are not updating the security policies at the same time, this can end badly.

As with every new feature, new ports need to be opened. There is a chance of using new software tools as well. Both of those mean new vulnerabilities. You need to treat the entire IT stack as a well-coordinated system and understand how a change in one component might affect the system as a whole. When you add a new server, you have to add security/network policies at the same time. It's the same principle.

The microservices architecture is the latest way of doing things faster and better. Netflix is often considered the frontrunner of this type of architecture, and soon there are a lot of companies implementing it.

So, what are microservices? Traditionally, engineers built everything around a monolithic software system and tied the processes to an application. They mostly ran on the same server. According to the bandwidth, you could scale up the servers with more CPU, more RAM, more NICS, etc. There is a big issue with this design, as it makes the server a critical point in the entire data center, so you have to make sure that the server is up and running all the time. If the server reboots or crashes, your application is not available.

As per Murphy's Law, everything that can go wrong will go wrong. So one day, this server is going to fail. In traditional architectures, the common way of preventing this is to add another passive server to take over the primary ones in case of any failures. Previously, you needed only one server, but now your critical server list increased to two. You also need monitoring systems and regular DR drills to make sure everything is working fine. This means additional effort and resources, but the problem remains as it is.

The flaw with this kind of design is that it doesn't take failures into account. Hardware will fail, disks will crash, networks will get disconnected. These things happen on a weekly, if not on a daily, basis in any data center. If the design has not taken this into account, you are in for many nasty surprises.

The competing architecture that emerged as an alternative is based on the principle that takes failures as normal. The microservices architecture splits the monolithic software structure into small services, and these services communicate with each other through REST/RPC interfaces. This can result in an explosion of traffic inside the DC, which means that filtering unwanted traffic inside the DC is a priority. This is called a pet vs. cattle design approach to IT. The microservices based architecture treats your servers similar to cattle. A certain controlled amount of loss won't affect the overall functioning of the systems, meanwhile, you have to give utmost care to your pet servers to keep them running.

Virtual Machines and Containers

Modern applications reside inside virtual machines or containers. Containers are gaining in popularity, as they are the easiest way to deploy software based on the microservices architecture. A container can be started and killed faster compared to the longer boot time and additional unwanted software loaded as part of normal operating systems. Containers are very specific. One feature or function is typically implemented on a container and can run on any available computer. Software security built around the operating system needs to reliably change according to these new requirements and make sure the system as a whole is effectively filtering out unwanted traffic and threats.

Changes in the Cloud and the Need for End-to-End Automation

Another factor that adds to the latest trend is the exponential adoption of the cloud. The cloud changes the way we do things and, along with that, it changes the security settings. The public/private cloud system contains security groups that help filter traffic on a VNIC level. I discuss this in more detail later, including how VMware implements Zero Trust security.

Infrastructure automation, as well as tools like Terraform and Cloud Formation, are gaining traction. Immutable infrastructure, as people call this model, is the process of bringing up new load balancers, security groups, networks, and volumes with every new deployment. This enables you to automate the entire infrastructure creation, which would have taken months based on a traditional build. As you might have noted, creating security groups and policies is part of the automation process, so any security tools used inside the DC have to play nice with the infrastructure automation tools. Otherwise, there might be dangerous scenarios where there is a mismatch of security VM migration, even across locations. This can be achieved with an L2 extension and there are multiple ways of implementing this type of architecture using VMware. One main issue you have to keep in mind is that your security policies also have to move along with the change in locations.

Isolating threats and creating better quarantine policies are parts of the new generation of security systems.

Summary

This chapter covered the perimeter security model in practice and discussed its advantages and disadvantages. It explained how a network attack can progress and included a discussion of some real-life incidents. The intent here is to get a feel for the current defense architecture. The next chapter explains in more detail how this perimeter security system is not sufficient and how a Zero Trust network can provide much better security.

CHAPTER 2

Microsegmentation and Zero Trust: Introduction

When you implement Zero Trust micro-segmentation, all ingress/egress traffic hitting your virtual NIC cards will be compared against a configured list of firewall policies. The packet will be dropped if there is no rule matching the specific traffic flow. A default deny rule at the end ensures that all unrecognized traffic is denied at the vNIC itself. From a security perspective this is called *whitelisting* or a *positive security model,* whereby only things that are specifically allowed are accepted—everything else is rejected.

In a traditional perimeter-based setup, deploying a Zero Trust architecture requires an enormous amount of work and time. All packets have to go through the perimeter firewall, where the filtering will take place based on the configured firewall's rules. The packet has to travel up to the perimeter firewall, only to get dropped by the deny rule.

A common setup for this is to group the servers into different zones based on their functions. All management servers are grouped under the management zone, whereas monitoring servers are grouped under a different monitoring zone. The demilitarized zone (DMZ) contains servers

© Sreejith Keeriyattil 2019
S. Keeriyattil, *Zero Trust Networks with VMware NSX,*
https://doi.org/10.1007/978-1-4842-5431-8_2

that require special protection. Zones can be quite large; you can even put all the Windows workstations in a particular zone and apply similar policies to them all. This is logical, as most workstations require similar access settings.

All servers within the same security zone trust each other. This is the default behavior, because servers in the same zone have the same accessibility requirements. In such a scenario, there is nothing that stops a compromised server inside a zone from reaching the open ports in other servers inside the same zone. For SMB file share access, the common approach is to allow access to ports 135/445 from Windows workstations. As mentioned, nothing stops a vulnerable workstation from scanning and infecting other workstations in this case.

You can see how trust, even among servers in the same zones, can lead to disaster. Zero Trust eliminates all these concerns, as there is no default allow policy. Every packet is scrutinized against a set of rules, and it is allowed to pass only if it matches a specific allow rule.

This offers a multitude of advantages. The first one is that all flows will be logged and if an attack happens, you can identify the flow. This makes auditing easier. The Zero Trust model is tailored to meet modern threats.

Host-Based Firewalls

Traditional IT systems configure a host-based firewall (see Figure 2-1). The host-based firewall runs inside the operating system. It augments the perimeter firewall security. Together, they act as a perfect deterrent to malicious threats.

Managing host-based firewalls is much more time-consuming. Even with centralized tools, there is no easy way to apply the rules across the servers and keep them updated routinely.

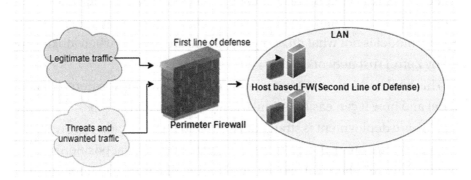

Figure 2-1. *Traditional model*

In a common production setup like the one shown in Figure 2-1, the perimeter and the host-based firewall act in unison to achieve the desired result.

How Zero Trust Can Be Deployed

Any new feature that requires a complete revamp of the IT systems is challenging to implement. Given the mission-critical applications running on the production system, this would be a strenuous task.

In general, any Zero Trust security system should be able to blend into the current architecture effortlessly. There are many ways you can use the core idea of the Zero Trust policies. Reference architecture from Google details how they removed the use of VPN and integrated the infrastructure stack to a policy-based Zero Trust network. With this implementation, users are granted access based on the device they are in and their access permissions. All user traffic is authenticated, authorized, and encrypted.

This approach is a big deviation from the current enterprise architecture. As discussed, anything that has a large impact on the IT system as a whole is tricky to implement in an already running production setup. Beyondcorp can fulfill most of these modern-day challenges and can be used in a variety of ways. It even has a Google tag, as they have been using this model for many years. However, an end-to-end change to the security model is not what most organizations are seeking when looking to deploy Zero Trust networks.

This book talks about VMware's way of implementing the Zero Trust model and how it can easily assimilate into your existing setup.

VMware deployment is straightforward and has a decade-long record of working with enterprise customers. VMware is in a great position to develop a model where you can have a product that is easy to implement and meets all the standard requirements.

Apart from the Google and VMware implementations of the Zero Trust model, there are multiple ways to implement it. This book discusses VMware's way of doing it and how to deploy it in an enterprise architecture in which a VMware-based stack is already running. Along with that, you can see how automating security policies and integrating them with third-party providers can give you tighter security. I will discuss integrating third-party products later in this book.

Prerequisites of Zero Trust

This section covers the prerequisites of Zero Trust.

Scalable Infrastructure

An infrastructure based on virtualization is a proven and mature design approach used in enterprise IT. There is no debate going on as to whether to virtualize or not to virtualize. Zero Trust requires an infrastructure built on a virtual layer. This doesn't mean that you can never achieve the target using physical servers. There are models that can do that, but virtualization gives you a lot of advantages. You can add a rule based on a larger subset, and filter based on resource groups, virtual machines names, and cluster names. In a physical setup, these choices are not available.

Another advantage of a virtual layer is the limitless opportunity for automation. Without automation, given the pace at which application delivery is heading, you won't be able to survive or manage a satisfactory IT infrastructure with up-to-date security settings. We are in the age of "Infrastructure as Code" and to make all these possible in the least disruptive way possible, you need a well-matured virtual layer.

Application Dependency Mapping

To create infallible security rules and policies, you need to know the dependencies and application flows. This is a must when you're designing an IT infrastructure, especially when using Zero Trust networks. You are in the business of designing a security model where only the trusted flows are allowed. Security architects should know more about the application and their behavior in a broad sense. For example, does Application A need access or connectivity (even ICMP access) to Application B? Does this connectivity occur anywhere in the application flow if they are in different VLANs? If they need to be in the same VLAN, do they need L2 connectivity between them?

These questions have to be asked during the design phase. Only when all these questions are properly answered should you proceed with the later steps. Remember that there is a default deny at the bottom of the security rules. If you are not careful about this during the design phase, you might end up in trouble later.

Ports and Services

The straightforward way is to use third-party tools like Tuffin is to understand the different connectivity patterns. Ports used for ingress/egress traffic for the application have to be recorded. Other information—like management traffic and traffic to log servers and monitoring servers—needs to be taken into account when considering the flows.

Current Perimeter Firewall Policies

You can't entirely exclude the perimeter firewall. In other words, you don't break down the castle wall and abandon the gates once you determine that the door locks are strong enough. You have to configure the required Northbound security rules in the perimeter firewall, where the necessary initial filtering takes place, before the traffic enters the DC.

There are multiple options available, such as using a virtual firewall VM, where the VM acts like the perimeter firewall and does all the filtering. This can be useful according to the requirements and design approach. If traffic flow is high, nothing can beat the power of a hardware appliance.

Monitoring Logs

This section covers why you need log servers and how to monitor logs.

Why do you need a log server? Logs are critical components of any security infrastructure. You need logs for various purposes, like auditing and monitoring. Traditional methods, like sending the logs to the syslog or FTP server, have their shortcomings. With all the advancements in analytics, you are not looking just to store the logs; you need to analyze and get meaningful information from the data. This requires a modern log server setup. You can use any of the open-source log server systems, like the ELK stack, or you can go with options like VMware Log Insight.

Log server stacks based on the latest models will make your life a lot easier, with intelligent API queries where you can look for specific details and information.

Tools for Log Analysis

This book discusses the VMware log analysis offering called VMware Log Insight. Log Insight is a very useful tool when it comes to analyzing and creating reports on data trends. You can promptly find out a lot of information from the dashboard. You can even filter the logs specific to one ESXi server and logs related to the packets that hit a specific distributed firewall rule. When you use it with the right queries, it turns out to be a really powerful tool that will make your life easier. Chapter 7 is dedicated to log analysis and discusses this topic in more detail.

Auditing Purpose and Log Backup

The security auditor can audit security in any organization that has a healthy security practice. Critical logs need to be analyzed and stored for future reference and use. This data will be stored on a tape drive for long-term retention. A log server can make auditing tasks a lot easier. It provides an analytics dashboard on certain incidents and reports on the overall health of the system. This makes the job of the security administrator a lot easier in terms of generating reports.

Adding a New Application to an Existing Infrastructure

The process should be simple, straightforward, and automated. A design that enforces a lot of manual restrictions and processes in order to add a new resource isn't scalable. Given the scale at which virtual machines are being created, this would soon become a very cumbersome process if you didn't have any groupings or tags. VMware helps with the usage of tags and security groups. Virtual machines can be grouped under a wide range of options, and this can happen automatically if you create a virtual machine with a specific tag. The security rules associated with that tag are then applied to the vNIC.

You can learn about VMware's way of doing this, as well as the best practices, in more detail. As a rule of thumb, any Zero Trust system should follow any features that will make the system easier to deploy and manage.

Geomigration for the virtual machine workload is achievable in an active-active data center setup. In such cases, there can be an L2 extension across the DC with a dark fiber cable. This setup will enable seamless migration of the workload between data centers along with a GSLB (Global Server Load Balancer).

In such a design, when the VM is migrated to the other DCs (such as from DC-A to DC-B), the security rules should also move. If any of these changes require manual attention, you will be looking at a huge mess in the future. As the migration itself can be automated according to the load, if your rules are not being migrated across, this can lead to security issues in the future. Fortunately, VMware has features like distributed firewall rules, that do this. As the security rules are applied to the virtual machine's NIC, it moves along with the virtual machines, irrespective of the location or specific computers.

VMware NSX

Software-defined networking (SDN) is now becoming a standard. SDN enables better infrastructure automation and configuring networks through API interfaces. Given the movement toward immutable infrastructure, automation capabilities are a must for all infrastructure components. SDN enables you to virtualize the network layer by separating the control plane from the data plane.

Traditional network switch design combines the control plane and the data plane into the hardware switch and loads a proprietary OS like CISCO IOS or JUNIPER Junos to configure the networking stack. This worked fine for years. As the need for virtualizing the network stack arose, this model wouldn't scale, leading to the SDN movement.

The VMware SDN stack provides end-to-end network virtualization by virtualizing infrastructure components like the firewall, router, load balancer, and VPNs into virtual functions. As mentioned, this is a prerequisite to creating an immutable infrastructure. To automate the application stack creation, you have to create networks, load balancers, and security rules. Virtualizing it makes it easier to automate these layers as well.

VMware provides a REST API interface to configure the network functions. This makes it easier to integrate the features into an existing automation tool. The book discusses these points more in later chapters.

Overlay: VXLAN

The Overlay protocol is used with modern SDN solutions. VLAN, given its advantages, is not always well suited to cloud-based solutions. Along with the technical limitations of 4096 VLAN per infrastructure, there are other limitations. For example, it's not well suited to network automation and virtualizations. Overlay protocols are tunneling protocols. The tunnel has a source IP address and a destination IP address. The idea is simple when you want a packet to travel from Compute-1 to Compute-2. The actual packet created by the virtual machine will be encapsulated into additional headers and L4 layer flags. Once the packet is encapsulated, the original packet created by the virtual machine will be added as a payload for the compute NIC interface. Because of this additional header size, MTU size requirements across the networks with overlay might have to be changed. GRE and VXLAN are two of the more well known protocols. (See Figure 2-2.)

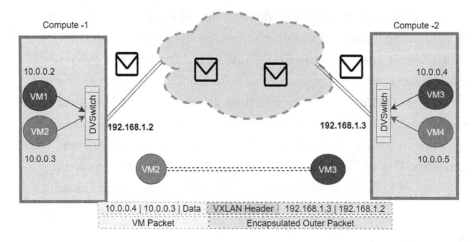

Figure 2-2. *Overlay packet flow*

VXLAN is used as an overlay network in VMware NSX. VXLAN is a tunneling protocol. Encapsulation of network packets and adding VXLAN headers happens at the VTEP port. The encapsulated packet travels through the network underlay as a normal IP packet. After reaching the destination, the packet will be decapsulated and sent to the right vNIC.

VXLAN Headers

The VXLAN header (see Figure 2-3) is a 24-bit identifier attached to the VM packet. VXLAN uses VNI to identify different packets. VNI is similar to a VLAN tag, but it has more range than a 12-bit VLAN tag.

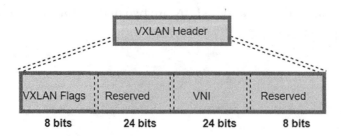

Figure 2-3. *VXLAN header*

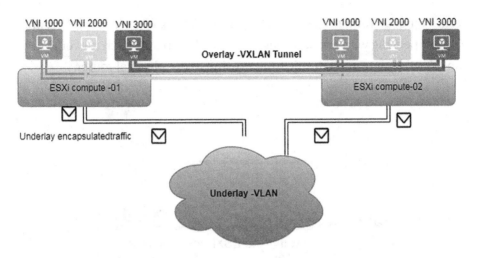

Figure 2-4. *Communication over a VXLAN tunnel*

In Figure 2-4, VNI 1000, VNI 2000, and VNI 3000 are the VXLAN networks attached to the virtual machines. VM packets, while coming out of the vNIC, will be encapsulated into these VNI IDs. The packet from the virtual machine will be the payload for the Compute-01 NIC. Once it reaches the Compute-02 NIC, decapsulation will happen at the VTEP port and the packet will be forwarded to the vNIC with the right VXLAN ID. If the flow is from VNI 1000 to VNI 2000, routing will happen at the compute where the packet originates. DLR will do the routing of the packet inside the computer hosts.

Distributed Router

A distributed logical router is shown in Figure 2-5. This is a feature in NSX that reduces the routing traffic inside the data center. DLR is deployed as a kernel module in the ESXi host. DLR provides a virtual router instance inside the ESXi host. This prevents the network packet from traveling to the physical router for routing to the desired destination. DLR needs a control VM, whereby the BGP/OSPF routing paths are exchanged with the perimeter edge router. The control VM is not sitting in the data path; it only helps in peering with the edge devices. This design approach prevents a considerable amount of traffic from flowing to the physical router.

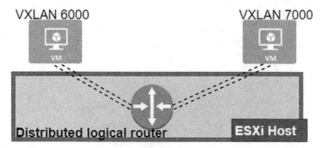

Figure 2-5. *DLR-based routing inside ESXi*

VMware NSX Distributed Firewall

VMware DFW is a kernel-based firewall installed in the ESXi kernel space. DFW is a stateful firewall, which means it will keep track of the connections and will act in accordance with its previous decision. This capability gives stateful firewall packet filtering features to the VMware distributed firewall. DFW firewall rules will be applied per vNIC; each packet originating from the VM has to pass through the filtering module before the packet even reaches outside the ESXi. This helps block the traffic in the virtual machine space itself. In the case of a traditional perimeter firewall, the packet has to travel up to the perimeter firewall, only to be denied by the perimeter security rules. This drastically reduces the East-West traffic and hair pinning concerning security flows. (See Figure 2-6.)

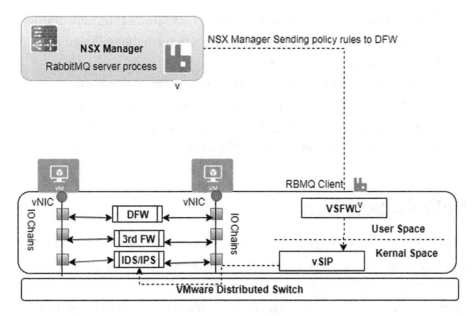

Figure 2-6. *DFW internal view*

The NSX Manager is the central management console for all the VMware NSX SDN-related configurations, including micro-segmentation. Even though other VMware toolsets can aid in creating the ruleset, the configuration should be done through the NSX Manager. The NSX Manager has to be integrated with VMware vSphere. After the integration, the NSX Manager can be accessed via a separate tab in the VMware vSphere interface.

Micro-segmentation rules can be configured from the VMware NSX Network and Security tab. VMware uses the RabbitMQ messaging bus to push the firewall rules to other computer nodes that host the application VM. During the ESXi host preparation, the DFW kernel module will be installed on all computer hosts in the cluster. The NSX Manager will send the policy actions to the RabbitMQ server process, which in turn pushes all the policies to the RB MQ client, which in this case is the vsfwd process. The vsfwd process receives the message and sends it to vSIP, which is a

VIB that's included in the host preparation. The VMware Internetworking Service Insertion Platform's (VSIP) function is to push the policy rules to all DFW filters in the virtual machines.

There is a possibility to integrate a third-party firewall into the VMware's IO chain. The IO chains are used to redirect the packet according to the intended configuration. Third-party IDS/IPS FW can easily be integrated into the VMware NSX suite using this method.

DFW Packet Flow

A distributed firewall instance per vNIC will have two tables—a rule table and a flow table. The rule table contains the firewall policies applied to that vNIC and the flow table (the connection tracker) contains the cached entries of the permitted flows. The firewall rule will be applied from top to bottom and the practice is to use a default deny rule at the bottom to secure the VM from unwanted traffic.

Consider Table 2-1. For new traffic originating from Webserver-1 and Webserver-2, there will be no flow entries. The rules applied to these webservers are only for reference purposes. In reality, this has to be augmented with multiple other rules to create a valid application traffic flow.

Table 2-1. *Rule Table*

DFW Rules	Source	Destination	Service	Action	Applied To
Rule 1	All	Webserver-1	HTTPS	Allow	DFW
Rule 2	All	Webserver-2	HTTPS	Allow	DFW
Rule 3	Webserver-1	Webserver-2	Any	Deny	DFW

You can allow the external users to access Webserver-1 and Webserver-2's HTTPS port. When the traffic starts flowing through the vNIC, it has to go through the IO chains. As there are no flow entries in the cache for the flow, DFW has to go through the ruleset and determine that Rule 1 and Rule 2 allow HTTPS traffic from an external user. This then updates the flow table, and further flows can be permitted through the cache.

As you can see, the Zero Trust approach includes a deny rule at the bottom by default, and it's not explicitly mentioned in the ruleset. You don't need communication flow between Webserver-1 and Webserver-2; the default deny rule blocks this traffic.

This feature can contain the spread of any attacker trying to attack a webserver. If one webserver is compromised, you can be sure that the attacker can access only the valid ports in this instance. This effectively contains the spread of many modern virus attacks, like Notpetya for example.

Summary

This chapter discussed the VMware NSX features and the internal details of the VMware distributed firewall. The next chapters go in-depth into implementing these security practices in a real-time infrastructure. You will learn more about adding distributed firewall rules and security groups.

CHAPTER 3

Zero Trust Networks with VMware NSX: Getting Started

This chapter continues the journey of Zero Trust networks using VMware NSX. This chapter explains how to create firewall rules in VMware NSX. This includes setting up the NSX Manager, deploying a NSX distributed firewall, and configuring firewall rules. You can do all this through VMware vSphere after integrating with VMware's NSX Manager. You can use REST API calls to automate the configuration as part of the infrastructure automation.

NSX has a wide range of use cases. This book focuses only on security-related use cases.

The chapter does a deep dive of the various configuration options for a VMware distributed firewall. This configuration might differ from version to version, but the main feature set remains the same. To learn more about the version related configuration, refer to the VMware official docs. As a rule of thumb, the chapter refers to configuring VMware NSX version 6.3 and above.

© Sreejith Keeriyattil 2019
S. Keeriyattil, *Zero Trust Networks with VMware NSX*,
https://doi.org/10.1007/978-1-4842-5431-8_3

NSX Manager Installation

Prerequisites

The NSX Manager is packaged in an OVA file template, which can be imported directly into the running VMware vSphere environment. The import process is straightforward, as with any other OVA templates. As the NSX Manager is the centralized management service for all the SDN features, deploying the virtual machine in a cluster configured with high availability and DRS brings an added advantage. For enterprise setup, it is always recommended to use a high-availability cluster for NSX Manager deployments. Table 3-1 lists the ports that need to be opened as a prerequisite before installing the NSX Manager.

Table 3-1. *Ports that Need To Be Opened as a Prerequisite Before Installing the NSX Manager*

From	To	Port
Client PC	NSX Manager	443
Client PC	NSX Manager	80
ESXi Host	NSX Manager	5671
NSX Manager	NSX Controller	443
NSX Manager	vCenter Server	443
NSX Manager	vCenter Server	902
NSX Manager	ESXi Host	443
NSX Manager	ESXi Host	902
NSX Manager	ESXi host	48656
NSX Manager	DNS Server	53
NSX Manager	Syslog Server	514
NSX Manager	NTP Time Server	123
vCenter Server	NSX Manager	80
REST Client	NSX Manager	443
ESXi Host	NSX Manager	8301, 8302
NSX Manager	ESXi Host	8301, 8302
Guest Introspection VM	NSX Manager	5671

NSX Manager Installation

Once the required port is opened, the OVA file can be imported using the vCenter client. Log into vCenter and then, from the VM and templates, select Deploy OVF Template.

The NSX Manager to vCenter relationship is 1: 1, which means there can be only one NSX Manager attached to one vCenter. The NSX Manager deployed using the OVA file has a unique UUID. If the same template is used to deploy another site, the UUID will remain the same, which can cause further synchronization issues.

Once the appliance is up and running, you can log in to the NSX Manager web interface.

There are multiple options you can set in the NSX Manager, but you won't do much of your work using the NSX Manager dashboard. The primary objective is to integrate the NSX Manager with VMware vSphere, where you can manage all NSX components.

From the login dashboard, you can get statistics about the CPU/RAM usage. The NSX Manager has the option to stop/start services like RabbitMQ and PostgreSQL from the dashboard.

The RabbitMQ process is the messaging queue channel that NSX uses to push firewall policies to the VFW daemon listening to the ESXi host. To have a working synchronized firewall service, the RabbitMQ service should be running on the NSX Manager (see Figure 3-1).

Figure 3-1. *The NSX Manager dashboard*

Registering the NSX Manager with vCenter is a straightforward process. You simply need to enter the FQDN and the credentials in the NSX Management service box, as shown in Figure 3-2.

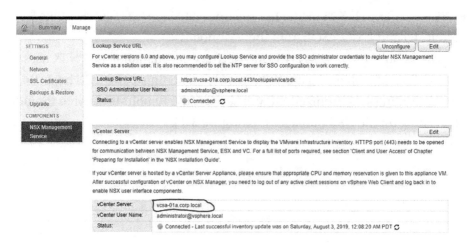

Figure 3-2. *The NSX Manager and vCenter integration*

If all goes well, the status will show that it's connected with a green button. Registration can be verified by logging in to the vCenter. (See Figure 3-3.)

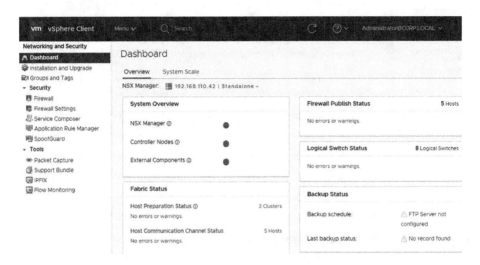

Figure 3-3. *The NSX system overview from vCenter*

vCenter can be used for further configuration on NSX. You can verify from the dashboard that the NSX services are in the running state and the registered NSX Manager is in standalone mode. This can change to primary/secondary for CrossVC NSX Implementation. (See Figures 3-4 and 3-5.)

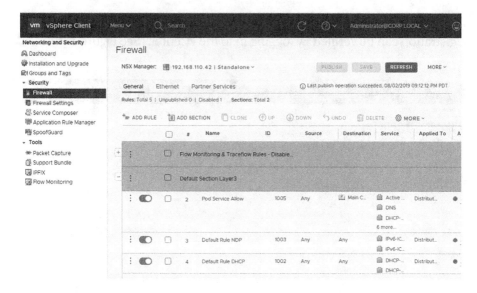

Figure 3-4. *The DFW rules window*

```
nsxmgr-01a> show dfw cluster all
No.  Cluster Name     Cluster Id        Datacenter Name   Firewall Status    Firewall Fabric Status
1    RegionA01-MGMT01  domain-c141       RegionA01         Enabled            GREEN
2    RegionA01-COMP02  domain-c201       RegionA01         Enabled            GREEN
3    RegionA01-COMP01  domain-c26        RegionA01         Enabled            GREEN
```

Figure 3-5. *DFW enabled cluster status from ESXi*

Firewall Policy Update Process

NSX Manager RabbitMQ Server Process

RabbitMQ is a message broker service that implements the AMQP
messaging protocol. RabbitMQ communicates with the client using the
TCP protocol. The connection from the NSX Manager to the ESXi host is
SSL encrypted. VSFWD receives the message from the server and pushes
the rules to the DFW kernel modules (see Figure 3-6).

```
[root@nsxmgr-01a /etc/rabbitmq]# ps -ef |grep rabbit
root      2694  2177  0 10:12 pts/0    00:00:00 grep rabbit
root      4145     1  0 06:56 ?        00:00:00 /bin/sh /usr/local/sbin/rabbitmq-server
root      4380  4145  0 06:56 ?        00:01:12 /usr/lib/erlang/erts-9.0/bin/beam.smp -W w -A 64 -P 1048576 -t 5000000 -stbt
db -zdbbl 128000 -K true -B i -- -root /usr/lib/erlang -progname erl -- -home /root -- -pa /usr/local/rabbitmq_server-3.6.11/
ebin -noshell -noinput -s rabbit boot -sname rabbit@localhost -boot start_sasl -config /etc/rabbitmq/rabbitmq -kernel inet_de
fault_connect_options [{nodelay,true}] -sasl errlog_type error -sasl sasl_error_logger false -rabbit error_logger {file,"/var
/log/rabbitmq/rabbit@localhost.log"} -rabbit sasl_error_logger {file,"/var/log/rabbitmq/rabbit@localhost-sasl.log"} -rabbit e
nabled_plugins_file "/etc/rabbitmq/enabled_plugins" -rabbit plugins_dir "/usr/local/rabbitmq_server-3.6.11/plugins" -rabbit p
lugins_expand_dir "/common/rabbitmq/mnesia/rabbit@localhost-plugins-expand" -os_mon start_cpu_sup false -os_mon start_disksup
 false -os_mon start_memsup false -mnesia dir "/common/rabbitmq/mnesia/rabbit@localhost" -kernel inet_dist_listen_min 25672 -
kernel inet_dist_listen_max 25672
[root@nsxmgr-01a /etc/rabbitmq]#
```

Figure 3-6. *NSX Manager ➤ RabbitMQ server process ➤ (SSL/TCP)*
➤ VSFWD (RBMQ Client)

The running RabbitMQ process can be checked from the NSX Manager
CLI tools.

A vhost user named shield will be created for the DFW message
queue. (See Figures 3-7 and 3-8.)

```
[root@nsxmgr-01a /etc/rabbitmq]# rabbitmqctl list_vhosts
Listing vhosts
vshield
/
[root@nsxmgr-01a /etc/rabbitmq]#
```

Figure 3-7. *RabbitMQ vhost status*

```
=INFO REPORT==== 3-Aug-2019::07:01:08 ===
accepting AMQP connection <0.1123.0> (192.168.110.55:41806 -> 192.168.110.42:5671)

=INFO REPORT==== 3-Aug-2019::07:01:08 ===
connection <0.1123.0> (192.168.110.55:41806 -> 192.168.110.42:5671): user 'vse_50086cbb-1c39-777a-43d1-8c7e591f1681' authenti
cated and granted access to vhost 'vshield'

=INFO REPORT==== 3-Aug-2019::07:01:10 ===
accepting AMQP connection <0.1141.0> (192.168.110.54:27639 -> 192.168.110.42:5671)

=INFO REPORT==== 3-Aug-2019::07:01:10 ===
connection <0.1141.0> (192.168.110.54:27639 -> 192.168.110.42:5671): user 'vse_5008cced-c7f3-79d0-fae3-335373bb1aef' authenti
cated and granted access to vhost 'vshield'
```

Figure 3-8. *RabbitMQ connection verification*

vhosts are a logical grouping of the RabbitMQ resources that can be
used to separate the objects that are using the RabbitMQ resources.

The RabbitMQ options listed here are purely for information purposes;
it is not advisable to change the configuration of any production systems.
There won't be root login access to the NSX Manager server in an
enterprise setup.

ESXi Host VSFW (RabbitMQ Client)

Policies created from the NSX Manager will be sent from the RabbitMQ server process to the VSFWD listening to the ESXi hosts. Communication will happen over the 5671 port (see Figure 3-9).

```
[root@esx-01a:~] esxcli network ip connection list |grep 5671
tcp         0         0  192.168.110.51:19096        192.168.110.42:5671   ESTABLISHED      68255  newreno  vsfwd
tcp         0         0  192.168.110.51:62947        192.168.110.42:5671   ESTABLISHED      68255  newreno  vsfwd
tcp         0         0  192.168.110.51:13519        192.168.110.42:5671   ESTABLISHED      68255  newreno  vsfwd
[root@esx-01a:~] 
```

Figure 3-9. *Communication over the 5671 port*

Connection status in ESXi indicates that the VSFW is listening on the 5671 port for any messages from the NSX Manager. The VFFWD configuration can be verified using the `esxcfg-advcfg -g /UserVars/ RmqIpAddress` command. The NSX Manager's IP address has to be listed in the output.

You have verified all the required components for NSX. A distributed firewall has been installed and configured to make further use of the system.

Firewall Rule Creation

You can create firewall rules from the NSX Manager by choosing the Firewall tab.

In the Firewall configuration tab, there are multiple options that can be used to configure specific features in NSX. The General tab is where all L3 packet control rules are placed. The Ethernet tab is used to configure L2 rules.

VMware NSX has partnered with different security providers to enable the integration of multiple firewall products with VMware. You can integrate third-party products like Palo Alto Firewall and Trend Micro into the NSX ecosystem. Having the ability to integrate a wide variety of third-party tools into the NSX environment makes NSX a perfect fit as a complete end-to-end security and network offering.

Adding Sections

You can segregate the firewall rules into sections. Managing firewall rules is as important as creating them. Without a straightforward and easy-to-use approach to creating firewall rules, you will be risking "firewall rule explosion". You can group sections logically. They can be divided based on the applications or various departments in the organizations. It is always good practice to divide the rules into different sections, as this makes it easy to apply changes across the sections all at once.

To create a section, choose Firewall ➤ Add Section. There are few options you can configure in the Add Section window, apart from the section name.

1)   Enable user identity at source.

This option can be useful for a VDI setup. If you are enabling users to share sessions in a remote desktop, this means two users can use the same virtual machine and the same IP address. In such cases, there needs to be a way to segregate access requirements. Consider a scenario where User-1 and User-2 use the same VDI desktop in different sessions. If User-1 needs an Internet connection and User-2 doesn't, there has to be a set of rules applied to the firewall policies to enable this. This scenario is difficult to implement in a traditional firewall setup.

With NSX, you can set up identity-based rules. For this prerequisite, you need to enable active directory integration with NSX (this procedure is explained in the VMware docs). Guest introspection services have to be configured in clusters.

After AD integration, you can create security groups based on the directory group information. Once you are done creating security groups, you can create firewall sections with the Enable User Identity at the Source option. This will filter packets based on the user's identity. User-1 and User-2 use the same VDI and IP address, but they have different access restrictions.

2) Enable TCP strict.

The TCP protocol uses a three-way handshake to establish a session.

1. The client sends a SYN packet to the server asking it to establish a session.

2. The server replies with an SYN/ACK message to the client.

3. The client responds with an ACK, completing the handshake process and establishing a session.

If you enable TCP strict in the sections, DFW will only allow packets that have completed the handshake process. If a random packet arrives at DFW and a handshake has not been registered before, that packet will be dropped.

3) Enable stateless firewall.

DFW by default acts as a stateful firewall, which means it will keep track of the active connections. Packets matching an existing connection will be allowed by the firewall and any new packet will be checked against the configured firewall rules.

By enabling stateless firewall, you can negate this
property. DFW won't keep track of the connections.
This has to be enabled based on the application
requirements.

These options will be enabled only for general rules, not for L2 rules.

You can only enable either TCP strict or stateless firewall for any
section, not both at the same time. A user identity service cannot be
enabled with a stateless firewall. DFW has other options, like merging
sections, which can be used if you want to club firewall rules for two
different departments into a single place, because of a change in an
application model or for other business reasons.

Adding Firewall Rules

You can add rules to sections through the Firewall ➤ Add Rule path. See
Figure 3-10.

Figure 3-10. *Adding DFW rules*

Name and ID

The firewall rule can have a user-friendly name so you can quickly identify
it. You can enable/disable the rule with a simple button on the right side.

Source and Destination

In a traditional perimeter firewall, most of the L3 filtering happens based on IP address matching. With NSX, you have multiple options available in addition to that. You can add vCenter objects as a source in the firewall rule. You have a wide range of options to choose from:

- Security groups

- IP sets

- Cluster

- Data center

- Distributed port group

- Logical switch

- Resource pool

- Virtual machine

- vNIC

Options for selecting vCenter objects—such as Distributed Port Group and Logical Switch—provide a lot of adaptability concerning rule creation. You can apply the same set of firewall rules to all servers in the management cluster. You can even create a rule that limits a specific logical switch that's based on VXLAN traffic. You can use a logical switch in the source and the destination and control how VMs in certain VXLAN segments communicate with another. VXLAN is a tunneling protocol, so this DFW feature set provides flexibility in that you can use multiple options and apply rules on a granular level.

Security Groups

Security groups in general terms are groups of servers in which you need to apply a specific policy set. You can group all webservers belonging to a certain application into a webserver security group, for example. Security groups allow you to either include or exclude certain groups of servers based on the particular rule where you are using those security groups.

Security Tags

You can assign metadata attributes to the virtual machine using tags. Tags can be created with a specific name, and each tag belongs to a certain category. Your operations servers can be on one category and can identify different types of servers with the label. You can use syslog label for all the servers in the log cluster, a monitoring label for monitoring virtual machines, etc. Using context labels provides an even more efficient and easier approach to security as well.

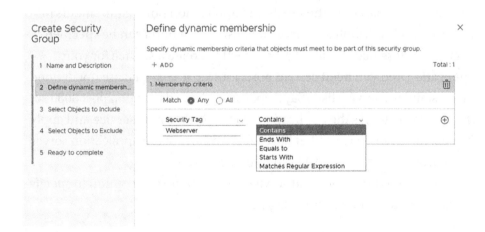

Figure 3-11. Dynamic membership options

You can create security groups based on a security tag. If this is used with dynamic inclusion (see Figure 3-11), every time a server with the tag "webserver" is deployed in the data center, rules will be automatically applied to the virtual machine, giving you an automated way of applying the rules. When you are dealing with large enterprise infrastructures and creating and deleting virtual machines according to requirements, tags can make the task easier.

There are options to use Boolean expressions like equals, with, etc. They can be used based on the application or security requirements.

Negate Destination

For the Negate Destination option, rules will be applied to traffic going to the destination, except the ones you specify in the destination field.

Services

Services often deal with protocol and port-level filtering. New services can be created based on the needs and application port requirements of the layer 3/4/7 attributes. Source and destination ports can be specified to create a classified service. Say you need to create a service for your application and you need certain ports for web access that are not defined in the standard service lists. Say Application A needs to open port 8080 so the client can access the application. You can add a new service and apply it to clients. Then packets that have an IP address of the application server A and a destination port of 443 should be allowed.

Apart from the service and service groups, there is an option to specify raw port/protocol details. (See Figure 3-12.)

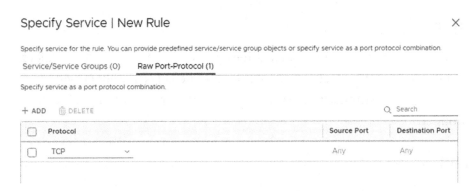

Figure 3-12. *Adding a raw protocol to DFW rules*

Applied To

This option specifies where to apply the firewall rules (see Figure 3-13).

Specify Applied To | New Rule

Specify containers on which this rule will be applied

☑ Apply this rule on all clusters on which Distributed Firewall is installed

☐ Apply this rule on all the Edge gateways
   (For Edges with version 6.1.0 and higher)

Select one or more objects for the applied to field of the firewall rule

Available Objects (1)	Q Search
☐ Name	
☐ ⚏ Perimeter-Gateway-01	
1 - 1 of 1 objects	

Selected Objects (0)	Q Search
☐ Name	Object Type
0 objects	

Figure 3-13. *Applying rules to VMware objects*

You can also use this window to apply the rule you created in the perimeter gateways.

Action

Based on the rules, DFW can take three actions on a packet—Allow, Reject, and Block. The difference between Block and Reject is that Block will silently drop the traffic, whereas Reject will notify the client that it is getting dropped.

Log

You can enable/disable logging of the selected security rule with this option. Ideally, you should log the rules that can be used to analyze the traffic in case you have any concerns. When there are situations where you don't need to log, you can use this option.

Saving Firewall Rules

Firewall rules can be saved and exported for backing up. In addition to this, you can load the exported security rule; this option is available in the same window (see Figure 3-14).

Figure 3-14. *Loading a saved configuration option in NSX*

Saved configurations can be exported from the NSX Manager tab as well (see Figure 3-15).

Figure 3-15. *Saved configuration list*

Exclusion List

You can place the virtual machines where you don't want any of the security policies to be applied in the exclusion list. No DFW rues apply to the virtual machines in the exclusion list. This can come in handy when you want to apply the rules to a cluster, but want to avoid only a select set of virtual machines.

Configuring DFW on a Live Network

This section shows you how to configure the first firewall rule and then apply it to the virtual machines. Consider a live production network with a pool of webservers receiving a request on a standard HTTP port and serving the request from the backend pool of the application and database servers. This is a traditional standard three-tier model. Using the distributed firewall approach, if you want to implement a Zero Trust network, you need to provide granular security rules in the network. In a perimeter-based firewall model, you can group the webservers in a webserver zone and apply the webserver-specific policies to all the webservers. This will work fine. If you don't want the webservers to have access to each other, you can limit the access of each server in the zone. That way, if an attacker tries to compromise a webserver, you can limit his ability to reach other servers.

- Webserver-1: 172.16.10.11

- Webserver-2: 172.16.10.12

In a traditional setup, Webserver-1 and Webserver-2 can be in the same zone and can access each other (see Figures 3-16 and 3-17).

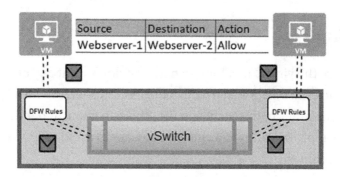

Figure 3-16. *Traditional setup*

```
root@web-02a [ ~ ]# ping 172.16.10.11
PING 172.16.10.11 (172.16.10.11) 56(84) bytes of data.
64 bytes from 172.16.10.11: icmp_seq=1 ttl=64 time=0.886 ms
64 bytes from 172.16.10.11: icmp_seq=2 ttl=64 time=1.07 ms
^C
--- 172.16.10.11 ping statistics ---
2 packets transmitted, 2 received, 0% packet loss, time 1133ms
rtt min/avg/max/mdev = 0.886/0.982/1.079/0.101 ms
root@web-02a [ ~ ]#
```

```
root@web-01a [ ~ ]# ping 172.16.10.12
PING 172.16.10.12 (172.16.10.12) 56(84) bytes of data.
64 bytes from 172.16.10.12: icmp_seq=1 ttl=64 time=0.920 ms
64 bytes from 172.16.10.12: icmp_seq=2 ttl=64 time=0.751 ms
64 bytes from 172.16.10.12: icmp_seq=3 ttl=64 time=0.932 ms
^C
--- 172.16.10.12 ping statistics ---
3 packets transmitted, 3 received, 0% packet loss, time 2347ms
rtt min/avg/max/mdev = 0.751/0.867/0.932/0.089 ms
root@web-01a [ ~ ]#
```

Figure 3-17. *Traditional setup*

Quick Start Guide to Dart Programming

Create High-Performance Applications for the Web and Mobile

Sanjib Sinha

Apress®

Quick Start Guide to Dart Programming

Sanjib Sinha
Howrah, West Bengal, India

ISBN-13 (pbk): 978-1-4842-5561-2   ISBN-13 (electronic): 978-1-4842-5562-9
https://doi.org/10.1007/978-1-4842-5562-9

Managing Director, Apress Media LLC: Welmoed Spahr
Acquisitions Editor: Nikhil Karkal
Development Editor: Matthew Moodie
Coordinating Editor: Divya Modi

Cover designed by eStudioCalamar

Cover image designed by Pixabay

Distributed to the book trade worldwide by Springer Science+Business Media New York, 233 Spring Street, 6th Floor, New York, NY 10013. Phone 1-800-SPRINGER, fax (201) 348-4505, e-mail orders-ny@springer-sbm.com, or visit www.springeronline.com. Apress Media, LLC is a California LLC and the sole member (owner) is Springer Science + Business Media Finance Inc (SSBM Finance Inc). SSBM Finance Inc is a **Delaware** corporation.

For information on translations, please e-mail rights@apress.com, or visit www.apress.com/rights-permissions.

Apress titles may be purchased in bulk for academic, corporate, or promotional use. eBook versions and licenses are also available for most titles. For more information, reference our Print and eBook Bulk Sales web page at www.apress.com/bulk-sales.

Any source code or other supplementary material referenced by the author in this book is available to readers on GitHub via the book's product page, located at www.apress.com/978-1-4842-5561-2. For more detailed information, please visit www.apress.com/source-code.

Printed on acid-free paper

*To Arun Sengupta and Dipali Sengupta,
my elder brother and sister-in-law, the people closest to my
heart. Although we are locationally challenged, living in
different places, we are separated only by space. Wherever
we live, we will always be together in our minds.*

Table of Contents

About the Author

 **Sanjib Sinha** is an author and tech writer. Being a certified .NET Windows and web developer, he specializes in Python security programming and Linux and in many programming languages such as C#, PHP, Python, Dart, Java, and JavaScript. Sanjib won Microsoft's Community Contributor Award in 2011, and he has written the following books for Apress: *Beginning Ethical Hacking with Python, Beginning Ethical Hacking with Kali Linux, Beginning Laravel 5.8* (first and second editions), and *Bug Bounty Hunting for Web Security.*

About the Technical Reviewer

Abir Ranjan Atarthy is an Offensive Security Certified Professional (OSCP), Certified Ethical Hacker (CEH), and Certified Hacking Forensic Investigator (CHFI).

He has deep expertise in the domain of cybersecurity and different programming languages with more than 10 years of hands-on experience in the areas of network security, vulnerability analysis, penetration testing, web security, security analytics, malware protection, cryptography, data protection, and digital forensics.

He has coded many scripts in Python, Ruby, etc., and has mentored numerous students to create tools/applications in different areas of cybersecurity.

Abir has authored several technical articles that have been published in IT security journals and is frequently invited to speak at cybersecurity conferences and forums. He has been quoted by leading newspapers and TV channels on several occasions as a subject-matter expert.

In addition, he has conducted several workshops and training/certification programs on cybersecurity, Python, secure coding framework, etc., for large corporations, different universities, and engineering colleges.

He has an M.Sc. in computer applications and has finished short-term programs in object-oriented programming in Java and C++, data structure, and aspects of software engineering at the Indian Institute of Technology – Kharagpur.

Currently he is with TCG Digital Solutions Pvt. Ltd.

CHAPTER 1

Getting Started with Dart

So, why the Dart language? Well, Dart is a great fit for both mobile apps and web apps. Dart is free and open source, and the repository is available at `https://github.com/dart-lang`. You can also get a feel of the language at the official web site: `https://www.dartlang.org/`. The advantage of Dart is, since it is a client optimized programming language for apps on multiple platforms, you can use it for as many purposes as Desktop, Mobile, backend, and web applications. Another advantage is it can be transcompiled into JavaScript, if you want.

In this introductory chapter, let's try to understand why learning the Dart language is important for building mission-critical mobile apps on iOS and Android. If you already have a working knowledge in Object Oriented Language like Java or Python, it will be much easier for you to understand the core concepts because using C-style syntax, Dart is a class-defined, garbage collected language.

Developers around the world use Dart to create high-quality apps for iOS and Android and the Web. It is feature rich so that client-side development is also possible. As we progress throughout the book, you will see how correct this statement is.

If you want to learn how to build native iOS and Android mobile apps and web apps using Dart, then this book serves as a good introduction because it is designed to give you a complete picture of how Dart works.

© Sanjib Sinha 2020
S. Sinha, *Quick Start Guide to Dart Programming*,
https://doi.org/10.1007/978-1-4842-5562-9_1

Though building a full mobile app is beyond the scope of this book, you will build a simple web app in Chapter 9.

The Core Features of Dart

Figure 1-1 shows the core features of the Dart programming language.

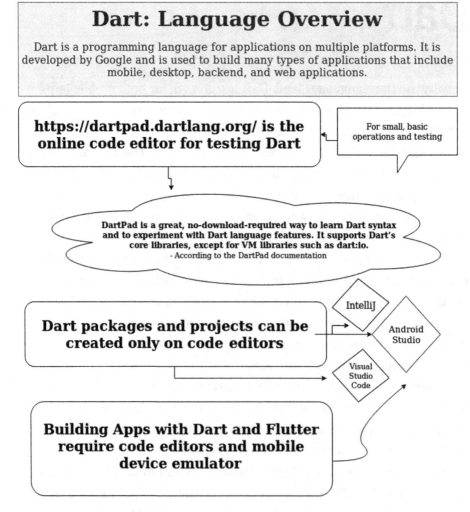

Figure 1-1. *The Dart language overview and how we can use code editors*

For small operations, you can use the online code editor at https://
dartpad.dartlang.org. However, for building packages and creating
projects, you need a code editor like Android Studio or IntelliJ IDEA
Community Edition. Visual Studio Code also has Dart language testing
support. But using Android Studio or IntelliJ IDEA Community Edition
is recommended. They make it easy to install the required plugins;
furthermore, if you want to build mobile applications using Dart and
Flutter, these tools are more useful.

Note   These code editors are known as *integrated development
environments* (IDEs). They have lots of features that make writing
code easy and efficient. In other words, they are designed to make
your coding life easier.

First, Dart is extremely productive. If you already know an object-
oriented programming language such as C++, C#, or Java, it will not take
you more than a few days to learn the Dart language. If you are an absolute
beginner, then it is good that you are starting to learn Dart as your first
programming language because it has a clear and concise syntax. It also
has rich and powerful core libraries and supports thousands of packages.
As an absolute beginner, you don't have to worry about the libraries right
now. You will learn to use them later in the book when the time comes.

Syntax-wise, Dart has similarities with C, C#, Python, Java, and
JavaScript (Figure 1-2).

Dart Language Features

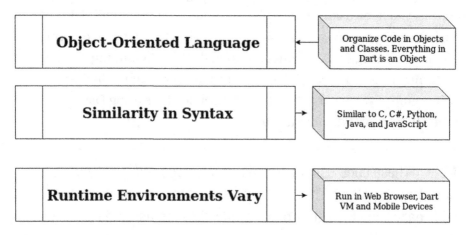

Figure 1-2. *Dart language features at a glance*

Dart is fast and furious, and the performance is high across mobile devices and the Web. In addition, its portability rate is extremely good. It compiles to ARM and x86 code so that Dart mobile apps can run on iOS and Android and beyond.

Beginners should note that there is a difference between ARM and X86 processors; the ARM processors follow a Reduced Instruction Set Computer (RISC) architecture, while x86 processors are Complex Instruction Set Architecture (CISC). Because of these features, x86 processors are considered to be faster than ARM processors.

In addition, for web apps, Dart has a close relationship with Flutter, which is implemented by using Dart code.

Using an IDE for Dart

You can use any good IDE; however, my choice is either IntelliJ IDEA Community Edition or Android Studio. Both are free and can be easily downloaded on Windows, Linux, and Mac.

For the code in this book, you will find IntelliJ IDEA Community Edition the easiest to use. It is designed for general development, whereas Android Studio is designed for mobile development. This means it's easy to start a simple Dart app in IntelliJ but not in Android Studio. In fact, Android Studio does not even have that option. It will allow you to create only a Flutter mobile app. If your goal is mobile development, I recommend you use IntelliJ to learn Dart from this book and then switch to Android Studio for your first Flutter app.

Tip   One work-around to this approach is to create a Dart app in IntelliJ IDEA Community Edition and then open it in Android Studio (with the Dart plugin installed). Android Studio will run the app no problem; it's creating one in the first place that is difficult. You will see I have taken this approach in the book.

There are two options for both IDEs, as Android Studio is basically a customized version of IntelliJ.

- Installing the IDE to test your code with the Dart SDK on your local system.

- Installing Flutter and the Dart plugin in any IDE. In this case, you don't need the Dart SDK on your operating system.

Installing either IDE in Windows is relatively easy. Download the .exe file from the official web site and double-click to launch it. This is the recommended way. You can also download the ZIP file and unpack it to the program files. You will find the bin folder where you can launch the respective .exe files. However, downloading the .exe file from the official web site and launching it online is recommended.

Installing an IDE on a Mac is not a complicated process. You need to launch the DMG file and then drag and drop the app into the Applications folder. After that, the launching process is easy; the setup wizard will guide you through the rest.

I recommend you use Linux as the main operating system; Android as a framework will always execute better on top of the Linux kernel, and it's likely you'll want to use Dart for Android development. Installing the Dart SDK in Linux is also easy.

Why do you need the Dart SDK? Well, it has the libraries and command-line tools that you need to develop all kinds of Dart applications—web, command-line, or server apps. To develop only mobile apps, you don't need the Dart SDK. The Flutter plugins in the IDE will work.

To install Dart on Linux, first open your terminal, and then you can issue the following commands:

```
//code 1.1
sudo apt-get update

sudo apt-get install apt-transport-https

 sudo sh -c 'curl https://dl-ssl.google.com/linux/linux_
 signing_key.pub | apt-key add -'

 sudo sh -c 'curl https://storage.googleapis.com/download.
 dartlang.org/linux/debian/dart_stable.list > /etc/apt/sources.
 list.d/dart_stable.list'
```

After that, install the stable release of the Dart SDK.

```
//code 1.2
sudo apt-get update

 sudo apt-get install dart
```

After that you can check your Dart version.

```
//code 1.3
$ dart --version
Dart VM version: 2.4.0 (Unknown timestamp) on "linux_x64"
```

The Dart SDK includes a lib directory for the Dart libraries that you will use in the IDE. In addition, the Dart SDK has a bin directory that has the command-line tools. It helps run the console inside your IDE, and you can also have the terminal output, if you want. For that, you can go to the project's bin folder and run the main.dart file.

Installing IntelliJ IDEA Community Edition

Installing IntelliJ IDEA Community Edition is easy. You can install it from the Ubuntu Software Center. Open the Software Center and type **IntelliJ Community Edition**. It will show up. Click the Install button (Figure 1-3).

***Figure 1-3.** Launching IntelliJ*

You can also install IntelliJ IDEA Community Edition through the command line on the terminal.

```
//code 1.4
sudo snap install intellij-idea-community –classic
```

The applications in the Ubuntu Software Center are snap packages; therefore, if you already have snap packages installed in your machine, you can install it through the terminal. After the primary installation is done, don't forget to install the Dart plugins, either from the Configure option at startup or from File ➤ Settings ➤ Plugins within the IDE (Figure 1-4).

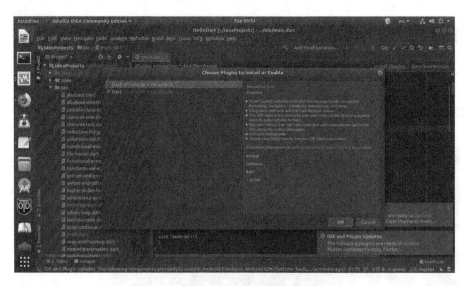

Figure 1-4. *Installing or enabling the Dart plugins*

Finally, IntelliJ IDEA Community Edition is ready for action. Figure 1-5 shows some projects from the book. You can keep your Dart files in the bin folder and run the program by pressing Shift+F10 or selecting Run ➤ Run from the menu bar. Most of the example code will print to the console at the bottom of the IDE.

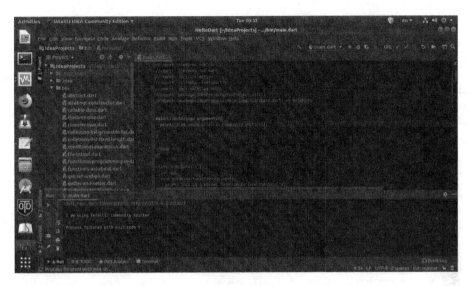

Figure 1-5. IntelliJ IDEA Community Edition and the console

Installing Android Studio

Installing Android Studio on Linux is quite simple and user friendly, though not as straightforward as installing IntelliJ IDEA Community Edition.

You don't have to issue any command-line instructions. Download the ZIP file and unpack it to either /usr/local/ or /opt/ for shared users. Now, navigate to the /android-studio/bin/ directory and execute the studio.sh file with the help of this command:

```
//code 1.5
./studio.sh
```

If it asks you to install the required libraries for 64-bit Linux machines, install them. If you are a first-time user of Android Studio, you can import the previous Android Studio settings or you can skip this by clicking the OK button.

The Android Studio wizard will guide you to set it up; remember, this setup includes downloading Android SDK components that are required for development; in the Configure option when you start the IDE, you can install the Flutter and Dart plugins (or select File ➤ Settings ➤ Plugins when the IDE is open).

Figure 1-6 displays Android Studio.

Figure 1-6. *The Android Studio IDE and the Dart files in the bin folder*

To get maximum use of Android Studio on a 64-bit Linux machine, say Ubuntu, you need to install some 32-bit libraries with the following command-line instructions. You can access these libraries through your project's lib folder. The bin folder consists of command-line tools, as I have mentioned earlier.

```
//code 1.6
sudo apt-get install libc6:i386 libncurses5:i386
libstdc++6:i386 lib32z1 libbz2-1.0:i386
```

The command will ask you for the root password. For the 64-bit Fedora, the command is different.

```
//code 1.7
sudo yum install zlib.i686 ncurses-libs.i686 bzip2-libs.i686
```

Now, you are ready to work in Android Studio.

Writing Some Dart Code

Let's look at our first Dart code. Put the following code into your main.dart file in your IDE. main() is the entry point, not only for Dart; if you build mobile apps using Flutter, you will find that in Flutter, this is the entry point as well.

```
//code 1.8
main() {
  print("Hello World!");
}
//output
Hello World!
```

In Android Studio or IntelliJ, you can press Shift+F10 to run the code.

Let's write some more console-based code to get a feel for Dart. At the same time, you will see the most basic syntax and how the commands work together.

```
//code 1.9
main() {
  print("Hello World!");
  //calling a function
  doSomething();
}
```

```
//define a function
doSomething(){
  print("Do something!")
  //calling a function inside another function
      lifeIsShort();
}
//defining another function
lifeIsShort(){
  print("Life is too short to do so many things.");
}
```

We have started our code with the top-level function main(); it is required and special in nature because this is how the application executes. So, inside the main() function, we have called a function doSomething(), which in turn calls the lifeIsShort() function.

Each function gives a display output with print(); this is a handy way to display any output. We have covered many things in our first program. Now run the code (Shift+F10).

You'll see there is a mistake in our code. It is an intended mistake so that you understand how debugging takes place in Dart.

Take a look at the output:

```
//output of code 1.9
bin/main.dart:12:24: Error: Expected ';' after this.
  print("Do something!")
```

We have forgotten to place a semicolon after displaying the output.

```
//code 1.10
//define a function
doSomething(){
  print("Do something!");
```

```
//calling a function inside another function
lifeIsShort();
}
```

Let's correct it and run the program again.

```
//output of code 1.10
Hello World!
Do something!
Life is too short to do so many things.
```

Now it is OK. You have learned many things with this first code; most important is that we can learn from our mistakes.

You should always be careful about syntax errors. Missing a semicolon or a dollar sign before a variable can be a big game-changer.

You have seen how we comment on our code with // characters, as shown here:

```
//calling a function inside another function
lifeIsShort();
```

Anything on that line is ignored when the program runs. Try to contribute as much comments as possible to make clear your viewpoint so that when another person reads your code, they will understand it and visualize it as you have visualized your code while writing it. The person who reads your code in six months may well be you, so be kind to your future self.

If you are a complete beginner, you may be at a loss to understand these explanations. You may feel puzzled about words such as *function, comment, output*, etc. Therefore, the next few sections are dedicated to beginners.

Variables, Operators, Conditionals, and Control Flow

In this section, we will discuss some initial key concepts of Dart that are absolutely necessary for beginners. First, like Python, Dart is an object-oriented programming language. Everything is an object here.

Consider a whole number like 2. In nature, it is an integer. In Dart, all integers are objects. Even functions and null are objects. I know, the term *object* may fill a beginner with bewilderment. We will discuss object-oriented programming at the right time. Before that, you will learn what variables, constants, and functions are.

Note   Briefly, null means that a data value does not exist. Since Dart considers every value type as an object, a null class has also been created to use that instance where no value is provided.

Variables Store References

Variables store references to objects. In other words, you may say, a variable is a spot in the memory or a container that contains some references to some values. As indicated by the name *variable*, the reference can change.

Like other programming languages, Dart has several types, such as integers, strings, Booleans, etc. Although Dart is strongly typed language, it also allows you to use duck typing, meaning that Dart can use a type as long as that type is suitable for that use ("If it walks like a duck and quacks like a duck, it is a duck").

Data types are types of data that we can represent in a programming language, such as an integer is a nonfractional numerical value like 1, 2, and so on. Later when needed, we can also manipulate these values in our program. For example, in a calculator we do lots of numerical operations such as additions, subtractions, etc. The default value of most data types is null. So, we need to mention what data type we are going to use.

We use variables to reference those types that are actually stored in memory. Consider the following:

```
int a = 1;
```

This means we first store the type of integer value 1 in our memory, and then we assign that value to the variable a. The equal sign (=) is the assignment operator in Dart, so it assigns values to variables. Later, we call a to grab 1 for any kind of mathematical operations.

In normal circumstances, in Dart, we mention what type we are going to use. If we use integers and strings, we write it like this:

```
//code 1.11
int myAge = 12;
String myName = "John Smith";
```

In the previous examples, we have explicitly declared the type that should be used. In the next example, we do the same thing, but implicitly.

Therefore, you can also write the same code in this way:

```
//code 1.12
var myAge = 12;
var myName = "John Smith";
```

Now, the question is, with a change of reference, does the type also change?

Please read on.

In the previous code snippets, variable myAge stores the value 12 and references it as an integer object. The same way, the myName variable stores the value John Smith and references it as a String object. The type of the myName variable is inferred to be string-specific, but you can change it. If you don't want a specific or restricted type, specify Object or dynamic type.

```
dynamic myName = "John Smith";
```

If you don't initialize a variable, the default value is set to be null. Let's consider the following code:

```
int myNumber;
```

Although it is an integer, it is not initialized. Therefore, the default value is Null. Let's run the code and take a look at the output.

```
//code 1.13
main() {
  print("Hello World!");
  int myNumber;
  print(myNumber);
}
```

The output is as expected:

```
Hello World!
null
```

Let's talk about the built-in types in Dart. So far you have seen some of the types, such as number and string. You have not seen the others.

Built-in Types in Dart

The Dart language has special support for the following types, and you can always follow the strongly typed or duck typed pattern to initialize them:

- Numbers

- Strings

- Booleans

- Lists (also known as arrays)

- Sets

- Maps

- Runes (for expressing Unicode characters in a string)

- Symbols

You can initialize an object of any of these special types using a literal. For example, Hello John Smith is a string literal, and false is a Boolean literal.

Consider this code:

```
//code 1.14
main() {
  String saySomething = "Hello John Smith";
  var isFalse = true;
  if(saySomething == null){
    print("It is ${isFalse}");
  }else print("It is not ${isFalse}");
}
```

Since the string variable is not null, the output should be as follows:

```
It is not true
```

Note   We use $\{\}$ to include the value of an expression in a string. In this case, it is the value of a variable converted to a string. Including the value of an expression in this way is called *string interpolation*. I'll cover that later in the chapter.

You will encounter the first four built-in types most often. You will learn how to use other built-in types as the situation demands.

Suppose You Don't Like Variables

Well, in some cases, you need the value to be constant. There are two techniques that you can follow when you don't intend to change the value of a variable.

- You can use const instead of var or a String, int, or bool type declaration.

- You can also use final; but remember, the final variable can be set only once.

So, there is a difference between these two keywords: const and final. We will come back to this topic when we discuss object-oriented programming. Note that an instance variable can be final but not const.

Consider this code:

```
//code 1.15
main() {
  const firstName = "Sanjib";
  final lastName = "Sinha";
  String firstName = "John";
  String lastName = "Sinha";
}
```

Look at the output full of errors:

```
//output
bin/main.dart:8:10: Error: 'firstName' is already declared in
this scope.
  String firstName = "John";
         ^^^^^^^^^
bin/main.dart:5:9: Context: Previous declaration of 'firstName'.
  const firstName = "Sanjib";
        ^^^^^^^^^
bin/main.dart:9:10: Error: 'lastName' is already declared in
this scope.
  String lastName = "Sinha";
         ^^^^^^^^
bin/main.dart:6:9: Context: Previous declaration of 'lastName'.
  final lastName = "Sinha";
```

When you want a variable to be a compile-time constant, use const; use final for an instance variable that you will never change.

As a quick review, we will first check the numbers. Then one after another, you will learn about string, Booleans, and other types.

Dart numbers are of two types: integers and decimals. You write them as int and double. Integers are numbers without decimal points. Examples are 1, 2, 22, etc. Doubles do have a decimal point like this: 1.5, 3.723, etc.

Playing with Number and Double

Both int and double types are subtypes of num. The num type includes basic operators such as +, -, /, and *; and they represent plus, minus, division, and multiplication, respectively. You can call them arithmetic operators. There is also modulo, that is, remainder, and the sign is %.

Let's see some interesting examples:

```
//code 1.16
main() {
  var one = int.parse('1');
  print(one);
  if(one.isOdd){
    print("It is an odd number.");
  } else print("It is an even number.");
}
```

We have converted a string into an integer, or number.

```
//output
1
It is an odd number.
```

We can also turn a string into a double number. Let's change the previous code a little bit.

```
//code 1.17
main() {
  var one = int.parse('1');
  var doubleToString = double.parse('23.564');
  print(one);
  print(doubleToString);
  if(one.isOdd && doubleToString.isFinite){
    print("The first number is an odd number and the second one
    is a double ${doubleToString} and a finite number.");
  } else print("It is an even number and the second one is not
  a double ${doubleToString} and a non-finite number.");
}
```

The output is quite expected. Both statements are true, so the relational operation gives this output:

```
//output
1
23.564
A first number is an odd number and the second one is a double
23.564 and a finite number.
```

We can do the reverse too. We are going to turn an integer to string here:

```
//code 1.18
main() {
  int myNUmber = 542;
  double myDouble = 3.42;
  String numberToString = myNUmber.toString();
  String doubleToString = myDouble.toString();
  if ((numberToString == '542' && myNUmber.isEven) &&
  (doubleToString == '3.42' && myDouble.isFinite)){
    print("Both have been converted from an even number
    ${myNUmber} and a finite double ${myDouble} to string. ");
  } else print("Number and double have not been converted to
  string.");
}
//output
```

Both have been converted from the even number 542 and the finite double 3.42 to a string.

As we progress, we will find that Dart is an extremely flexible language, and the syntax is simple to remember with lots of help from the core libraries.

Understanding Strings

A Dart string is a sequence of UTF-16 code units. For absolute beginners, I'll briefly describe UTF-8, UTF-16, and UTF-32. They all store Unicode but use different bytes. Let's first try to understand the advantages of using UTF-16 code over the other two. Let's learn about UTF-8.

In places where ASCII characters represent the majority of text, UTF-8 has an advantage. ASCII is meant for English only because it started in the United States. Later it spread all over the world, and other countries were eager to get strings to work on their languages. Like ASCII, UTF-8 encodes all characters into 8 bits.

Where ASCII is not predominant (in cultures where English is not predominant), UTF-16 has an advantage.

Using 2 bytes (16 bits) enables us to encode 65,536 distinct values. If you are serious about understanding encodings and character sets, please visit this link:

```
http://kunststube.net/encoding/
```

UTF-16 remains at just 2 bytes for most characters. However, UTF-32 tries to cover all possible characters in 4 bytes, which means that processors have extra load, making UTF-32 pretty bloated. Simply put, it is all about supporting as many languages as possible.

Unicode support makes Dart more powerful, and you can create your mobile and web applications in any language. Let's see one example where I have tried some Bengali script.

```
//code 1.19
main(List<String> arguments) {
  String bengaliString = "বাংলা লেখো";
  String englishString = "This is some English text.";
  print("Here is some Bengali script - ${bengaliString} and
  some English script ${englishString}");
}
```

```
Here is some Bengali script - বাংলা লেখো and some English script
This is some English text.
```

While handling strings, you should remember a few things. You can use both single quotes (") and double quotes ("").

```
//code 1.20
main(List<String> arguments) {
  String stringWithSingleQuote = 'I\'m a single quote';
  String stringWithDoubleQuote = "I'm a double quote.";
  print("Using delimiter in single quote -
  ${stringWithSingleQuote} and using delimiter in double
  quote - ${stringWithDoubleQuote}");
}
```

You can use the delimiter in both cases, but the double quote is more helpful in such cases. Look at the output:

```
//output of code 1.21
Using delimiter in the single quote - I'm a single quote and
using delimiter in the double quote - I'm a double quote
```

We have put the value of the expression inside a string by using our variable in this way: ${stringWithSingleQuote}. As noted earlier in the chapter, this is called *string interpolation*.

If you simply want to express the value of a variable, you do not have to use {}. You can use the variable in this way:

```
print("$stringWithSingleQuote");
print(stringWithSingleQuote);
```

String concatenation and even making it multiline is quite easy in Dart. Consider this code:

```
//code 1.22
main(List<String> arguments) {
  String stringInterpolation = 'string ' + 'concatenation';
  print(stringInterpolation);
  String multiLIneString = """
      This is
      a multi line
      string.
   """;
  print(multiLIneString);
}
```

You use the + operator for concatenation, meaning you join two strings together. Looking at the output here, we have used a triple quote with either single or double quotation marks:

```
//output
string concatenation
      This is
      a multi line
      string.
```

If you want to store some constant value inside a constant string, the value cannot be variables. Consider this code:

```
//code 1.23
main(List<String> arguments) {
  const aConstantInteger = 12;
  const aConstantBoolean = true;
  const aConstantString = "I am a constant string.";
```

```
  const aValidConstantString = "this is a constant integer:
  ${aConstantInteger}, a constant boolean: ${aConstantBoolean},
  a constant string: ${aConstantString}";
  print("This is a valid constant string and the output is:
  $aValidConstantString");
}
```

We have created a valid constant string by storing a constant value inside them. The output is perfectly OK.

```
//output
This is a valid constant string and the output is: this is a
constant integer: 12, a constant boolean: true, a constant
string: I am a constant string.
```

This will not work if you want to hold variable data inside a constant string. We have changed the previous code listing to this:

```
//code 1.24
main(List<String> arguments) {
  var aConstantInteger = 12;
  var aConstantBoolean = true;
  var aConstantString = "I am a constant string.";
  const aValidConstantString = "this is a constant integer:
  ${aConstantInteger}, a constant boolean: ${aConstantBoolean},
  a constant string: ${aConstantString}";
  print("This is a valid constant string and the output is:
  $aValidConstantString");
}
```

Here is the output, which is full of errors:

```
//output
```

```
bin/main.dart:9:63: Error: Not a constant expression.
  const aValidConstantString = "this is a constant integer:
  ${aConstantInteger}, a constant boolean: ${aConstantBoolean},
  a constant string: ${aConstantString}";
                                           ^^^^^^^^^^^^^^^^
bin/main.dart:9:104: Error: Not a constant expression.
  const aValidConstantString = "this is a constant integer:
  ${aConstantInteger}, a constant boolean: ${aConstantBoolean},
  a constant string: ${aConstantString}";
                                           ^^^^^^^^^^^^^^^^
bin/main.dart:9:144: Error: Not a constant expression.
  const aValidConstantString = "this is a constant integer:
  ${aConstantInteger}, a constant boolean: ${aConstantBoolean},
  a constant string: ${aConstantString}";
```

It did not work. As we progress, you will learn more about strings. Understanding them is important in the context of making mobile and web applications.

In the next section, you will learn about Booleans, which also play a vital role in building algorithms.

To Be True or to Be False

You have already seen that Dart has a type called bool. The Boolean literals true and false have the type bool. They are compile-time constants.

This is an extremely important concept in computer science because you can use control structures to alter the flow of your program that depends on whether a statement is true or false. We will cover this in Chapter 2.

Introduction to Collections: Arrays Are Lists in Dart

An *array*, or an ordered group of objects, is the most common collection in every programming language. In Dart, arrays are List objects. We will call them *lists* in our future discussions.

Dart is designed to compile to JavaScript to run across the modern Web; therefore, if you have a working knowledge of JavaScript, you will find some similarities in this type of collection.

Here is some sample code to consider so you can understand why this concept is important:

```
//code 1.25
main(List<String> arguments) {
  List fruitCollection = ['Mango', 'Apple', 'Jack fruit'];
  print(fruitCollection[0]);
}
```

Consider another piece of code:

```
//code 2.15
main(List<String> arguments) {
  List fruitCollection = ['Mango', 'Apple', 'Jack fruit'];
  var myIntegers = [1, 2, 3];
  print(myIntegers[2]);
  print(fruitCollection[0]);
}
```

What is the difference between these two code snippets? In code 2.14, we have explicitly mentioned that we are going to declare a collection of fruits. And we can pick any item from that collection using the key. In an array, the key is not mentioned in the definition; it is automatically inferred that the key starts from 0. Therefore, the output of code 2.14 is Mango. In the second instance, we do not have any explicit declaration about the type of the myIntegers list. We have written this:

```
var myIntegers = [1, 2, 3];
```

However, Dart infers that the list has type List<int>. Let's see the output of code 2.15:

```
//output
3
Mango
```

If we try to inject noninteger objects to the myInteger list, what happens?

```
//code 2.17
main(List<String> arguments) {
  List fruitCollection = ['Mango', 'Apple', 'Jack fruit'];
  var myIntegers = [1, 2, 3, 'non-integer object'];
  print(myIntegers[3]);
  print(fruitCollection[0]);
}
```

This did not raise any error. See the output, shown here:

```
//output of code 2.17
non-integer object
Mango
```

However, remember that Dart lists use zero-based indexing like all the other collections you may have seen in other programming languages. Just think of a list as a key-value pair, where 0 is the index of the first value or element. As we progress, we will discuss lists because there are other useful methods that we will use when we build our first mobile application. Dart lists have many handy methods.

Get, Set, Go

In Dart, a Set is an unordered collection of unique items. There are small differences in syntax between List and Set.

Let's look at an example first to know more about the differences.

```
//code 1.26
main(List<String> arguments) {
  var fruitCollection = {'Mango', 'Apple', 'Jack fruit'};
  print(fruitCollection.lookup('Apple'));
}
//output
Apple
```

We can search a set using the lookup() method. If we search for something else, it returns null.

```
//code 1.27
main(List<String> arguments) {
  var fruitCollection = {'Mango', 'Apple', 'Jack fruit'};
  print(fruitCollection.lookup('Something Else'));
}
//output
null
```

When we write the following, it does not create a Set, but a Map:

```
var myInteger = {};
```

The syntax for map literals is similar to that for set literals. Why is this? Because map literals came first. The literal {} is a default to the Map type. We can prove this by using this simple test:

```
//code 1.28
main(List<String> arguments) {
  var myInteger = {};
```

```
  if(myInteger.isEmpty){
    print("It is a map that has no key, value pair.");
  } else print("It is a set that has no key, value pair.");
}
```

Look at the output:

```
//output of code 2.20
```

This is a map that has no key-value pair. It means the map is empty. If it were a set, we would have gotten the output in that direction. We will see lots of examples of sets in the future, while we build our mobile application. For now, just remember that, in general, a map is an object that associates keys with values. The set has also keys, but they are implicit. In cases of sets, we call them *indexes*.

Let's see one example of the Map type by mapping literals. While writing keys and values, it is important to note that each key occurs only once, but you can use the same value many times.

```
//code 1.29
main(List<String> arguments) {
  var myProducts = {
    'first' : 'TV',
    'second' : 'Refrigerator',
    'third' : 'Mobile',
    'fourth' : 'Tablet',
    'fifth' : 'Computer'
  };
  print(myProducts['third']);
}
```

The output is obvious, as shown here:

```
'Mobile'
```

Dart understands that myProducts has the type Map<String, String>(Map<Key, Value>); we could have made the key integers or numbers, instead of a string type.

```
//code 1.30
main(List<String> arguments) {
  var myProducts = {
    1 : 'TV',
    2 : 'Refrigerator',
    3 : 'Mobile',
    4 : 'Tablet',
    5 : 'Computer'
  };
  print(myProducts[3]);
}
```

The output is the same as before: mobile.

Can we add a Set type collection of values inside a Map? Yes, we can. Consider this code:

```
//code 1.31
main(List<String> arguments) {
  Set mySet = {1, 2, 3};
  var myProducts = {
    1 : 'TV',
    2 : 'Refrigerator',
    3 : mySet.lookup(2),
    4 : 'Tablet',
    5 : 'Computer'
  };
  print(myProducts[3]);
}
```

In the previous code, we injected a collection of the Set type, and we also looked up the defining value through the Map key. Here, inside the Map key-value pair, we have added the set element number 2 in this way: 3 : mySet.lookup(2). Later we tell our Android Studio editor to display the value of the Map type myProducts.

The output is quite expected: 2.

You can create the same products list by using the Map constructor. For beginners, the term *constructor* might seem difficult. We will discuss this term in detail in Chapter 7. Consider this code:

```
//code 1.32
main(List<String> arguments) {
  var myProducts = Map();
  myProducts['first'] ='TV';
  myProducts['second'] ='Mobile';
  myProducts['third'] ='Refrigerator';
  if(myProducts.containsValue('Mobile')){
    print("Our products list has ${myProducts['second']}");
  }
}
```

Here is the output:

```
//output
Our products list has Mobile
```

Since we have an instance in code 1.32 of the Map class, a seasoned programmer might have expected new Map() instead of only Map().

As of Dart 2, the new keyword is optional. You will learn about it in detail in Chapter 7.

You will also learn more about collections in Chapter 7, where you will learn more about List, Set, and Map.

Operators Are Useful

Simply put, programming is about processing variables. This processing might be to perform a mathematical calculation or to concatenate two strings, for example. For that purpose we need operators. The simplicity of Dart is the + operator adds two integer operands (variables) and produces a result. At the same time, we may use the + operator to concatenate two strings (as shown in code 1.22).

In Dart, when you use operators, you actually create expressions.

Here are some examples of expressions: a++, a + b, a ∗ b, a/b, a~/b, a%b, and so on.

There are many types of operators in Dart. Even absolute beginners probably have heard of arithmetic operators. Relational operators are extremely useful for the control structures.

We will take a look at them one after another.

The usual arithmetic operators are - add (+), subtract (-), multiply (∗), divide (/), and modulo or remainder (%); a special operator, divide, returning an integer looks like this: ~/.

Let's see one example:

```
//code 1.33
main(List<String> arguments) {
  int aNum = 12;
  double aDouble = 2.25;
  var theResult = aNum ~/ aDouble;
  print(theResult);
}
//output
5
```

Note this special operator has displayed an integer, not a double. However, if we had divided it in a plain fashion, it would look like this:

```
//code 1.34
main(List<String> arguments) {
  int aNum = 12;
  double aDouble = 2.25;
  var theResult = aNum / aDouble;
  print(theResult);
}
```

Here is the output:

```
//output of code 2.26
5.333333333333333
```

One key feature of Dart is that it supports both prefix and postfix increment and decrement operators.

Here, a prefix means ++variable or --variable. These either add 1 or subtract 1 from the variable value, respectively. The postfix does the same; only the syntax changes, like this: variable++ or variable--.

Let's see an example:

```
//code 1.35
main(List<String> arguments) {
  int aNum = 12;
  aNum++;
  ++aNum;
  int anotherNum = aNum + 1;
  print(anotherNum);
}
```

The output is as expected: 15. Both prefix and postfix work in the case of -- also.

Relational Operators

Relational operators are also called *equality operators* because == means "equal," and other relational operators usually check for equality in various forms.

Let's consider some code snippets that will show us many types of relational operators in one glance.

```
//code 1.36
main(List<String> arguments) {
  int firstNum = 40;
  int secondNum = 41;
  if (firstNum != secondNum){
    print("$firstNum is not equal to the $secondNum");
  } else print("$firstNum is equal to the $secondNum");
}
//output
40 is not equal to the 41
```

In the previous code, the != operator stands for "not equal." It comes out true if the operands are not equal. So, we're saying "If firstNum does not equal secondNum, execute the code between {}. Otherwise, execute the code after the else."

Let's change this code a little bit:

```
//code 1.37
main(List<String> arguments) {
  int firstNum = 40;
  int secondNum = 40;
  if (firstNum == secondNum){
    print("$firstNum is equal to the $secondNum");
  } else print("$firstNum is not equal to the $secondNum");
}
```

Here we're saying "If firstNum equals secondNum, execute the code between {}. Otherwise, execute the code after the else." Let's add some more logic to our code, as shown here:

```
//code 1.38
main(List<String> arguments) {
  int firstNum = 40;
  int secondNum = 40;
  int thirdNum = 74;
  int fourthNum = 56;
  if (firstNum == secondNum || thirdNum == fourthNum){
    print("If choice between 'true' or 'false', the 'true' gets
    the precedence.");
  } else print("If choice between 'true' or 'false', the
  'false' gets the precedence.");
}
//output
If choice between 'true' or 'false', the 'true' gets the
precedence.
```

This time we're saying "If firstNum equals secondNum OR if thirdNum equals fourthNum, execute the code between {}. Otherwise, execute the code after the else." We use the OR (||) operator to implement this logic. So if one side of the OR operator is true, the whole statement is true.

This is not the case for the AND (&&) relational operator. Look at this code:

```
//code 1.39
main(List<String> arguments) {
  int firstNum = 40;
  int secondNum = 40;
  int thirdNum = 74;
  int fourthNum = 56;
```

```
if (firstNum == secondNum && thirdNum == fourthNum){
  print("If choice between 'true' or 'false', in this case
  the 'true' gets the precedence.");
} else print("If choice between 'true' or 'false', in this
case the 'false' gets the precedence.");
}

//output
If choice between 'true' or 'false', in this case the 'false'
gets the precedence.
```

We have used the && relational operator, and here the expression is false because both sides have to be true in the case of the AND operator. The ! sign has many roles. Consider this code snippet:

```
//code 1.40
main(List<String> arguments) {
  int aNUmber = 35;
  if(!(aNUmber != 150) && aNUmber <= 150){
    print("It's true");
  } else print("It's false.");
}
```

Can you guess what the output would be? The first statement is false because we have negated a true statement by using the ! sign.

```
!(aNUmber != 150)
```

The second statement is true; the value is less than or equal to 150.

```
aNUmber <= 150
```

Since the logical operator is AND (&&) here, the whole expression will be false.

```
!(aNUmber != 150) && aNUmber <= 150
```

Had we used the OR (||) logical operator, the output would have come out as true.

Just to remind you, the >= operator means greater than or equal to. It is > for greater than, or it is < for less than. Take some time to play around your logical or relational operators because this is one of the main pillars of computer science.

Type Test Operators

The as, is, and is! operators are handy for checking types at runtime.

Consider this code:

```
//code 1.41
main(List<String> arguments) {
  int myNumber = 13;
  bool isTrue = true;
  print(myNumber is int);
  print(myNumber is! int);
  print(myNumber is! bool);
  print(myNumber is bool);
}
```

The first one is true, the second one is false, and so on.

```
//output
true
false
true
false
```

Assignment Operators

While assigning a value, we use the = operator. What happens when the assigned-to variable is null? We use a special type of operator: - ??=.

Consider this code:

```
//code 1.42
main(List<String> arguments) {
  int firstNum = 10;
  int secondNum;
  if(firstNum == 10) print("The value of ${firstNum} is set.");
  if (secondNum == null) print("It is true.");
  secondNum ??= firstNum;
  print(secondNum);
}
```

Now look at the output:

```
//output
The value of 10 is set.
It is true.
10
```

In code 1.42, we have assigned the value of firstNum to 10, and the type is an integer. So, we can say, the value of firstNum is set. At the same time, we have not assigned any value to secondNum, so by default, it is null. After that, we assign the integer to the variable that held null by this special operator: ??=.

Almost the same thing happens in the case of compound assignment operators. Now we are going to write the previous code in this way:

```
//code 1.43
main(List<String> arguments) {
  int firstNum = 10;
```

```
  int secondNum;
  if(firstNum == 10) print("The value of ${firstNum} is set.");
  if (secondNum == null) print("It is true.");
  secondNum ??= firstNum;
  print(secondNum);
  print("After using an assignment operator, the value changes.");
  secondNum += secondNum;
  print(secondNum);
  print("After using an assignment operator, the value changes
  again.");
  secondNum -= secondNum;
  print(secondNum);
  if (secondNum == null) print("It is true.");
  else print("it is false, because the 'secondNUm' has the
  value of ${secondNum} now.");
}
```

Look at this output where it is evident that we have changed the value of secondNum consecutively:

```
//output
The value of 10 is set.
It is true.
10

After using an assignment operator, the value changes.
20

After using an assignment operator, the value changes again.
0

it is false, because the 'secondNUm' has the value of 0 now.
```

As we progress, you will see more examples of operators.

Summary

Numbers, strings, and Booleans—they are all literals in Dart. Consider these literals: 1, 2.3, "Some Strings", true, false.

We need to remember a few things, such as the following:

var isValid = true;

- var is the data type.

- isValid is the variable name (or spot in memory).

- true is a literal.

You can mention the data type of a variable as int, double, String, or bool. If you don't, you can simply refer to them as var. In that case, when it's not mentioned, the data type is inferred.

String interpolation is a good practice. Don't use the + sign to add two strings.

Use an expression for operators, such as ${number1 + number2}.

What will be your choice? final or const? It is a difficult choice. You need to remember a few things: when you choose final, it is initialized, and when it is accessed, the memory is allocated for it. The const is implicitly final; this means when it is compiled, it is initialized, and the memory is allocated for it.

CHAPTER 2

Flow Control and Looping

Controlling the flow of your code is important. Programmers want to control the logic of their code for many reasons; one of the main reasons is that the user of the software should have many options open to them.

You may not know the conditions beforehand, in which way your programming logic should move, though. You can only guess, so as a developer, you should open as many avenues for the user as possible. There are several techniques you can adopt to control the flow of the code. For example, the if-else logic is popular.

if-else

Let's look at a simple example of controlling the flow of the code. After that, we will delve deep into the logical consequences of this approach. An if can be followed by else if the Boolean statement tested by the if block comes out as false.

```
if(it is true){
The program executes
}
Else {
This block will not execute then
}
```

© Sanjib Sinha 2020
S. Sinha, *Quick Start Guide to Dart Programming*,
https://doi.org/10.1007/978-1-4842-5562-9_2

Just the opposite happens when the expression tested by if is false.

```
if(it is false){
The program will not execute
}
Else {
This block will execute then
}
```

In programming, this testing mechanism depends on a variety of relationships. In the previous chapter, you saw some of them. You will see more here.

```
//code 2.1main(List<String> arguments) {
  bool firstButtonTouch = true;
  bool secondButtonTouch = false;
  bool thirdButtonTouch = true;
  bool fourthButtonTouch = false;

  if(firstButtonTouch) print("The giant starts running.");
  else print("To stop the giant please touch the second button.");

  if(secondButtonTouch) print("The giant stops.");
  else print("You have not touched the second button.");

  print("Touch any button to start the game.");

  if(thirdButtonTouch) print("The giant goes to sleep.");
  else print("You have not touched any button.");

  if(fourthButtonTouch) print("The giant wakes up.");
  else print("You have not touched any button.");
}
```

```
//output of code 21
The giant starts running.
You have not touched the second button.
Touch any button to start the game.
The giant goes to sleep.
You have not touched any button.
```

Now you can make this small code snippet more complicated, as shown here:

```
//code 2.2
main(List<String> arguments) {
  bool firstButtonTouch = true;
  var firstButtonUntouch;
  bool secondButtonTouch = false;
  bool thirdButtonTouch = true;
  bool fourthButtonTouch = false;
  firstButtonUntouch ??= firstButtonTouch;
  firstButtonUntouch = false;

  if (firstButtonUntouch == false || firstButtonTouch == true)
  print("The giant is sleeping.");
  else print("You need to wake up the giant. Touch the first
  button.");

  if(firstButtonTouch == true && firstButtonUntouch == false)
  print("The giant starts running.");
  print("To stop the giant please touch the second button.");

  if((secondButtonTouch == true && thirdButtonTouch == true)
  || fourthButtonTouch == false) print("The giant stops.");
  else print("You have not touched the second button.");

  print("Touch any button to start the game.");
```

```
if(thirdButtonTouch) print("The giant goes to sleep.");
else print("You have not touched any button.");

if(fourthButtonTouch) print("The giant wakes up.");
else print("You have not touched any button.");
}
```

Your output will vary, as shown here:

```
//output of code 2.2
The giant is sleeping.
The giant starts running.
To stop the giant please touch the second button.
The giant stops.
Touch any button to start the game.
The giant goes to sleep.
You have not touched any button.
```

For if-else logic, always remember the following golden rules. These are for the AND condition:

1. When both conditions are true, the result is true.

    ```
    statementOne = TRUE;
    statementTwo = TRUE;
    if(statementOne and statementTwo){
       the statement will execute, as it stands for TRUE
    }
    ```

2. When both conditions are false, the result is false.

    ```
    statementOne = FALSE;
    statementTwo = FALSE;
    if(statementOne and statementTwo){
       the statement will not execute, as it stands for FALSE
    }
    ```

3.   When one condition is true and the other condition
     is false, the result is `false`.

```
statementOne = TRUE;
statementTwo = FALSE;
if(statementOne and statementTwo){
   the statement will not execute, as it stands for FALSE
}
```

Now here are the rules for the OR condition:

1.   When one condition is true or one condition is false,
     the result is `true`.

```
statementOne = TRUE;
statementTwo = FALSE;
if(statementOne or statementTwo){
   the statement will execute, as it stands for TRUE
}
```

2.   When both conditions are false, the result is `false`.

```
statementOne = FALSE;
statementTwo = FALSE;
if(statementOne or statementTwo){
   the statement will not execute, as it stands for
   FALSE
}
```

You should now have an idea of how you can use `if-else` logic when you need it. It can become complex when you start adding relational operators.

Finally, before leaving this section, I will show you another code snippet where the existing set of rules or principles has been changed. Rearranging the order of the AND and OR logic will give you an idea of how the output can change.

```
//code 2.3
main(List<String> arguments) {
  bool firstButtonTouch = true;
  var firstButtonUntouch;
  bool secondButtonTouch = false;
  bool thirdButtonTouch = true;
  bool fourthButtonTouch = false;
  firstButtonUntouch ??= firstButtonTouch;
  firstButtonUntouch = false;

  if (firstButtonUntouch == false || firstButtonTouch == true)
  print("The giant is sleeping.");
  else if (thirdButtonTouch) print("You need to wake up the
  giant. Touch the first button.");
  else if(firstButtonTouch == true && firstButtonUntouch ==
  false) print("The giant starts running.");
  else if (secondButtonTouch) print("To stop the giant please
  touch the second button.");
  else if((secondButtonTouch == true && thirdButtonTouch
  == true) || fourthButtonTouch == false) print("The giant
  stops.");
  else if (thirdButtonTouch) print("You have not touched the
  second button.");
  else if (secondButtonTouch) print("Touch any button to start
  the game.");
  else if(thirdButtonTouch) print("The giant goes to sleep.");
  else if (firstButtonUntouch) print("You have not touched any
  button.");

  if(fourthButtonTouch) print("The giant wakes up.");
  else print("You have not touched any button.");
}
```

Here is the output of the previous code:

```
The giant is sleeping.
You have not touched any button.
You can change the pattern and see what happens.
```

Let's consider the first line of code, shown here:

```
if (firstButtonUntouch == false || firstButtonTouch == true)
print("The giant is sleeping.");
```

firstButtonUntouch was initially NULL. After that we used the special ??= operator and assigned its value to firstButtonTouch, which was initially true. Therefore, firstButtonUntouch is now true. Now the set of axioms between false or true? It comes out true. And we have the output.

Conditional Expressions

Dart has two conditional expressions that can replace the if-else clause when testing small expressions. Consider this code:

```
//condition? exp1 : exp2;
int num1 = 20;
int num2 = 30;
int smallerNumber = num1 < num2? num1 : num2;
// it is expected that num1 will always be smaller
```

Here we compare num1 to num2. If num1 is smaller (num1 < num2 is true), we assign num1 to the variable. If num1 < num2 is false, we assign num2. The general form is as follows, where expression1 is returned if condition is true and expression2 is returned if condition is false:

```
condition? expression1 : expression2
```

The other form deals with `nulls`.

```
int smallNumber = num1 ?? num2";
```

If num1 is not null, we assign it to smallNumber. If it is null, we assign num2 to smallNumber.

Looking at Looping

In computer programming, when we need to repeat a given section of code a certain number of times until a particular condition is met, we use a *loop*. This is a control structure that is repeated until a certain condition is met.

for Loop

The general syntax of the for loop looks like this:

```
for(var x = 0; x <= 10; x++){
    //iteration from 0 to 10 happens in between
}
```

In the previous code, the value of x starts at 0. Then we test if the loop is going to execute (x <= 10;). If that expression returns true, the loop executes, and we carry out the last instruction in the for clause (x++), adding 1 to x. The for loop then tests to see whether it should run again; if it does, then x++ runs again too. This continues until x <= 10 returns false.

The for loop is necessary for iterating any collections of data. Here is a typical example of the for loop:

```
//code 2.4
main(List<String> arguments) {
    var proverb = StringBuffer('As Dark as a Dungeon.');
```

```dart
for(var x = 0; x <= 10; x++){
    proverb.write("!");
    print(proverb);
  }
}
```

In the previous code, we used two built-in functions.

They are `StringBuffer()` and `write()`. We get these from Dart libraries.

The output is as follows:

```
//output of code 2.4
As Dark as a Dungeon.!
As Dark as a Dungeon.!!
As Dark as a Dungeon.!!!
As Dark as a Dungeon.!!!!
As Dark as a Dungeon.!!!!!
As Dark as a Dungeon.!!!!!!
As Dark as a Dungeon.!!!!!!!
As Dark as a Dungeon.!!!!!!!!
As Dark as a Dungeon.!!!!!!!!!
As Dark as a Dungeon.!!!!!!!!!!
As Dark as a Dungeon.!!!!!!!!!!!
```

In our future discussions, we will use the `for` loop quite extensively, so currently, let's stop here. You should understand the concept of why the exclamatory sign has increased from 0 to 10. It stops when the certain condition (here x=10) is met.

I am now going to cover an interesting feature of iterating collections, namely, using `Set` and `Map`. When the object you are going to iterate is `Iterable`, you can use the `forEach()` method. We are about to present two sets of collections; one is `Set`, and the other is `Map`.

```
//code 2.5
main(List<String> arguments) {
  Set mySet = {1, 2, 3};
  var myProducts = {
    1 : 'TV',
    2 : 'Refrigerator',
    3 : mySet.lookup(2),
    4 : 'Tablet',
    5 : 'Computer'
  };
  var userCollection = {"name": "John Smith", 'Email':
  'john@sanjib.site'};

  myProducts.forEach((x, y) => print("${x} : ${y}"));
  userCollection.forEach((k,v) => print('${k}: ${v}'));
}
```

As you see in the previous code, there are two sets, `myProducts` and `userCollection`. In both sets, a key=>value pair is declared. In the first case, 1 is key, and TV is the value. Now, Dart has a built-in `forEach(key:value)` method that can be used to give the output. In the first instance, x is the key, and y represents the value. After that, we use string interpolation to give the output.

Here is the output:

```
//output of code 2.5
1 : TV
2 : Refrigerator
3 : 2
4 : Tablet
5 : Computer
name: John Smith
Email: john@sanjib.site
```

When you do not know the current iteration counter, the forEach() method is a good option. In usual cases, Iterable classes, such as List and Set, also support the for() loop form of iteration.

Consider this code:

```
//code 2.6
main(List<String> arguments) {
  var myCollection = [1, 2, 3, 4];

  for(var x in myCollection){
    print("${x}");
  }
}
```

Here is the output:

```
//output of code 2.6
1
2
3
4
```

while and do-while

On a given Boolean condition, the while loop controls the flow and repeatedly executes the value. It loops through a block of code, as long as the specified condition is true.

Consider this simple example to understand the structure:

```
while (condition) {
  // code block to be executed
}
```

Here's a simple example that prints out from 0 to 10:

```
int x = 0;
while (x <= 10) {
  print("The output: ${x}");
  x++;
}
```

I hope you can see the similarity between the for and while loops. The syntactical structure is just different.

Be careful about handling the while loop. Since a while loop evaluates the condition before the loop, you must know how to stop the loop at the right time before it enters into infinity.

```
//code 2.7
main(List<String> arguments) {
  var num = 5;
  var factorial = 1;
  print("The value of the variable 'num' is decreasing this
  way:");

  while(num >=1) {
    factorial = factorial * num;
    num--;
    print("'=>' ${num}");
  }
  print("The factorial  is ${factorial}");
}
```

In the previous code, before the loop begins, the while loop evaluates the condition. Since the value of the variable num is 5 and it is greater than or equal to 1, the condition is true. So, the loop begins. As the loop begins, we have also kept reducing the value of the variable num; otherwise, it would have entered into an infinite loop.

The value of the variable reduces this way:

```
//output of code 2.8
The value of the variable 'num' is decreasing this way:
'=>' 4
'=>' 3
'=>' 2
'=>' 1
'=>' 0
The factorial is 120
```

In the case of a do-while loop, it evaluates the condition after the loop.

```
//code 2.9
main(List<String> arguments) {
  var num = 5;
  var factorial = 1;

  do {
    factorial = factorial * num;
    num--;
    print("The value of the variable 'num' is decreasing to :
    ${num}");
    print("The factorial  is ${factorial}");
  }
  while(num >=1);
}
```

We have slightly changed the code snippet so that it will show the reducing value of the variable, and at the same time it will show you how the value of the factorial increases.

```
//output of code 2.10
The value of the variable 'num' is decreasing to : 4
The factorial  is 5
```

```
The value of the variable 'num' is decreasing to : 3
The factorial  is 20
The value of the variable 'num' is decreasing to : 2
The factorial  is 60
The value of the variable 'num' is decreasing to : 1
The factorial  is 120
The value of the variable 'num' is decreasing to : 0
The factorial  is 120
```

Once you understand the pattern of loops, you can easily choose between for, while, and do-while. Let's look at that now.

Patterns in Looping

I have met many students who feel confused about the while loop. I cover the looping structure in this section so that you can understand it.

People often do not know that a for loop can also turn into an infinite loop if it is not handled properly.

Actually, some concepts of loops are the same for every loop, be it for, while, or do-while. There are three things to remember.

- Counter variable

- Condition checking

- According to the condition, increment or decrement

Let's consider the code snippet:

```
void forLoopFunction(){
  for(var i = 0; i <= 5; i ++){
    print(i);
  }
}
```

```
void whileLoopFunction (){
  var i = 0;
  while(i <= 5){
    print(i);
    i++;
  }
}
// in doWhileLoop the execution part comes before the specified
condition. The concept is same.
void doWhileLoopFunction (){
  var i = 0;
  do{
    print(i);
    i++;
  } while(i <= 5);
}

main(){
  //print(smallerNumber);
  //print(smallNumber);
  forLoopFunction();
  print("");
  whileLoopFunction();
  print("");
  doWhileLoopFunction();
}
```

Here is the output:

```
0
1
2
3
```

4

5

0

1

2

3

4

5

0

1

2

3

4

5

Let's consider the for loop first.

```
for(var i = 0; i <= 5; i ++){
  print(i);
}
```

We have started with the counter variable, here i = 0. Then we have checked the condition, as shown here:

```
i <= 5
```

After the second step, we have incremented the value: i++.

The steps are quite logical. We could not have decremented the value. It would have taken us to an infinite loop because after starting at 0, the value of i would decrease, and the specified condition would remain true forever. If we had decremented the value of i, by writing i--, the condition checking would have never stopped until our computer's memory permitted. A hang or freeze occurs when the program ceases to respond to code.

Now we have done the same thing in the while loop. The steps are just a little bit different.

```
var i = 0;
while(i <= 5){
  print(i);
  i++;
}
```

In the previous code, the counter variable comes before the while loop starts. The while loop starts with the condition checking, as shown here:

```
i <= 5
```

We saw the same thing in the second step of the for loop. After that, according to the condition, we incremented the value of i inside the while loop. Once the value of i equals 6, it immediately stops responding to the inputs. It gives output from 0 to 5.

Now let's look at the do-while loop code. We start with the counter variable, and then we increment or decrement the value.

```
var i = 0;
do{
  print(i);
  i++;
} while(i <= 5);
```

In the last stage, we check the condition inside the while loop.

You may ask which loop is better. Actually, it depends on the context. In some situations, the for loop is enough. In fact, in most cases, we can manage with the for loop. If we want to know how many times a given number can be divided by 2 before it is less than or equal to 1, the while loop is better to use.

for Loop Labels

In some situations, we use nested for loops. Inside a for loop, we can run another for loop; and in many cases, this is essential. In Dart, there is a concept called a *label* that allows us to handle the outer loop and the inner loop separately. With the help of continue and break, we can jump to labels. Let's look at the code first; after that, I will explain what is happening:

```dart
void labelsLoop (){
  outerloop: for(var x = 1; x <= 3; x++){
    print("One cycle of outerloop with $x starts and the whole
    innerloop runs.");

    innerloop: for(var y = 1; y <= 3; y++){
      if(x == 1 && y == 1){
        print("Since outerloop $x and innerloop $y both are 1,
        it gives no output.");
        break innerloop;
      }
      print(y);
    }

    print("One cycle of outerloop ends with $x");
  }
}
main(List<String> arguments){
  labelsLoop();
}
```

If you look at the output shown here, you can understand how it works:

```
One cycle of the outer loop with 1 starts and the whole inner
loop runs.
Since outer loop 1 and inner loop 1 both are 1, it gives no
output.
```

```
One cycle of the outer loop ends with 1
One cycle of the outer loop with 2 starts and the whole inner
loop runs.
1
2
3
One cycle of the outer loop ends with 2
One cycle of the outer loop with 3 starts and the whole inner
loop runs.
1
2
3
One cycle of the outer loop ends with 3
```

We can also use break in normal cases, without a label.

Consider this code:

```
void main() {
  for (var j = 0; j < 5; j++) {
        if (j > 3 ) break ;
    print(j);
  }
}
```

Here is the output:

```
0
1
2
3
```

As you see in the previous code, where we have used labels, the counter variable, condition checking, and increment parts are the same in both the outer loop and the inner loop. So when the outer loop starts with 1, the inner loop inside the outer loop also starts with 1, and it should have completed the whole cycle. But we have injected an if statement and told the program that when the value of the outer loop and the inner loop both are 1, break the inner loop. We have used the labels outerloop and innerloop to demarcate the loops. Using the if statement, that particular cycle of innerloop could not complete the whole cycle. However, after that, it goes on as usual.

A label is a distinctive concept of Dart.

Continue with the for Loop

You have just seen how we have explicitly broken the inner loop and stopped one cycle of the inner loop. So, break is an important concept while using the for loop. At the same time, the continue keyword also plays a key role in the for loop.

Let's consider this code snippet:

```
void loopContinue(){
  for(var num = 1; num <= 5; num++){
    if(num % 2 == 0 ){
      print("These are all even numbers. $num");
      continue;
    } print("These are all odd numbers. $num");
  }
}
main(List<String> arguments){
  loopContinue();
}
```

Take a look at the output, and you will understand how the keyword continue works. It takes us out of the current loop to the start of the next one.

Currently there are no security rules relating to this application. You need to create the rules and publish them to the webserver called vNICS (see Figure 3-18).

Figure 3-18. *DFW rules created using NSX*

This simple rule will block all traffic from Webserver-1 to Webserver-2. The Source field contains the IP address of Webserver-1 and the Destination field contains the IP address of Webserver -2 (see Figure 3-19).

```
root@web-01a [ ~ ]# ping 172.16.10.12
PING 172.16.10.12 (172.16.10.12) 56(84) bytes of data.
From 172.16.10.12 icmp_seq=1 Destination Host Prohibited
From 172.16.10.12 icmp_seq=2 Destination Host Prohibited
From 172.16.10.12 icmp_seq=3 Destination Host Prohibited
^C
--- 172.16.10.12 ping statistics ---
3 packets transmitted, 0 received, +3 errors, 100% packet loss, time 2129ms
```

Figure 3-19. *IP and destination addresses*

You then enable the Block option (see Figures 3-20 and 3-21).

```
root@web-01a [ ~ ]# ping 172.16.10.12
PING 172.16.10.12 (172.16.10.12) 56(84) bytes of data.
^C
--- 172.16.10.12 ping statistics ---
10 packets transmitted, 0 received, 100% packet loss, time 12304ms
```

Figure 3-20. *Enabling the block*

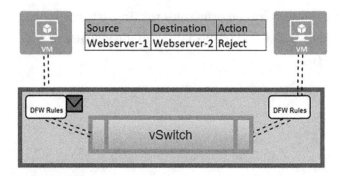

Figure 3-21. *Enabling the block*

To review, when you create a firewall rule using the NSX Manager, the message will be sent to the RabbitMQ server process, which has to be sent to the client process. VSFWD and the RabbitMQ client will be listening on the port for any active connections or any messages from the NSX Manager. Once it receives the message, it is pushed to the DFW kernel module, which in turn will apply the rule on the vNIC of Webserver-1.

The packet will be dropped before it has a chance to enter the network. In a perimeter firewall, the packet has to travel up to the hardware appliance only to get dropped. As the firewall module is in the kernel of the ESXi host, this can perform near to the line rate.

The process of verifying the DFW rules in the ESXi host is shown in Figure 3-22.

```
world 69504 vmm0:web-01a_corp.local vcUuid:'50 08 2c 51 03 bb 8f 21-d6 8b f9 d5 44 5b 47 63'
  port 33554443 web-01a_corp.local.eth0
  vNic slot 2
    name: nic-69504-eth0-vmware-sfw.2
  agentName: vmware-sfw
    state: IOChain Attached
    vmState: Attached
    failurePolicy: failClosed
    slowPathID: 2
    filter source: Dynamic Filter Creation
  vNic slot 1
    name: nic-69504-eth0-dvfilter-generic-vmware-swsec.1
  agentName: dvfilter-generic-vmware-swsec
```

Figure 3-22. *Verifying the rules*

You can find the `dvfilter` name from this output.

`nic-69504-eth0-vmware-sfw.2`

With this information, you can now find the rules corresponding to the vNIC in Webserver-1 (see Figure 3-23).

```
[root@esx-02a:~] vsipioctl getrules -f nic-69504-eth0-vmware-sfw.2
ruleset domain-c26 {
  # Filter rules
  rule 1007 at 1 inout protocol any from ip 172.16.10.11 to ip 172.16.10.12 drop with log;
  rule 1005 at 2 inout protocol tcp from any to addrset ip-ipset-2 port 464 accept;
  rule 1005 at 3 inout protocol tcp from any to addrset ip-ipset-2 port 53 accept;
  rule 1005 at 4 inout protocol udp from any to addrset ip-ipset-2 port 67 accept;
  rule 1005 at 5 inout protocol udp from any to addrset ip-ipset-2 port 53 accept;
  rule 1005 at 6 inout protocol udp from any to addrset ip-ipset-2 port 123 accept;
  rule 1005 at 7 inout protocol udp from any to addrset ip-ipset-2 port 464 accept;
  rule 1005 at 8 inout protocol tcp from any to addrset ip-ipset-2 port 1024 accept;
  rule 1005 at 9 inout protocol udp from any to addrset ip-ipset-2 port 123 accept;
  rule 1005 at 10 inout protocol udp from any to addrset ip-ipset-2 port 68 accept;
  rule 1003 at 11 inout protocol ipv6-icmp icmptype 136 from any to any accept;
  rule 1003 at 12 inout protocol ipv6-icmp icmptype 135 from any to any accept;
  rule 1002 at 13 inout protocol udp from any to any port 67 accept;
  rule 1002 at 14 inout protocol udp from any to any port 68 accept;
  rule 1001 at 15 inout protocol any from any to any accept;
}

ruleset domain-c26 L2 {
```

Figure 3-23. *The rules corresponding to the vNIC in Webserver-1*

The drop rule is listed in the ruleset rule 1007.

This rule will be automatically removed when you disable or delete the DFW rule (see Figure 3-24).

```
[root@esx-02a:~] vsipioctl getrules -f nic-69504-eth0-vmware-sfw.2
ruleset domain-c26 {
  # Filter rules
  rule 1005 at 1 inout protocol tcp from any to addrset ip-ipset-2 port 464 accept;
  rule 1005 at 2 inout protocol tcp from any to addrset ip-ipset-2 port 53 accept;
  rule 1005 at 3 inout protocol udp from any to addrset ip-ipset-2 port 67 accept;
  rule 1005 at 4 inout protocol udp from any to addrset ip-ipset-2 port 53 accept;
  rule 1005 at 5 inout protocol udp from any to addrset ip-ipset-2 port 123 accept;
  rule 1005 at 6 inout protocol udp from any to addrset ip-ipset-2 port 464 accept;
  rule 1005 at 7 inout protocol tcp from any to addrset ip-ipset-2 port 1024 accept;
```

Figure 3-24. *Automatic removal of the rule*

The Application Rule Manager (ARM)

The Application Rule Manager (ARM) is a handy tool that comes to the rescue when you want to create micro-segmentation policies for a new infrastructure. Using the Zero Trust, aka micro-segmentation, approach, there is a need to know every connection that the server takes to the outside. This can be achieved using third-party tools. Starting with the latest NSX versions, you can access the Application Rule Manager. Virtual machines can be added to the Application Rule Manager to monitor traffic. The ARM will analyze the traffic and suggest the security rules that have to be created for that particular server. In this example, I added Webserver-1 to the Application Rule Manager to monitor the traffic in and out of Webserver-1. Monitoring has to be enabled for a certain period to collect useful data for analyses. (See Figure 3-25.)

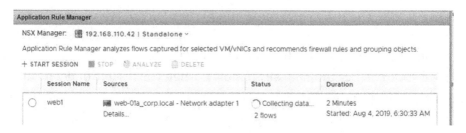

Figure 3-25. *Application Rule Manager (ARM) flow analysis*

After collecting the data, the ARM will display the flows it discovered and automatically suggest which rules should be added to the DFW. The best practice is to watch/monitor all new applications before adding them directly to the DFW ruleset. There is a chance that some flows might be missed in the ruleset, which means the deny rule will drop the packet, thinking that it is not legitimate (see Figures 3-26 and 3-27).

Figure 3-26. *The ARM's flow statistics*

Figure 3-27. *The ARM-recommended flows*

NSX Perimeter Gateway

A wide range of the NSX features can be configured through the
NSX Perimeter Gateway. This Perimeter Gateway acts similarly to a
traditional perimeter firewall. In NSX terms, you can call it an *edge*,
as this will sit in the outer boundary of your NSX environment. On
the NSX Edge tab, there will be at least two NSX edges—one for DLR

and the other for the Perimeter Gateway. The DLR edge serves as a distributed logical routing feature in the NSX. The Perimeter Gateway has a wide variety of use cases:

- Firewall

- DHCP

- NAT

- Routing

- Load balancer

- VPN

- SSL VPN

You can use additional edge devices to enable the load balancer feature according to the bandwidth requirements. A VPN service can be enabled on the edge device, which enables a secure communication to other endpoints (see Figure 3-28).

Figure 3-28. *The NSX Perimeter Gateway*

Summary

This chapter explained the VMware NSX distributed firewall rules and policies. You created webservers and applied security policies to them using DFW. During the verification process, you saw how the rules are added to the ESXi host DFW kernel module and how the message is transferred from the NSX Manager to the ESXi hosts.

This information sets the basis for the journey toward setting up an infrastructure based on Zero Trust. The next chapter focuses on the use case of a service composer and the automation. It discusses creating security policies using a service composer and third-party integration. It discusses integration with Trend Micro and how this can help you build a Zero Trust network.

CHAPTER 4

NSX Service Composer and Third-Party Integration

You have learned about basic rule creation and the features you can enable using the NSX web interface. With a user-friendly interface, NSX gives you the option to configure nearly all the essential features. When it comes to automation, not everything can be accessed via the GUI. There is a practical limit on how much can be stacked together in a single window. You will learn about the NSX REST API calls and options in later chapters. The NSX Service Composer is a powerful feature that enables you to compose security models in NSX with just a few clicks.

Service Composer enables you to build security policies and apply them to security groups. Modern IT architectures require that you model the security framework with ease. Service Composer gives you an easy way of achieving a lot of things. You can configure and integrate security policies built in third-party products to security groups in NSX. With Service Composer, this is an out-of-the-box task.

This chapter discusses how NSX integrates third-party products into the NSX environment. NSX is an end-to-end feature-rich networking security tool. There are occasions when traditional vendors, with their decades-long experience, have a mature way of solving the problems.

© Sreejith Keeriyattil 2019
S. Keeriyattil, *Zero Trust Networks with VMware NSX*,
https://doi.org/10.1007/978-1-4842-5431-8_4

For example, intrusion detection systems and anti-malware systems are well developed, and this space has many competent products. If NSX we to enter that market, that could include reinventing the wheel. To meet such requirements, NSX has integration options that seamlessly integrate third-party products into the NSX environment.

Service Composer

Service Composer provides you with an easy way to compose security models and apply them to security groups. It also provides the flexibility to integrate third-party products and apply them to VMware objects. The two main components are the security groups and the security policies. You'll create security policies using Service Composer and apply them to security groups. You learned about security groups as a way to organize servers into separate groups according to your needs.

A security group can be made up of the following:

- Other security groups

- IP sets

- MAC sets

- Security tags

- Clusters

- Data centers

- Directory groups

- Distributed port groups

- Legacy prot groups

- Logical switches

- Virtual machines

- vNIC

Given the options, what makes NSX security groups stand out is their ability to add VMware objects. This provides the flexibility to use the same grouping you used at a cluster/data center level in vCenter and apply it to the security model.

Security groups in layman terms refer to "what you want to protect". There are different combinations of this:

- Security groups can be nested inside another security groups

- The virtual machine can be part of multiple security groups

- Security group membership can be changed any time

- There is an exclude option that you can use to prevent adding certain objects from secure groups

You can also add members dynamically. When a newly created virtual machine meets a certain defined expression, it can be automatically added to the security group.

Security Policies

A security policy, by definition, is a group of network and security services. There are mainly Guest Introspection services and network introspection services used to create security policies, which can later be applied to virtual machines. Policies are rules and security groups can have multiple policies. In such cases, the weight of the security policy determines its precedence. You will use security policies to integrate policies configured and created on third-party products. Once you register and deploy the service VM, the policies can be configured in the third-party products and can be included in the NSX security policy.

Guest Introspection Services

Guest Introspection offloads antivirus and anti-malware functionalities to dedicated service virtual machines. These dedicated virtual machines (which are often connected to a third-party partner like Trend Micro) can then update and deploy the latest security signatures. Trend Micro can be installed and configured, even without NSX. The advantage of using NSX with Trend Micro is the tight integration and centralized configuration control you get. This chapter discusses integrating Trend Micro with VMware NSX. There are other third-party tools that can be combined with NSX. The configuration flow and integration process would be similar in all those cases, except for the partner configuration GUI/CLI process.

The Guest Introspection service has the following components.

- *MUX module:* When you install Guest Introspection on a vCenter cluster, a new VIB will be added to all the ESXi hosts in the cluster. This module, called a MUX module in simple terms, acts as a switch between the thin agent running inside the Guest VM (this can be Windows or Linux) and the Partner Service virtual machine. The module is also used by the Guest Introspection service VM for configuration updates. Traffic switching happens through the MUX module. The installed VIB can be verified on the ESXi host where the Guest Introspection service is deployed. This VIB would not be included in the normal host preparation process and is only installed when there is a Guest Introspection service required on the cluster.

- *Guest Introspection VM:* Used for communication from the NSX Manager to the ESXi host. The GI VM receives the configuration from the NSX Manager REST call.

- *Partner SVM:* It's vendor-specific and uses the EPSEC library for communication with the MUX module. As with the Guest Introspection service VM, Partner SVM will be deployed on all the hosts in the cluster. You need an IP set that has to be configured into these service VMs for the configuration from the partner management software.

  Traffic that's leaving the virtual machine will be intercepted and sent to this partner SVM for analysis. Any discrepancies found will be checked against the configured set of policies and against the latest virus and malware signatures. Packets are discarded if a malware virus is detected in the process.

An important point to keep in mind is that Guest Introspection will come into effect after the filtering of the distributed firewall rules. So if there is a rule that blocks the packet flow, there is a chance that the packet won't reach the third-party product SVM. Figure 4-1 illustrates the internal flow.

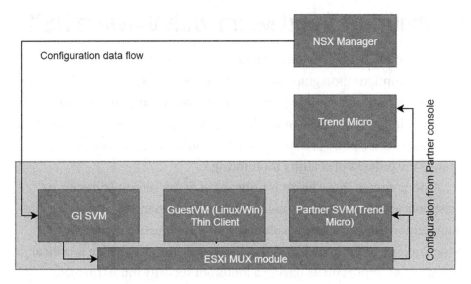

Figure 4-1. *NSX Manager-Partner SVM integration*

Configuration Flow

Once you have integrated the Partner VM, you can use the NSX Manager to configure the security policies into security groups. As mentioned, the Service Composer can be used to accomplish this. The NSX Manager will send the configuration data from the NSX Manager VM to the Guest Introspection virtual machines that will be installed on all the computers in the cluster. The Guest Introspection virtual machine, in turn, uses the configuration data received from NSX to configure the ESXi MUX module and then sends a health report back to the NSX Manager.

The thin client that's installed on the guest VM as part of the VMware tools intercepts the requests from the VM to modify any file context or security-related information. The data will then be sent to the partner SVM for analysis. It will check the data against known security signatures. The file will be in the locked state during that process. Once the analysis is complete, the partner product will command the thin client to perform the necessary actions.

Configuring Trend Micro with VMware NSX

End-to-end configuration and integration of Trend Micro with NSX is best left to the configuration guide and the docs from both parties. This section discusses how can these integrations can be useful. High-level information about the integration, as illustrated in Figure 4-2, is discussed. This section also shows an example of how Service Composer and security policies change the process of security monitoring.

Automation at these levels is unheard of in the security domain, as most policies are applied manually. The need for manual monitoring and intervention during a threat is often regarded as one of the reasons that organizations suffer huge losses during attacks. Response time is critical and is just as important as having a foolproof security infrastructure.

The Zero Trust model, by default, provides a lot of features and granularity. But it won't give you this all in one model. The security defined in the system has to be based on a feedback model. A warning detected anywhere in the infrastructure has to be cascaded to the other tools and components. For example, when Trend Micro detects a threat, it has to be synced with the entire NSX environment for you to safely say that the entire data center is protected. If this is not syncing up, the different security models will work as islands and there is a huge chance of a resulting disaster.

Chapter 3 discussed how a basic Zero Trust model is set up. It discussed a very simple ruleset that was defined to block webservers in a group from communicating with each other. You also learned how a remote desktop user can be separated based on user sessions. All these examples attempt to trim down the security rules to the bare minimum so that only the necessary flows are permitted.

Recall that one of the primary purposes of the Zero Trust model is to limit the spread of an attack. If one webserver is affected, the attacker should not be able to create havoc on the remaining webservers, which could result in crashing all the webserver groups.

This section discusses the same isolation in the context of the Service Composer.

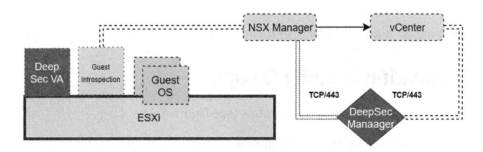

Figure 4-2. *Trend Micro/NSX integration overview*

This example uses Horizon virtual machines. The users are logged in to do their daily tasks and actions. If the concerned virtual machines belong to the sysadmin group, they will be using them to configure and manage tasks on the IT infrastructure. Now, what would happen if a virus infected one of the virtual machines?

As a rule of thumb, you should always assume that there is a good chance that one of your VMs will become infected by a virus or ransomware. These virtual machines are accessed by users who often don't have good security knowledge or habits. One day, a user will click on a malicious email attachment or on a malware link. There is no foolproof way to prevent such things from happening. What you can do is limit the spread of the virus when such a thing happens on a live network.

This example uses the Windows 10 VM, which is installed inside the VMware Horizon, as a testbed to contain a virus (see Figure 4-3). You'll then configure Service Composer to quarantine the VM, thereby reducing the potential spread.

Figure 4-3. *VMware Horizon dashboard*

Configuring Security Groups

This example uses two security groups (see Figure 4-4):

- Trend_micro_security_group
- Quarantine

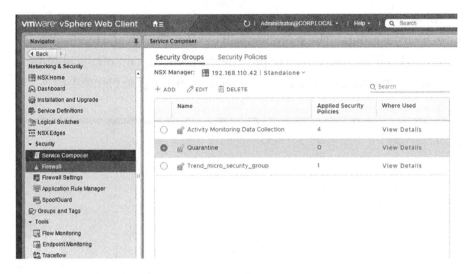

Figure 4-4. *Service Composer security groups*

All the virtual machines in this cluster will come under these security groups. This is where you apply the security policies that contain all the virtual machines that need to be monitored (see Figure 4-5).

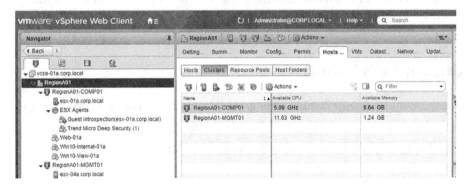

Figure 4-5. *Cluster with Trend Micro SVM deployed*

All servers falling under the RegionA01-COMP01 cluster will fall under these security groups. The members will be added in a static inclusion manner. This means you have to provide the condition manually in order for a virtual machine to be added to a security group (see Figure 4-6).

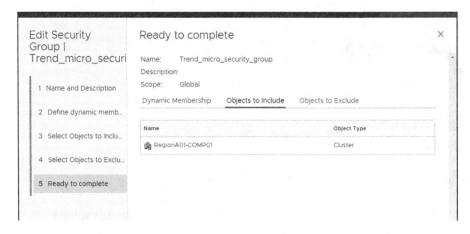

Figure 4-6. Adding a cluster to SG

The Windows 10 virtual machine used for testing is part of this same cluster.

Quarantine Group

The quarantine group is a security group that has a dynamic membership tagged to it, as shown in Figure 4-7. This means that virtual machines with the VM tag ANTI_VIRUS will automatically be added to the quarantine group. This feature is very useful.

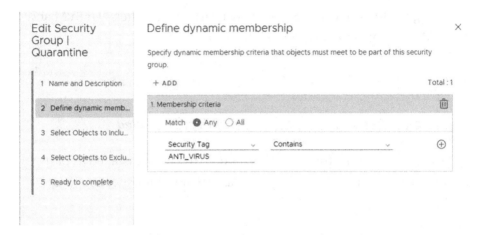

Figure 4-7. *Adding a security tag to define dynamic membership*

Verify the Trend Micro Integration and Setup

You now need to set up the cluster (see Figure 4-8).

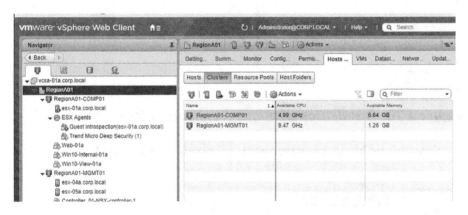

Figure 4-8. *Cluster setup with Introspection VM and Trend Micro SVM*

In Figure 4-9, you can see that the two virtual machines—GI SVM and TrendMicro SVM—are installed on the host.

```
[root@esx-01a:~] esxcli software vib list |grep mux
epsec-mux                 6.5.0esx65-8462817        VMware  VMwareCertified  2018-06-12
[root@esx-01a:~] █
```

Figure 4-9. *Two service virtual machines are installed*

You can also verify that the MUX module has been installed as part of the host preparation process for installing Guest Introspection (see Figure 4-10).

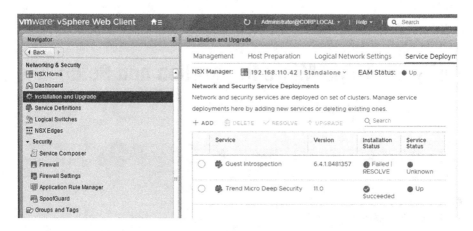

Figure 4-10. *Installation dashboard showing failed actions*

Resolve and status are successful, as shown in Figure 4-11.

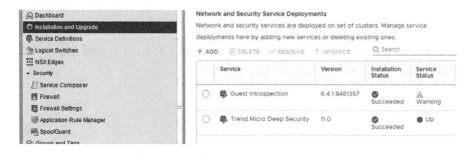

Figure 4-11. *Succeeded status after the Resolve step*

Log in to the Trend Micro Security console (see Figure 4-12) to check if Windows 10 has been added to the malware protection.

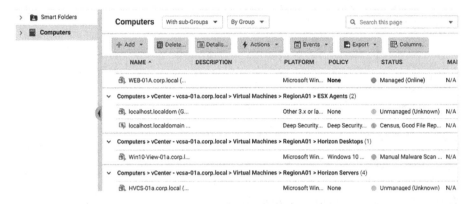

Figure 4-12. *The Trend Micro dashboard*

Windows 10 can be checked under the Computers tab in the Trend Micro security console. Trend Micro has been integrated with the vCenter, which makes it easier for Trend Micro to search for new virtual machines and apply the rules.

Infecting the Windows 10 VM

Log in to the Windows 10 Virtual machines, copy the `eicar.com` file, and paste it anywhere on the desktop.

The `eicar` file is an anti-malware test file provided by the European Institute for Computer Anti-Virus Research. It can be used to test how the VM reacts during a malware infection (see Figure 4-13).

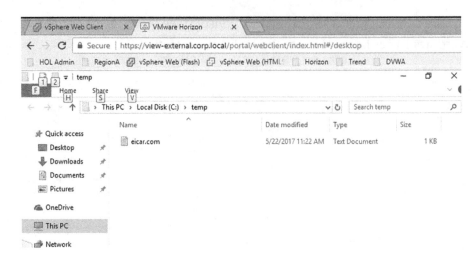

Figure 4-13. *Anti-malware test file*

Copy and paste the `eicar` file anywhere on the desktop (see Figure 4-14).

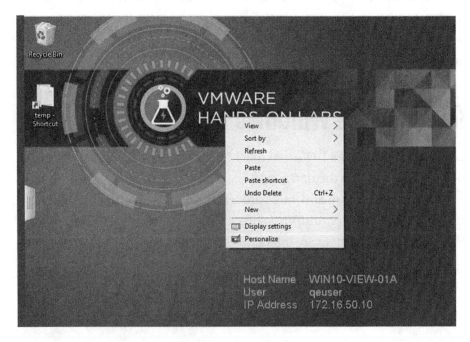

Figure 4-14. *Initiating a copy to the desktop*

You should immediately be prompted with a message that malware has been detected. This means that all the processes discussed in this chapter have happened like clockwork. The GI SVM has intercepted the task of copying the file to the desktop sent the action to Trend Micro SVM, where it was analyzed against existing security signatures. The file was detected as malware and this information was sent back to GI SVM. GI SVM informs the NSX Manager about the incident. It then tags the virtual machine with a different tag and adds the virtual machine to the quarantine security group.

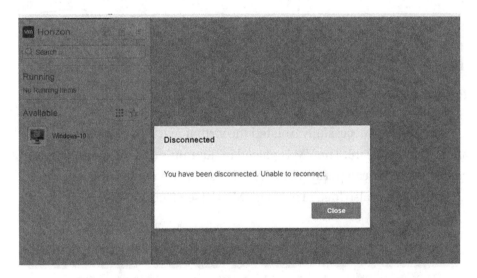

Figure 4-15. *VM has been automatically disconnected and moved*

The VM is disconnected (see Figure 4-15) and the security tag is automatically applied (see Figure 4-16). The virtual machine is then added to the quarantine security group.

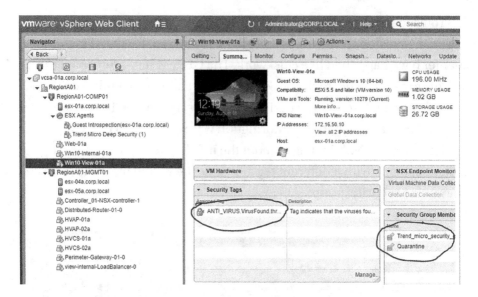

Figure 4-16. *VM assigned the dynamic tag automatically*

The system successfully isolated the virtual machine when it was affected by malware. The VM is placed in quarantine so the administrator can act on it. He can perform a scheduled scan and remove the malware.

The event is also logged in Trend Micro (see Figure 4-17).

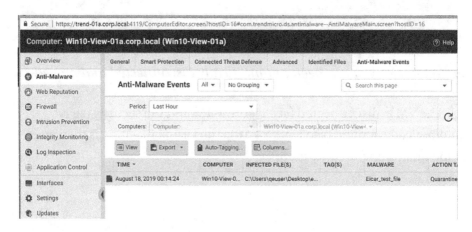

Figure 4-17. *Event logged in Trend Micro*

Figure 4-18 shows the full scan options for the Windows 10 VM.

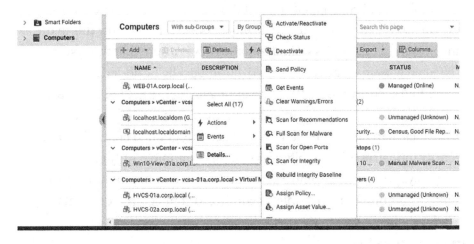

Figure 4-18. *Full scan options from Trend Micro*

Once the scan is completed and the malware has been removed, the VM is automatically removed from the quarantine group (see Figure 4-19).

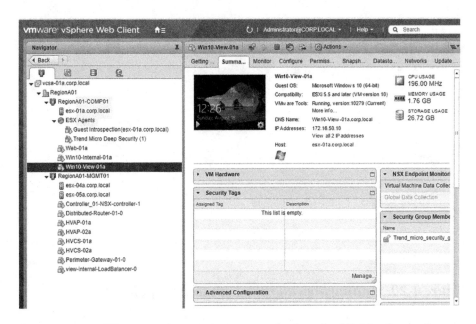

Figure 4-19. *The security tag is removed after the VM is cleaned up by removing malware file*

All these processes happen in the background. Once you have the initial setup, NSX will take care of the virtual machine. There is no manual intervention required to do any of this. You can apply this to the ransomware scenarios as well. When the NSX is aware that the system is affected with malware, they would automatically be added to the quarantine security group, thus preventing further spread of the attack.

When you use such automated policies in conjunction with the Zero Trust rules of micro-segmentation, you get fine-grained control of your security infrastructure. Needless to say, this example is only one of the many ways you we use Trend Micro and NSX in combination. There are multiple combinations possible, according to your setup requirements.

Firewall Rules

You can also add firewall rules along with the security policies (see Figures 4-20 and 4-21).

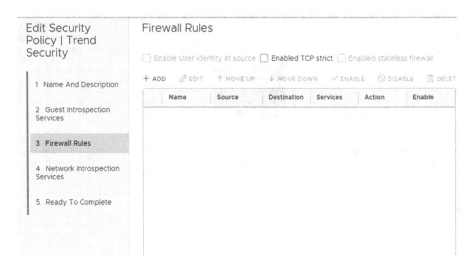

Figure 4-20. *Adding firewall rules with security policies*

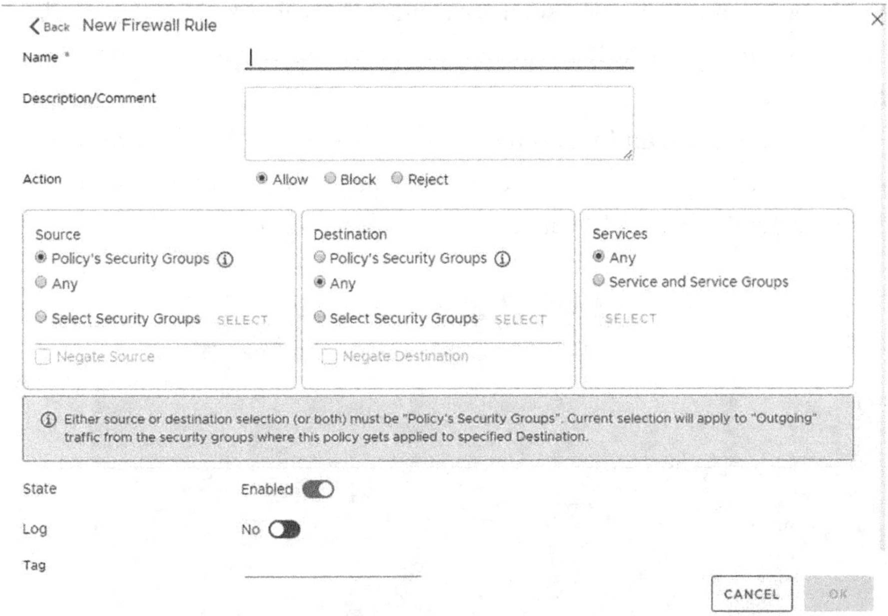

Figure 4-21. *Options for the firewall rule*

Network Introspection

Network introspection enables network services like IDS/IPS through a third-party product. Once you have enabled network introspection, a separate slot in the IO chain will be added for the virtual machines. Slots 4-11 will be used for this purpose and traffic will be redirected to the partner VM for processing. The decision regarding the packet flow will be made accordingly. This gives you a powerful feature where NSX can be used along with market-leading security vendors like Palo Alto to enable IDS/IPS functionality to the traffic of the virtual machine inside VMware NSX.

This section illustrates a wonderful example of a traditional network feature set working in sync with NSX. It will be integrated with NSX and will be used for advanced threat detection and avoidance. You could then integrate a well-known security vendor software like Palo Alto and Checkpoint into your NSX environment, thereby steering traffic to the partner solutions.

In order to get seamless management across multiple software systems, you have to integrate these third-party solutions, such as Palo Alto/Checkpoint, with VMware NSX (see Figure 4-22).

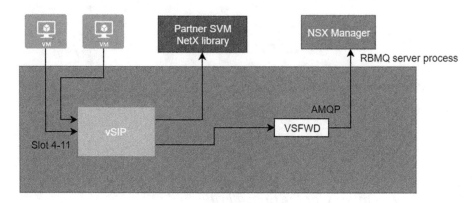

Figure 4-22. *Network introspection internal flow*

The packet flow happens as follows.

As a prerequisite, you need to deploy the partner service manager into the NSX Manager. Once the registration is complete, you will be ready to do the service virtual machine deployments on the relevant cluster. There will be a single SVM deployed on each host in the cluster you are selecting. You can exclude the management cluster according to this exercise. Service virtual machines need a gateway IP and you need to specify the IP set. Once the deployment is finished, you can see the status of the SVM on the NSX Manager tab. Make sure they are all in the green state and resolve any issues that are notified on the NSX Manager tab

The VMware Service Insertion Platform (VSIP) plays a crucial role in steering the traffic. You already learned that Slot-2 in VSIP will be used by DFW to filter traffic. The remaining slots (Slots 4-11) will be used for network introspection applications. When the packets come out of the virtual machine, they have to hit Slot-2 used by DFW first. Once the DFW checks the packet against the rules, it will divert the packet for further actions. If allowed, it will send the packet down the IO chains. In this case, if there is a network introspection service deployed, the packet will hit the first assigned slot, anywhere from Slot 4-11 and will be redirected to the SVM. The partner SVM will then do the necessary actions in the packet. If the packet is allowed to go, the partner SVM will return it to the vSIP for further processing. Otherwise, precautionary measures will be taken on the packet, such as dropping or blocking it.

You can use various security architectures to enable the SVM. There is no requirement to enable third-party control on all the virtual machines in the cluster. For this, you can create a separate security group and add the virtual machines to the specific groups.

Say you need a URL filtering functionality, such as to block YouTube on certain Horizon desktops. You can do this by grouping all the virtual machines in a separate security group. You then create a security policy on the third-party management console and apply the security policy to those security groups. There are third-party products, like Checkpoint, which can be integrated with VMware NSX.

Summary

In this chapter, you learned how powerful VMware third-party integration is and how you can use Service Composer in various use cases, all in sync with the DFW rules. All this will help you enable tight security controls in your infrastructure.

Coming chapters go into depth about building Zero Trust networks on a production network. Those chapters use the infrastructure of a fictional T-shirt company to teach you how to set up DFW rules in NSX.

CHAPTER 5

Bird's-Eye View of a Zero Trust Network

You have learned the basics of how to create distributed firewall rules as well as how to create security groups, service composers, etc. It's time to get ruthless with real-world scenarios. The intention here is to explain how you can implement a Zero Trust policy-based network on a real production system.

Introduction

Like any design, the architecture may differ according to the business requirements. A financial services company requires tighter security control than a company handling less critical business solutions. Every company needs a top-class security model deployed on its network. No company is looking for second-class solutions, but you'll often have a trade-off between cost and functionality. This forced you to choose a design that meets your company's greatest needs. For instance, a landlocked country doesn't need a heavy navy presence; instead, they focus their defense strategies on building a more dependable army and air force. You can always consider real-life examples when designing security models.

© Sreejith Keeriyattil 2019
S. Keeriyattil, *Zero Trust Networks with VMware NSX*,
https://doi.org/10.1007/978-1-4842-5431-8_5

A wide range of complicated attacks threaten Internet-facing companies today. Most fend off such threats only due to sheer luck. Sometimes companies are not even aware that data theft happened at all. They become aware only when the hackers threaten to release the data if they don't agree to their demands. You can argue that even cutting edge security models fail to protect some companies from being embarrassed in front of the world when they are exposed by hackers.

The Zero Trust model cannot completely prevent such attacks. Take into consideration Google's way of designing systems. Google always designs with failure in mind. For their infrastructure system, their rule of thumb is that hardware can fail at any time. They create strategies based on how the system will react when there is a failure. The application will be grouped according to business criticality and they spend more money on monitoring critical applications.

You can model your security infrastructure based on business requirements. It is important to discuss this with various stakeholders before committing to any design approach. If you are passionate about cars and you wanted to buy a new one, you would naturally go for the best available car in the market. What you might not consider due to your passion are the budget, affordability, mileage, and many other things.

As a security consultant, it is always easier to suggest the top-selling and latest security tool available in the market. There is an old saying in IT groups that states, "Nobody gets fired for buying IBM". There are many real examples where projects start with high expectations and, at the end, the budget skyrockets and the entire project wraps up before getting anything production-ready. This can happen when designing security systems as well if you are not careful.

As a security consultant, your job is to determine the requirements and priorities. You have to defend each extra penny the customer is paying. Setting up a cutting-edge defense system only to protect a blog or a less critical gaming application is not a good use of money or time.

This chapter focuses on how to design a general system based on the Zero Trust network.

It is important to understand the basic requirements and why you do things you'll do in NSX. This information can be carried on to other areas.

Stakeholder Meetings

Before going ahead with your design, it is important to have a detailed discussion with each of the application owners. As a security consultant, your job is to make sure all the relevant policies are applied to the system. For that, you might also need to know the kind of application you are protecting. There are multiple design approaches and deployment models available in the market and there are situations where models will differ across each team. You need to know:

- Kind of database and the data the application stores

- How the application is connected to other applications

- Whether the application is web facing

- How they are planning to take on load balancing

- Application upgrade model

Application Architecture

Application architecture can be quite complex and demanding. At first, it might seem this has nothing to do with the security model and its implementation. The application architecture defines how code reacts to certain events and how the servers are organized at different levels. This gives you an important piece of information about the data flow.

In Zero Trust networks, it is vital to understand the packet flow inside the data center. Application dependency mapping documents are sometimes the most difficult thing to achieve in any infrastructure project. As it happens, each application owner is very confident about how their application works in their isolated system. They have factored in all the possibilities and edge cases to make sure all the possible issues are addressed. When it's deployed to production, many are unaware of how the performance or changes in other applications impact their servers. You need to have a clear understanding of the business logic and application flow to segment these into firewall policies. There are different architecture models available in the market, several of which are discussed in the following sections.

Layered Architecture

Figure 5-1 shows one of the most commonly used web application architectures, the layered model. There is a two-tiered architecture and three-tiered architecture. The logic is separated into different layers and each layer has a particular purpose. The most common initial separation layer is the web tier, which ingests the user requests coming from the Internet. This is the only layer that is Internet-facing, and its responsibility is to cater to web requests.

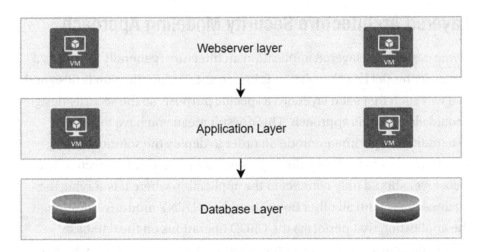

Figure 5-1. *Layered model*

As most of the user hits happen at this layer, the load balancing feature will have to be applied to this layer for extreme bandwidth scenarios. The web layer is mainly composed of the server, which has a stateless feature. This makes scaling webservers easy.

Next is the application tier, which contains the server that runs the business logic. Here, you take the user requests and run the logic and generate an expected result. As you see, this is one of the core components and has been designed and optimized for different scenarios.

The third layer is the database tier. You have already applied the logic to the user request, so the output might be doing a CRUD (Create, Read, Update, Delete operation) on a database that's sitting in the database tier.

Layered architecture can be quite useful in the quick development of the software, as the responsibilities are divided across different tiers. But often there are drawbacks with this design. Over time, there is a chance that the codebase will end up as a monolithic design and becomes difficult to manage and upgrade. A tiered architecture, in some cases, can make it difficult for anyone to understand the overall architecture, thereby making the entire system more complex.

Layered Architecture Security Modeling Approach

While designing a layered application architecture (generally known as a three-tier model layer), isolation is important. The application is designed in a way such that each layer has a specific purpose, so the security design should also use this approach. This doesn't mean you have to go back to a traditional perimeter model in order to deploy the solution. The flow from layer to layer should be properly identified and protected. The webserver should only connect to the application where it is serving the business logic, and all other flows should use DENY mode. In addition, the application that performs the CRUD operations on the database should be allowed to connect only to those specific ports. This will help in achieving real layer-based architecture in security modeling. As you can see, understanding the architecture helps you keep the application and security architecture in sync. This provides more scalable and more reliable security over time.

Event-Driven Architecture

Event-driven architecture, as the name suggests, waits for an event and takes specific actions when the event is generated. This type of architecture isn't the best or most generic type. But it's used with many modern web application architectures, notably e-commerce. For example, consider the communication between two web services in a typical e-commerce setup. You have an order application service listening for user requests. Once it receives a request, it will update its registry and publish an event to another application service.

The inventory application service will be subscribed to the order events. It receives the request, checks the database for inventory, and publishes a `no_stock` or `in_stock` reply. This kind of communication logic between services is quite common nowadays, particularly in cloud-based architectures.

Event-Driven Architecture Security Modeling Approach

Along with the Zero Trust generic approaches, event-based architecture ends with more intricate communication flow between services. There has to be a clear understanding of the requirements and the publish/subscribe process to events. A fundamental study should be made of the required flows. Fortunately, VMware NSX has well-designed tools to take care of this exhaustive task of identifying the flows. Using a combination of Application Rule Manager (ARM) and Log Insight, you can gain a fair understanding of the flows and create firewall rules based on them.

There are third-party tools like Tufin that do a similar job. Depending on the complexity of the setup, more in-depth analysis and care should be taken in the preparation phase of configuring NSX security.

Microservices Architecture

Microservices architecture is the new default cloud-based architecture. Designing microservices means splitting a monolithic application into smaller services. It's based on the UNIX philosophy "do one thing and do it well". You could arguably say that the microservices design pattern is a natural progression, where we have moved toward containers and cloud-based deployments. Both the user experience and the load in this current Internet era have increased. Where everything is online, there is a need to spur on demand by frequently adding new features. When you consider the same scenario a decade back, there wasn't such an urgent need to add new features and optimization. There was always an emphasis on security and optimization of resources. But as the Internet landscape has changed, the new generation is more willing to move on from one product to another without hesitation. If the product they are using doesn't meet their expectations, they quickly change from one e-commerce website to another, especially if the website slows or is not easy to use.

As a result, there are plenty of changes happening on the infrastructure and application sides. We can't consider security as isolated from all the changes happening outside. The security model has to incorporate the design changes happening elsewhere.

Microservices Architecture Security Model Approach

Designing a security model for a microservices-based architecture is time-consuming. There can be multiple REST API calls happening between applications at any given time. With Zero Trust, it is important to take every flow into account. This is where the automation and ease of configuration comes to assist. In such cases, you need to make heavy use of automation. NSX has a good feature set for automation in the name of label, service composer, and REST API integration. All these features can be used to add and remove virtual machines in to and out of the security groups based on the application's needs. Given the complex nature of microservice call flow, automation is a must when implementing security

Managing and Monitoring Servers

Take great care with the placement and security of your management servers. All your infrastructure management servers should be well protected and restricted by LDAP user access. Allowing admin and default credential access is probably the most irresponsible thing anyone can do. In a setup where they don't have well-defined processes and policies to commission hardware into, the data center will fall for this trap. Companies that are building new data centers usually end up missing some of these key points.

For instance, access to each computer or switch should be restricted only to a valid user. All these servers should be in another management network VLAN, but that is not a valid reason for allowing the default credential. The password-management policy should be followed across the hardware system.

I propose a jump server-based management setup. This simplifies applying all your firewall and access control to a single server or a group. The jump server can be properly deployed with tightened security controls and the latest patches applied and you can be 100% sure that there are no loopholes in it. Users with LDAP access log in to the jump server and, from there, they can navigate further to other servers for management purposes. Even then, only flows that are required should be allowed from these servers. A jump server shouldn't has full control over the infrastructure. You can divide jump server access according to the organization's division. The monitoring team that's accessing the jump server shouldn't have full control over the servers. Their job is to monitor and report any issues. Likewise, the security team, patching team, etc. should have required permissions only to do their roles. Figure 5-2 shows the access model view.

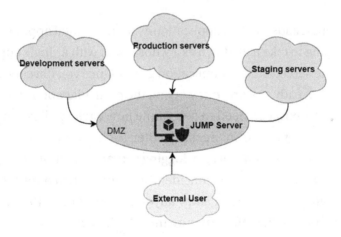

Figure 5-2. *Access model view*

With the introduction of DevOps, IT teams often have a blend of development and operations skillsets. In such models, you need to take extra care when giving control over the infrastructure to diverse teams. In deployment models, like deploying servers using infrastructure as a code, it is excellent in simplifying manual processes. At the same time, this gives more responsibility to the person who executes it. A manual error or grave mistake can lead to disaster in these cases.

Application Grouping

This chapter discussed the major application design architecture. There are other varieties of architecture that can be used for system design, like microkernel architecture and space-based architecture. The point is that you need to have an initial understanding of the application architecture before you jump into the Zero Trust security model design.

Once you have the information you need and initial discussion with the stakeholders, you can move into the design of the Zero Trust security model.

It is advantageous to use a application-wise, horizontal approach instead of trying to take it all down as a whole. Start with a single application. Register all the servers in that application group. Once you have the list of servers, you are ready to start your work on the particular applications.

In the next steps, you need to determine how each application interacts with other blocks in the data center, such as with other applications, management servers, logging servers, and monitoring and audit servers. It is important to consider the management applications, as well. By design, you should not allow anyone or any groups to have free access to any part of the infrastructure they don't need.

Security Groups

Security groups form a vital part of the NSX server grouping. You already read about how to create security groups. One of the initial steps in any design is to identify on what basis you will group the servers. This is important, as it forms a core part of the security system's design.

The grouping has to be scalable and reliable for a long time. Changing the grouping policies every time you add a new application or extend an existing application is not sound design.

The approach you use here can also depend on the application architecture in general. For a three-tier architecture, it is common to group webservers into one security domain and app servers into another. This method might not work if the application architecture doesn't strictly follow a layered model.

Naming also has importance in modeling. Most organizations use a naming convention and aren't detailed in the description of the names. This can work if the information is well documented and is updated regularly. Manual errors always begin with outdated documents. A new employee won't be able to identify the purpose of a security group if the name is not well defined.

Security groups (SGs) and service names have to be meaningful and should include the purpose and the application to which they apply. Also, take care so you don't end up with an SG overhaul. If you start creating a security group for each VM, you'll soon end up with too many SGs and it will be difficult to identify which ones need to be applied. A rule of thumb is to limit security groups to the web, app, and database application tiers.

The T-Shirt Company Example

You have read about the prerequisites and general recommendations to follow before trying to deploy the Zero Trust networks. Now it's time to delve more deeply into how all these pieces work together in a live production setup.

You have learned about security groups, services, service composers, DFW, third-party integrations, and other useful features. In a live production setup, these will act as an arsenal in the hands of a security consultant. Consultants have to use the right tools to get the right defense model per application. As discussed, there is no one size fits all approach in security. Even though you need to give equal importance to all applications, it is a fact that some applications are more critical than others.

This section uses a fictional T-shirt company to illustrate this process. It's an online e-commerce store that sells T-shirts.

Here are the assumptions about this example:

- This model is by no means a standard that can be applied everywhere.

- The use case creates some scenarios to help you understand how Zero Trust solves these problems.

- The problems can be solved using many techniques, but this example mentions only one of the best ways.

- This is by no means a standard design practice from VMware. For that, refer to the VMware designing guidelines.

- The Zero Trust model and VMware NSX design are evolving in each version. The versions have to be checked for any improvements or outdated features.

- This use case is security-focused and ignores other critical infrastructure components.

- The application architecture model mentioned here is generic and is by no means a standard e-commerce application architecture.

The first question is often, "why can't we put everything into a public cloud?". You could use AWS, Google Cloud, or Azure to achieve this. The question seems reasonable to a normal user, as the main advantage that public cloud vendors profess is that you don't need to manage your infrastructure any more. This will be done automatically by the service providers.

If you learn one thing and only one thing from this book, it's this—all the server, storage, application, databases, programming languages, and everything that is used to build an end-to-end web application must promote revenue to the funding company. No one uses a shiny new tool just because it is new and achieves some features that were not there before. The real question almost all CTOs will ask is how will it affect the bottom line. Can the company generate some percentage increase in revenue? Only if there is a financial benefit will most organizations go forward with expenditures.

The choice between a public cloud and an on-premise system depends on the business requirements and challenges. There is no one-size-fits-all solution.

Infrastructure for the T-Shirt Company

As portrayed in Figure 5-3, the T-Shirt company infrastructure is a scalable three-tier application. The application contains modules and services that do a specific job and help the overall system work seamlessly.

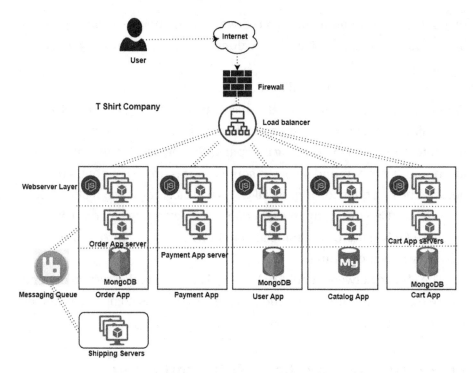

Figure 5-3. *T-Shirt company architecture*

On an individual component point of view, each service can act and run independently. For example, the catalogue application runs in a separate virtual machine and uses a separate database (or the same database that's shared across the application). The isolation you need purely depends on the applications.

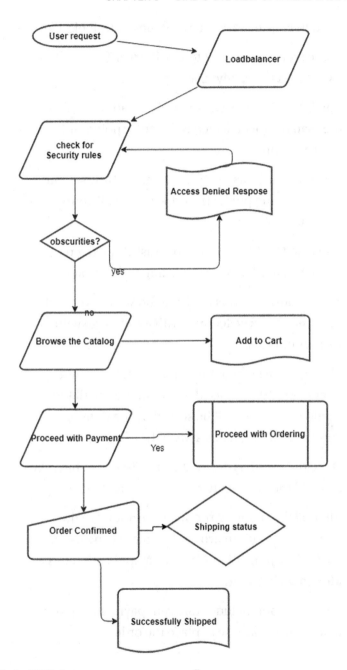

Figure 5-4. *T-Shirt company process flow*

As detailed in Figure 5-4, the user request flow looks like this:

1. A user requests the IP to DNS server for
   `www.tshirtcompany.com`.

2. The DNS responds with a public IP address of
   the load balancer, which is the entry point for the
   infrastructure.

3. Once the user has the IP address, the browser will
   connect to the public IP address and will connect to
   the load balancer.

4. The load balancer's job is to redistribute the request
   to the backend servers according to their load.

5. The request now hits the frontend webserver and
   the user will be welcomed with a web page with
   various options.

6. The user can search through the catalogue and
   filter the products based on her interests. All the
   catalogue entries will be served by the Catalog
   application, which has a MySQL DB backend.

7. Once the user has decided on the T-shirt to buy, she
   can add the product to the Cart application.

8. After all the required products are added to the
   cart, the user has to proceed with ordering using
   the Order application. The Order application has a
   MongoDB backend.

9. The Checkout includes different payments options
   that the user can use to place the order.

10. Once the order is complete, it will be shown on the order application page. This will also confirm the status of the request.

11. Separate applications can be used to track the shipping status and the successful completion of the request.

12. This can be used in conjunction with a messaging queue, which can subscribe to any events about the order status and display them accordingly.

13. The order is successfully shipped and marked as completed.

14. The user will be able to see the ordered products in her account. This includes relevant details, like the address of the shipment, and so on.

15. Options to create a new user, apply coupon codes, and so on, can be added to the design, as needed.

These points represent the request flow of an e-commerce application. According to the requirements, you can scale and add complexity to the application as you want. This job is up to the application developers and business owners as to how many features they need to attract new customers. In the modern e-commerce landscape, customers are looking for new and improved user experiences to keep them using the same website.

Say another competitor comes up with an amazing new product based on order history using AI and machine learning. Users might be tempted and gradually move toward other sites, as those competitors showed them products they have an affinity for. This simplifies their advertising costs and improves their margins.

The T-shirt company should be scalable and reliable enough to add such features with minimal effort. In a monolithic application, adding new features is a difficult task.

In this case study, the whole setup runs in a VMware SDDC setup. You are tasked to design the security model to protect these applications.

The T-shirt company purchased VMware NSX and a related toolset to better aid everyone involved in this project. The toolset includes the following:

- VMware vSphere license

- VMware NSX license

- VMware Log Insight

- VMware Network Insight

- TrendMicro/Panorama Checkpoint third-party product

License requirements and related information can easily be obtained from the VMware website. Refer to the VMware official website for information about licensing.

The coming sections analyze each application and the security rules required. You already read about creating rules and security groups. The focus here is on the type of rules that need to be created.

The setup here assumes that this is a *greenfield deployment.* That means that this is a new project and is not in production yet. Brownfield deployments are what you do on top of existing applications. Both have their challenges.

In a greenfield deployment, you are dealing with unknown facts. The setup is new and even the application developers might not be totally sure how their application behaves

In a brownfield deployment, you have an existing setup that you need to migrate. Activity will be done on a live production setup. You need to be sure about the DENY rules and packet flows. Migrating the existing firewall rules from a traditional firewall to NSX DFW is a challenge. You might need to rewrite the entire firewall rules in some cases.

This next step looks into the firewall rules that are required for the different services, such as those shown in Figure 5-5:

- Load balancer

- Frontend webservers

- Catalog application

- Order application

- User application

- Cart application

- Payment application

- Shipping application

- For MySQL databases

- For MongoDB databases

- RabbitMQ messaging queue

- Management and monitoring servers

	Listening Port
Load balancer	443
Frontend Webservers	80
Catalog Application Server	80
Order appication Server	80
Payment application Server	80
User applciation Server	80
Cart application Server	80
Shipping applciation Server	80
Mysql database	3306
MongoDB database	27017
RabbitMQ messaging Queue	5672
O&M servers	Port as per Req

Figure 5-5. *T-shirt company server inventory*

Load Balancer

This is the first entry point for all the requests that hit the T-shirt company (TSC) infrastructure. The load balancer can be physical or virtual. NSX has built-in functionalities of a load balancer. There is an option to enable multiple load balancer types in VMware NSX. Inline and one-arm load balancer models can be deployed within an NSX setup without any additional hassle. This will always depend on the use case. As discussed, some infrastructure needs to be extremely scalable and have resource-intensive operations like SSL offloading or complex health checks of the server pools. These options are shown in Figure 5-6.

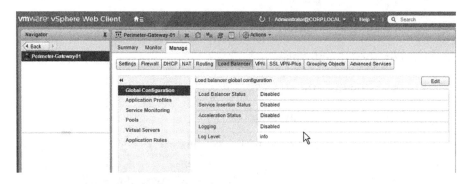

Figure 5-6. *NSX load balancer options*

If the frontend application demands resource-intensive operations, physical appliance-based load balancers like Citrix Netscaler or F5 have to be used. This resolves one problem, but you need to keep in mind that managing and maintaining these physical appliances is outside the scope of the NSX and you'll need to individually take care of these appliances. There are separate command sets and management tools for administering the load balancer.

For an end-to-end infrastructure automation, this might come as a roadblock. In an immutable infrastructure setup, the infrastructure automation tool should be capable of deploying the entire infrastructure stack using the scripted methods. In the case of the appliance, it won't be able to take part in the automation process.

All these points need to be kept in mind when you select your load balancing tools. The virtual appliance of popular load balancers can also provide most of the feature sets available in physical load balancers. Figure 5-7 shows the backend.

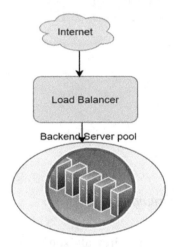

Figure 5-7. *Load balancer backend*

The load balancer has to forward the request using an algorithm that's best suited to the application. You can even use a round-robin algorithm where each request is forwarded in a round-robin fashion to the backend pool of servers. There would be a health check script, which can be based on a specific port or ICMP or HTTP request. The purpose is to identify whether the backend pool of servers is available and healthy to forward packets for further processing.

If the load balancer sits outside of NSX, the firewall rules have to be configured in the customer's firewall. In this case, you can configure the rule in the edge device, as the packets to a particular transport zone must enter through the edge appliances.

The idea is to drop the packet as early as you can, before allowing it to enter into the DC.

Edge Firewall Rules

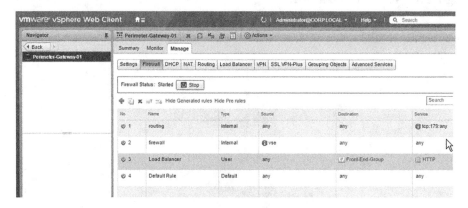

Figure 5-8. *NSX edge firewall*

The rules you define in the edge firewall (see Figure 5-8) will be matched against the packets that enter the NSX. Any other malformed packets will be discarded at this stage.

Here are the required steps:

1) Rule moves from the load balancer to the backend pools.

2) Define the ports on which the frontend webservers will be listening.

3) Create a service for those ports.

4)   Apply the rule in the edge firewall.

5)   There is a default DENY at the end, so any traffic
      that is not destined for the frontend servers will be
      dropped.

This example has only considered the production web frontend
servers. If there are other physical servers or monitoring servers outside
the VMware NSX environment, they have to be included in the rule.
Otherwise, the flow will be blocked by default.

Frontend Webserver Pool

Webservers sitting at the frontend are often the most targeted servers.
To access the application, you have to first get inside and then spread
through the system. Webservers are often placed in the demilitarized zone
with high levels of security. A hacker might target these webservers in
order to deface the website, thereby causing the company international
embarrassment. There may not be any intention to crash or steal assets,
but as you know, negative news can be just as harmful. If the incident is
faced by a financial company, this can be a big hit to their trust factor.

In most cases, you only have to focus on the ingress and egress
flow for the webserver pool. Frontend servers have to be extremely
scalable by design. When the load increases, the stateless nature of the
application should aid in creating multiple webserver copies according
to the incoming request bandwidth. Security should scale along with
this. Autoscaling is the most used word nowadays for distributed system
designs.

If you are enabling this kind of feature in your webserver design, be
sure to enable it on the security modeling too. For instance, if you have to
create an additional five webservers to feed bandwidth demands, make
sure all the servers are automatically included in the webserver security
groups, so that the polices are applied to the respective vNICs.

In doing so, you ensure that the security standards and policies are met. Figure 5-9 shows the frontend flow.

Application	Egress Server	Port	Appied to	Based on
Front End Webserver	Catalog Application Server	80	DFW	IP Sets/Sec Groups
Front End Webserver	Order appication Server	80	DFW	IP Sets/Sec Groups
Front End Webserver	Payment application Server	80	DFW	IP Sets/Sec Groups
Front End Webserver	User applciation Server	80	DFW	IP Sets/Sec Groups
Front End Webserver	Cart application Server	80	DFW	IP Sets/Sec Groups
Front End Webserver	Shipping applciation Server	80	DFW	IP Sets/Sec Groups
Front End Webserver	Mysql database	NA	DFW	IP Sets/Sec Groups
Front End Webserver	MongoDB database	NA	DFW	IP Sets/Sec Groups
Front End Webserver	RabbitMQ messaging Queue	NA	DFW	IP Sets/Sec Groups
Front End Webserver	O&M servers	Ports as per Req		

Figure 5-9. *Frontend webserver's connectivity flows*

You can apply the same process to a distributed firewall.

These are also micro-segmentation/Zero Trust policy rules.

Figure 5-10 shows the frontend rules.

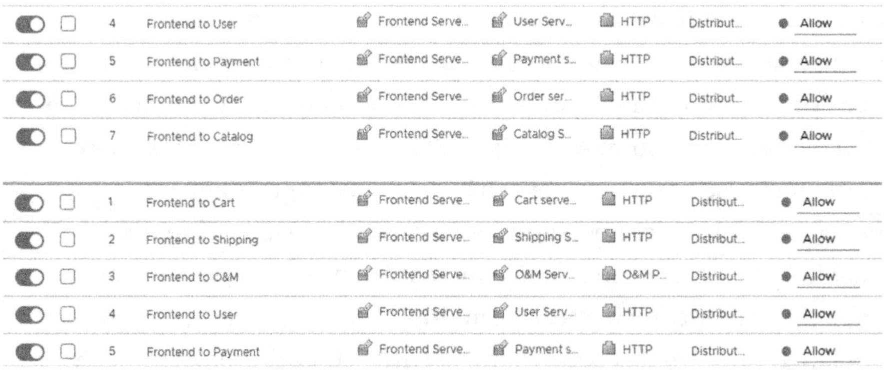

		4	Frontend to User	Frontend Serve..	User Serv..	HTTP	Distribut..	Allow
		5	Frontend to Payment	Frontend Serve..	Payment s..	HTTP	Distribut..	Allow
		6	Frontend to Order	Frontend Serve..	Order ser..	HTTP	Distribut..	Allow
		7	Frontend to Catalog	Frontend Serve..	Catalog S..	HTTP	Distribut..	Allow
		1	Frontend to Cart	Frontend Serve..	Cart serve..	HTTP	Distribut..	Allow
		2	Frontend to Shipping	Frontend Serve..	Shipping S..	HTTP	Distribut..	Allow
		3	Frontend to O&M	Frontend Serve..	O&M Serv..	O&M P..	Distribut..	Allow
		4	Frontend to User	Frontend Serve..	User Serv..	HTTP	Distribut..	Allow
		5	Frontend to Payment	Frontend Serve..	Payment s..	HTTP	Distribut..	Allow

Figure 5-10. *Frontend webserver's DFW rules*

Once a rule is published on all the hosts, the vNIC will start filtering packets based on the ruleset.

Catalog Application Server

Catalog application servers are responsible for listing inventory from the MySQL database in the backend. All inventory should be logged in to the database.

Inventory can be broken down into multiple sections. For example:

- New items

- T-shirts on discount

- Regular polo T-shirts

This can be designed and pushed into the schema of the database table. Because the webserver to application and then to database connectivity is a generic three-tier architecture, you need to understand which other applications need to access the catalog. The users need to log in and connect to the Catalog server to access the products. From the shipping agent's point of view, they need to be able to update the inventory and mark the product as out of stock when this is the case.

This applications have to talk to each other to keep others updated. As mentioned, the catalog has to be updated based on availability and quantity. If this synchronization process is not happening seamlessly, the whole system is going to break down sooner or later. Figure 5-11 shows the catalog flow.

Application	Egress Server	Port	Appied to	Based on
Catalog Application Server	Front End Webserver	80	DFW	IP Sets/Sec Groups
Catalog Application Server	Order appication Server	NA	DFW	IP Sets/Sec Groups
Catalog Application Server	Payment application Server	NA	DFW	IP Sets/Sec Groups
Catalog Application Server	User applciation Server	80	DFW	IP Sets/Sec Groups
Catalog Application Server	Cart application Server	80	DFW	IP Sets/Sec Groups
Catalog Application Server	Shipping applciation Server	80	DFW	IP Sets/Sec Groups
Catalog Application Server	Mysql database	3306	DFW	IP Sets/Sec Groups
Catalog Application Server	MongoDB database	NA	DFW	IP Sets/Sec Groups
Catalog Application Server	RabbitMQ messaging Queue	NA	DFW	IP Sets/Sec Groups
Catalog Application Server	O&M servers	Ports as per Req		

Figure 5-11. *Catalog server's connectivity flows*

The same rules can be deployed in DFW as micro-segmentation/Zero Trust policy rules.

Figure 5-12 shows the catalog server rules.

🔵	☐	1	Catalog to Front End	🗂 Catalog Servers	🗂 Frontend ..	📋 HTTP	Distribut..	●	Allow
🔵	☐	2	Catalog to User	🗂 Catalog Servers	🗂 User Serv..	📋 HTTP	Distribut..	●	Allow
🔵	☐	3	Catalog to Cart	🗂 Catalog Servers	🗂 Cart serve..	📋 HTTP	Distribut..	●	Allow
🔵	☐	4	Catalog to Shipping	🗂 Catalog Servers	🗂 Shipping S..	📋 HTTP	Distribut..	●	Allow
🔵	☐	5	Catalog to MySQL	🗂 Catalog Servers	🗂 MySQL Se..	📋 MySQL	Distribut..	●	Allow

Figure 5-12. *Catalog server's DFW rules*

The catalog server has direct connectivity to the database that stores all the inventory details. This can be treated as one of the critical connections points. Even with Zero Trust policy rules, all the required handling has to be done on a database level to ensure that there are no other vulnerable ports exposed in the system that can be accessed through the Catalog application.

Cart Application Server

Once the user determines which product she wants to buy, she usually adds the item to the cart. Users can add multiple items to their carts. Users then check out once they are finished shopping.

This means the cart needs to be stored somewhere. You can use a MongoDB database for this purpose. MongoDB is a document store database that has its own advantages compared to MySQL. You can use MySQL for the purpose as well.

There are multiple checkpoints to consider before adding the request to the cart. The system must first check the inventory/catalog for the availability of the stock. Then it determines how long it will take the product to reach the user. This means there is a bidirectional connection between the cart and the catalog applications. You can add other features, like a cart expiry, to the system. Since they don't impact the security model discussed here, this section skips those details. Figure 5-13 shows the cart application's server connectivity flows.

Application	Egress Server	Port	Appied to	Based on
Cart application Server	Front End Webserver	NA	DFW	IP Sets/Sec Groups
Cart application Server	Order appication Server	80	DFW	IP Sets/Sec Groups
Cart application Server	Payment application Server	NA	DFW	IP Sets/Sec Groups
Cart application Server	User applciation Server	80	DFW	IP Sets/Sec Groups
Cart application Server	Catalog Application Server	80	DFW	IP Sets/Sec Groups
Cart application Server	Shipping applciation Server	NA	DFW	IP Sets/Sec Groups
Cart application Server	Mysql database	NA	DFW	IP Sets/Sec Groups
Cart application Server	MongoDB database	270717	DFW	IP Sets/Sec Groups
Cart application Server	RabbitMQ messaging Queue	NA	DFW	IP Sets/Sec Groups
Cart application Server	O&M servers	Ports as per Req		

Figure 5-13. *Cart application's server connectivity flows*

These are also micro-segmentation/Zero Trust policy rules. Figure 5-14 shows the cart application's server DFW rules.

Figure 5-14. *Cart application's server DFW rules*

User Application Server

Once the user decides to check out, she has to verify the details before starting the order process. Users have to be registered at the site. If they are not logged in yet, they have to log in and access the cart. Users also have to update their address information if necessary. The user application server can save the user details on the MongoDB backend.

As discussed, there are many advanced features you can enable on a per user basis. You can even apply a discount for loyal users who place regular orders. You can encourage new users to visit regularly. All this will fall under the application design. From a security perspective, identifying the user credentials is important. All relevant measures have to be taken to ensure the database is hardened enough.

If the user is not registered, she has to be redirected to a registration page to enter the details.

Figure 5-15 shows the user application's server connectivity flows.

Application	Egress Server	Port	Applied to	Based on
User applciation Server	Front End Webserver	80	DFW	IP Sets/Sec Groups
User applciation Server	Order appication Server	80	DFW	IP Sets/Sec Groups
User applciation Server	Payment application Server	80	DFW	IP Sets/Sec Groups
User applciation Server	Cart application Server	80	DFW	IP Sets/Sec Groups
User applciation Server	Catalog Application Server	NA	DFW	IP Sets/Sec Groups
User applciation Server	Shipping applciation Server	NA	DFW	IP Sets/Sec Groups
User applciation Server	Mysql database	NA	DFW	IP Sets/Sec Groups
User applciation Server	MongoDB database	27017	DFW	IP Sets/Sec Groups
User applciation Server	RabbitMQ messaging Queue	NA	DFW	IP Sets/Sec Groups
User applciation Server	O&M servers	Ports as per Req		

Figure 5-15. *User application's server connectivity flows*

These are also micro-segmentation/Zero Trust policy rules.
Figure 5-16 shows the user application's DFW rules.

		1	User to Frontend	User Servers	Frontend ...	HTTP	Distribut...	● Allow
		2	User to Order	User Servers	Order ser...	HTTP	Distribut .	● Allow
		3	User to Payment	User Servers	Payment s...	HTTP	Distribut...	● Allow
		4	User to Cart	User Servers	Cart serve...	HTTP	Distribut...	● Allow
		5	User to MongoDB	User Servers	MongoDB ...	Mongo...	Distribut...	● Allow

Figure 5-16. *User application's DFW rules*

Order Application Server

The next step is to place the order. Necessary application checks have to be performed as well. This is also a business-critical application. A user who casually browses the catalog may not buy something every time. But when a user decides to check out, she is going to place an order.

The IT infrastructure has to be flawless and completely secure during this operation. This is an area where the company is getting revenue and the employees are getting paid. This process has to be secure and perfect.

The longer the user has to wait before ordering a product, the more she is going to be frustrated. No business wants to lose a purchase at this point.

All the order information will be again saved in a MongoDB database.

Figure 5-17 shows the order application's server connectivity flows.

Application	Egress Server	Port	Appied to	Based on
Order appication Server	Front End Webserver	NA	DFW	IP Sets/Sec Groups
Order appication Server	Cart application Server	80	DFW	IP Sets/Sec Groups
Order appication Server	Payment application Server	80	DFW	IP Sets/Sec Groups
Order appication Server	User applciation Server	80	DFW	IP Sets/Sec Groups
Order appication Server	Catalog Application Server	NA	DFW	IP Sets/Sec Groups
Order appication Server	Shipping applciation Server	80	DFW	IP Sets/Sec Groups
Order appication Server	Mysql database	NA	DFW	IP Sets/Sec Groups
Order appication Server	MongoDB database	270717	DFW	IP Sets/Sec Groups
Order appication Server	RabbitMQ messaging Queue	NA	DFW	IP Sets/Sec Groups
Order appication Server	O&M servers	Ports as per Req		

Figure 5-17. *Order application's server connectivity flows*

These are also micro-segmentation/Zero Trust policy rules.

Figure 5-18 shows the order application's server DFW rules.

		1	Order to Cart	Order servers	Cart serve...	HTTP	Distribut...	Allow
		2	Order to Payment	Order servers	Payment s...	HTTP	Distribut...	Allow
		3	Order to User	Order servers	User Serv...	HTTP	Distribut...	Allow
		4	Order to Shipping	Order servers	Shipping S...	HTTP	Distribut...	Allow
		5	Order to MongoDB	Order servers	MongoDB...	Mongo...	Distribut...	Allow

Figure 5-18. *The order application's server DFW rules*

Payment Application Server

The payment application usually forwards the request to the third-party banking interfaces. If the payment application saves the credit card details, there have to be enough security and encryption methods so that the user data is secure. There have been cases where user information (such as credit details) was stolen from websites. If you are going to save the data, make sure you have strict methods in place to secure it. The purpose of the payment application is to interact with the banking interface, do the transaction, and update the response.

The response of the banking interfaces are not in your control, but the necessary rules and ports need to be opened for this transaction to happen.

This section doesn't list all the details required for payment applications. Only general connectivity flows are listed, as shown in Figure 5-19.

Application	Egress Server	Port	Applied to	Based on
Payment application Server	Front End Webserver	NA	DFW	IP Sets/Sec Groups
Payment application Server	Cart application Server	NA	DFW	IP Sets/Sec Groups
Payment application Server	Order appication Server	80	DFW	IP Sets/Sec Groups
Payment application Server	User applciation Server	80	DFW	IP Sets/Sec Groups
Payment application Server	Catalog Application Server	NA	DFW	IP Sets/Sec Groups
Payment application Server	Shipping applciation Server	NA	DFW	IP Sets/Sec Groups
Payment application Server	Mysql database	NA	DFW	IP Sets/Sec Groups
Payment application Server	MongoDB database	NA	DFW	IP Sets/Sec Groups
Payment application Server	RabbitMQ messaging Queue	NA	DFW	IP Sets/Sec Groups
Payment application Server	O&M servers	Ports as per Req		

Figure 5-19. *Payment application's server connectivity flows*

These are also micro-segmentation/Zero Trust policy rules. Figure 5-20 shows the payment server's DFW rules.

		1	Payment to User	Payment servers	User Serv..	HTTP	Distribut..	Allow
		2	Payment to Order	Payment servers	Order ser..	HTTP	Distribut..	Allow

Figure 5-20. *Payment server's DFW rules*

Shipping Application

Once the order has been placed, the request has to be updated to the shipping application. It is the responsibility of the shipping application to keep track of the request updates. For this, you can use a messaging queue system as an asynchronous communication system for updates (see Figure 5-21).

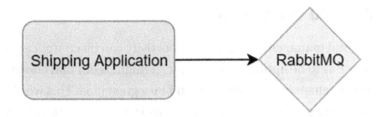

Figure 5-21. *The shipping application uses the RabbitMQ messaging queue*

A messaging queue is a system used in a distributed system for asynchronous communication. In this example, the application will be subscribed to a particular queue for any changes. If there are changes published to the queue by any connected application, they will be updated to all the subscribers. Figure 5-22 shows the shipping application's server connectivity flows.

Application	Egress Server	Port	Appied to	Based on
Shipping applciation Server	Front End Webserver	NA	DFW	IP Sets/Sec Groups
Shipping applciation Server	Cart application Server	NA	DFW	IP Sets/Sec Groups
Shipping applciation Server	Order appication Server	80	DFW	IP Sets/Sec Groups
Shipping applciation Server	User applciation Server	80	DFW	IP Sets/Sec Groups
Shipping applciation Server	Catalog Application Server	NA	DFW	IP Sets/Sec Groups
Shipping applciation Server	Payment application Server	NA	DFW	IP Sets/Sec Groups
Shipping applciation Server	Mysql database	NA	DFW	IP Sets/Sec Groups
Shipping applciation Server	MongoDB database	NA	DFW	IP Sets/Sec Groups
Shipping applciation Server	RabbitMQ messaging Queue	5672	DFW	IP Sets/Sec Groups
Shipping applciation Server	O&M servers	Ports as per Req		

Figure 5-22. *Shipping application's server connectivity flows*

These are also micro-segmentation/Zero Trust policy rules. Figure 5-23 shows the shipping application's DFW rules.

🔵	☐	1	Shipping to Order	🖼 Shipping Servers	🖼 Order ser...	🗔 HTTP	Distribut...	● Allow
🔵	☐	2	Shipping to User	🖼 Shipping Servers	🖼 User Serv...	🗔 HTTP	Distribut...	● Allow
🔵	☐	3	Shipping to RabbitM...	🖼 Shipping Servers	🖼 RabbitMQ ...	🗔 Rabbit...	Distribut...	● Allow

Figure 5-23. *Shipping application's DFW rules*

Database and O&M Servers

Operations and management server connectivity can be complicated. Port connectivity has to be application-specific. It might seem that allowing full access to management systems would be a great idea. This would most likely create a big loophole in your Zero Trust system. Hackers are normally looking for a management server to get easy access to your system, so this particular loophole could be dangerous and could act as a single point of failure.

Make security groups specific to management and monitoring servers and apply only required rules.

You have learned about each component and its respective flows. This sets you up for the requirements to designing better security solutions.

All servers can be added to the nested security groups. Another rule can be created for the traffic to management and monitoring servers (see Figures 5-24 and 5-25).

Figure 5-24. O&M DFW rules

Figure 5-25. Default DENY rule

Horizon VDI

In addition to the infrastructure server, what if the T-shirt company wanted to use an end-to-end VMware solution and a VMware horizon desktop infrastructure? You would need to add similar rulesets to make sure you are adding all the RDP sessions and scrutinizing the flows before requests enter the server farm.

An additional security group with Horizon clients can be included in the design; the required flows have to be decided based on the LDAP user types. For example, a normal user shouldn't have unrestricted access to all the servers in the system, but an administrator should be able to access the servers and perform maintenance tasks.

As discussed in the beginning of the chapter, most attacks originate from an internal network. Nowadays, most companies have mandatory security courses. But still, as this involves people from multiple backgrounds, not everyone is sufficiently aware of the security risks of clicking on an email attachment in spam. Most people think their security infrastructure or anti-virus software will take care of everything.

It is not the single desktop system you should be worried about. In most cases, the modern virus is created to have maximum impact. Unlike the previous generation of virus programs, new programs try to spread into the network first instead of crashing a single system.

Zero Trust policies and security groups have to prepare for these attacks along with their automated security.

Handling Scalability

Needing to add servers for scalability reasons happens almost instantly with any modern infrastructure. In the T-shirt application, you have to take these details into account when creating security groups. Each application can be added to a security group that has similar firewall rules.

If you use the service composer in conjunction with this approach, the results can be phenomenal. When you create a new webserver or a new application server, you can add specific tags that place the servers automatically in the security groups. The DFW policies are added to the vNIC automatically as well.

This should be applied to all application services. This practice has to be carried out across all the security groups. As the firewall policies increase with the number of servers, this will help you reduce manual tasks. Designing with automation in mind at the start can give you an advantage in later phases.

Brownfield Setup

In most scenarios, there are instances in which a customer wants to migrate from a traditional setup to a software-defined network architecture. The advantage in this case is that you know the existing setup, including its advantages and challenges and the problems you are trying to solve. But there should be a good amount of preparation to start the project. There is no plug-and-play solution, so you need to prepare and plan the phases and design changes.

Understanding the Current Architecture

One key point to mention is to make sure that all the relevant documentation is available and up to date before you even think about starting or changing things. Changing some part of the setup and trying to go back, only to find that there were no references or documentation on how you did it before is a disaster. So up to date documentation is the key.

Before tearing down the design, try to understand which part of the application works well and what advantages you're getting from this compared to a traditional perimeter appliance-based design. The performance of the hardware appliance would be great if you were using a separate physical server. They are firewall vendors with their own proprietary feature set, which can helpful in solving problems. This may not be available in NSX, but knowing what you don't have is as important as understanding what you do have. You are not looking to replace feature to feature. Identify the weaknesses in the design. When you have a comprehensive understanding of the strengths and weaknesses, you are in a good place to start planning.

An AS-IS and TO-BE detailing will always be helpful at the beginning of the project. Even SWOT analysis of the two methods will give you a fair idea of where you stand and where you are going to end up. This helps you convey a clear idea of what to expect, even to non-technical managers.

You could be bombarded with a lot of marketing terms and end up believing that the tool can do almost everything. In that case, you will end up being disappointed, even when the newly deployed stack is a considerable improvement in the design. Avoid such pitfalls by including all the stakeholders and ensuring that they understand what they are going to get at the end.

Be sure you back up the current configurations and the export options available in the firewall appliance. VMware NSX has very little support for the import feature from another firewall appliances. This ruleset, imported in a familiar format, will help create the distributed firewall rules.

Register the current requirements of auditing and logging. The same has to be implemented in a new setup, as the requirements for security audits are generic across the industry.

The latter part of the project can follow the greenfield system to design and model the security architecture based on Zero Trust networks.

How Zero Trust Helps: An Example

This section covers different kinds of attacks that can happen to any Internet company. There are distributed denial of service attacks happening daily all over the world. To coordinate such attacks, hackers typically take control of the network's infrastructure. Hackers sometimes get into the IoT network and use the IoT sensors to launch an attack.

They then illegally use your network. If a botnet was installed on your network and you were not aware, it can be used against any other Internet companies to launch a botnet attack. It is always crucial to have a defense mechanism against these common attack types.

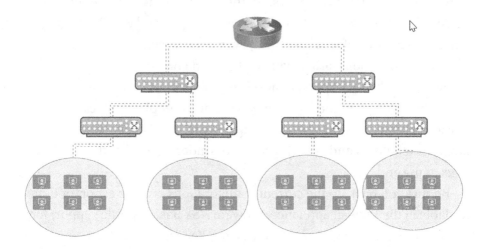

Figure 5-26. *Example infrastructure*

Consider Figure 5-26. You can even take the example of the T-shirt company's infrastructure.

Without Zero Trust

Without Zero Trust, there is no block of the lateral movement between the machines. Once a server/workstation is affected, the virus/ransomware can easily spread throughout the network (see Figure 5-27).

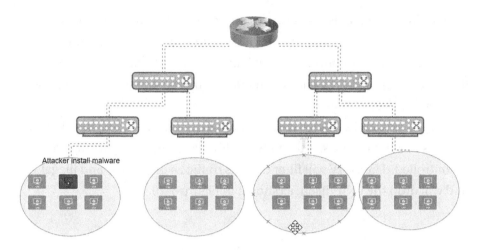

Figure 5-27. *Attacker gains access to the infrastructure*

Because the network is not segmented, the attacker can easily access across the network, unless he hits a firewall policy (see Figure 5-28).

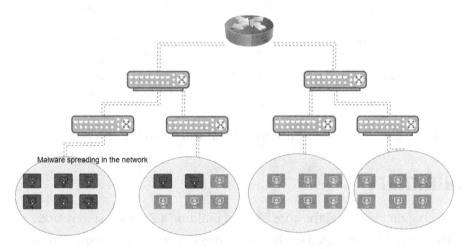

Figure 5-28. *Malware is spreading through the network*

Gradually, the malware looks for any kind of shared service or credential that can be used to hop into another server/workstation and launch attacks. This continues until it meets a definite policy that prevents this. In a network that has no segmentation, this type of attack can cause widespread destruction.

As you saw in the T-shirt company application, you deploy the firewall policies on all the vNICs. If the network is affected by malware, the spread is controlled. The DFW will filter out this traffic as unwanted and illegal and will drop the vNIC itself, as shown in Figure 5-29.

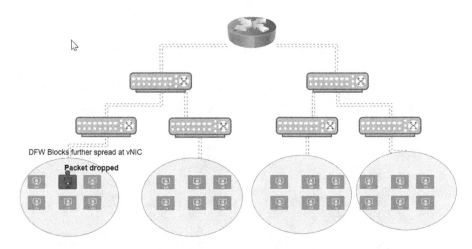

Figure 5-29. *DFW identifies the attack and stops the spread*

Summary

This chapter explained the core ideas of building a Zero Trust network. This idea can be reviewed further according to your project requirements and implemented across the VMware environment. The benefit you get from this design is very noticeable, as you have more control over your network. The next chapter discusses the tools that can aid you with this process. It covers the REST API and the automation options available with the NSX.

CHAPTER 6

The NSX REST API and PowerNSX

REST (Representational State Transfer) is an architectural style used to design APIs for various code builds. It's arguably the most popular API architecture choice at this time. Most products using an API interface use the REST API.

Suppose you built an awesome product that analyzes traffic data and suggests the best possible time to start a journey so that you can reach the destination with the least amount of traffic snarls. Your application is working great, and you are getting a lot of requests from third-party integrators asking you to provide an interface so that they can use the findings from your application.

These third-party partners have specific use cases. They can use the application to query for data, get the data, and then use it as input to their applications. If this seems complicated, consider that they just want to query the results from your application from time to time. This means you have to expose some part of your application to outside developers, which they can then use to target their queries.

© Sreejith Keeriyattil 2019
S. Keeriyattil, *Zero Trust Networks with VMware NSX*,
https://doi.org/10.1007/978-1-4842-5431-8_6

There are many models that can help build the API. REST-based API is one. There are specific requirements that need to be fulfilled for an API to be RESTful:

- Statelessness

- Client-server architecture

- Layered system

- Code on demand

These are the minimum criteria for a REST-based interface. Much more in-depth theory about the REST API can be found online. The intention here is not to design the API. VMware does the hard part for you. You need to know how to use the REST API interface for NSX.

The point to note is that even the GUI in the backend makes REST API calls to the NSX Manager and executes CRUD operations. So in short, you were using the REST API even though you weren't aware of it.

Another point is that any web application can expose its code through the REST API. For example, Twitter has exposed their API using the REST API interface; any user can search through the statistics that Twitter exposes globally using a REST client. For example, if you wanted to add the number of times a specific keyword is mentioned in tweets, you could do this using a RESTful call to the Twitter API. You can embed this information into your application code and your application will then seamlessly integrate with the Twitter API.

Most modern social media networks work this same way. Facebook and Instagram have their APIs exposed and third-party partners or advertising agencies can search through the information as needed. Of course, they don't expose their sensitive user information to everyone, but they are free to expose information that they think has monetary or advertising value.

```
These are all odd numbers. 1
These are all even numbers. 2
These are all odd numbers. 3
These are all even numbers. 4
These are all odd numbers. 5
```

break and continue are two important concepts not only in Dart but in every programming language.

Decision-Making with switch and case

In some cases, decision-making can be easier when you use switch instead of if-else logic. switch statements in Dart compare integers, strings, or compile-time constants using the double equal sign (==) behind the scenes; it maintains the rule, though, that the compared objects must be instances of the same class and not of any of its subtypes. (Don't worry, this will become clear when we get to classes later in the book.)

Consider this simple example first:

```
void main() {
   var marks = "A";
   switch(marks) {
      case "A": {  print("Very Good"); }
      break;

      case "B": {  print("Good"); }
      break;

      case "C": {  print("Fair"); }
      break;

      case "D": {  print("Poor"); }
      break;
```

```
    default: { print("Fail"); }
    break;
  }
}
```

The output is Very Good. Here the object marks is of the same class as in the case statements (String).

Let's look at another example:

```
//code 2.11
main(List<String> arguments) {
  //that could be the input value that would take inputs from
  users
  var startingTime = 5;
  switch (startingTime) {
    case 5:
      print("Printer Ready");
      break;
    case 6:
      print("Start printing");
      break;
    case 7:
      print("Stop for a second");
      break;
    case 8:
      print("Loading a tray and roll the paper.");
      break;
    case 9:
      print("Printer Ready, start printing.");
      break;
```

```
    default:
      print("Default ${startingTime}");
  }
}
```

The significance of break is that if the condition is met, the switch statement ends, and the program continues.

When someone starts the printer, it gives us output like this because startingTime is 5:

```
//output of code 2.11
Printer Ready
```

We have used a default clause to execute the code when no case clause matches.

Summary

Controlling the flow of code is essential for many reasons. This is the foundation of any algorithms that instruct computers to behave in a certain way. Building a mobile or web application needs many such instructions. Because these algorithms can be complex, they require an understanding of a few other key concepts such as functions and object-oriented programming.

In the next chapter, we will talk about functions first. After that, you will learn object-oriented programming thoroughly, and we will then return to the topic of features to discuss other key features of them.

CHAPTER 3

Functions and Objects

When we say functions are objects in Dart, it may seem confusing if you're a beginner. Basically, because Dart is an object-oriented language, even functions are objects and have a type called Function.

This means many things. First, you can assign a function to a variable, and you can even pass a function as an argument to other functions. You can also call an instance of a Dart class as if it were a function.

In this chapter, first you will now learn how a Dart function works. Then you will learn about objects. To understand objects, you need to have an understanding of object-oriented programming, which we'll also talk about in this chapter.

Functions

Let's see how functions work. This section is a basic introduction, and I will cover this topic more in-depth later when discussing methods in object-oriented programming.

© Sanjib Sinha 2020
S. Sinha, *Quick Start Guide to Dart Programming*,
https://doi.org/10.1007/978-1-4842-5562-9_3

Before writing a function, you need to remember these major points:

- It is a good practice to define the type of a function. So, type annotation is recommended.

- Although Dart recommends type annotation, a function still works without any type declaration. In other words, you can omit the type and write it straight. Dart uses type interference. Here's an example:

```
Map<String, dynamic> arguments = {'John': 'Smith',
'Chicago': 42};
Alternatively, you can use var and let Dart infer the
type:
var arguments = {'John': 'Smith', 'Chicago': 42};
// Map<String, Object>
```

- However, the most important thing to remember in Dart is that whatever value you want to return from a function, you need to change the type of that function accordingly. If you want an integer value to return, for example, you should change the type of the function to integer.

- Simply put, for void, nothing is returned from a function. So, whenever you use the keyword void before the function, you need to use print(object) to see what's happening inside that function.

The following are two simple functions with type annotations, and we have called them inside the main() function:

```
//code 3.1
main(List<String> arguments) {
  isTrue();
  isFalse();
}
```

```
void isTrue(){
  print("It's true.");
}
void isFalse(){
  print("It's false.");
}

//output of code 3.1
It's true.
It's false.
```

Let's omit the type and see how the same code works.

```
//code 3.2
main(List<String> arguments) {
  isTrue();
  isFalse();
}
isTrue(){
  print("It's true.");
}
isFalse(){
  print("It's false.");
}
```

This gives us the same result because according to the type of the value, it is automatically inferred. Here Dart knows they, here the types, are void because we are not using any return statements.

So, type annotations do not matter in such cases, but for API building (we will cover this part at the end of this book), type annotation is necessary.

Note   If you change this code by adding the type bool before the function name, it still works without giving any error. Dart just uses what you've written because there is no reason to display an error (we're not trying to return something that is not a bool). It's loose like that.

You can call another function inside a function, as shown here:

```
//code 3.3
main(List<String> arguments) {
  myName();
}
myName(){
  print("My name is John");
  myAge(12);
}
myAge(int age){
  print("My age is ${age}");
}
```

Later inside the function myName(), we have passed the age parameter or argument and get this output:

```
//output of code 3.3
My name is John
My age is 12
```

So, that was a short introduction to functions; it is evident that a function plays the same role that the verb plays in human languages. It is the action part of programming. You will understand it better when we discuss methods in object-oriented programming later in this chapter.

Before leaving this section, let look at another piece of code where we actually return a value, so the return type is important. We also use a different function syntax called *fat arrow*.

```
void withoutReturningValue(){
  print("We cannot return any value from this function.");
}

int anIntegerReturnTypeFunction(){
  int num = 10;
  return num;
}
//using Fat Arrow
String stringReturnTypeFunction(String name, String address) =>
"This is $name and this is $address and we have used the Fat
Arrow method.";

main(){
  withoutReturningValue();
  var returningInteger = anIntegerReturnTypeFunction();
  print("We are returning an integer: $returningInteger");
  print(stringReturnTypeFunction("John", "Jericho Town"));
}
```

First we use `int` as the return type of `anIntegerReturnTypeFunction()` and use the `return` keyword to specify the `int` that we're returning. This value is then assigned to a variable in `main()`.

Using the fat arrow method, we can return a value from a function in one line. This time we say it returns a `String` type. We will see more instances of fat arrow syntax later in the chapter.

The final type of function we should look at is the recursive function, shown here:

```
int getRecurse(int num)
{
    if (num > 1)
        return num * getRecurse(num - 1);
    else return 1;
}

main()
{
  print(getRecurse(5));
}
```

You can see that in main() we call getRecurse() with an int parameter of 5. Inside getRecurse(), we have an if clause to control the number of times we recurse. If the parameter is greater than 1, the code multiplies the parameter by the results of another call to getRecurse, with 1 subtracted from the parameter. This recursive call is repeated until the parameter equals 1. At that stage, the chain of recursion is wound up, and the final result is returned.

You can add some print statements to see the recursion in action.

```
int getRecurse(int num)
{
  if (num > 1) {
    print("In getRecurse and num is $num");
    return num * getRecurse(num - 1);
  } else return 1;
}
```

```
main()
{
  print(getRecurse(5));
}
```

The output is as follows:

```
In getRecurse and num is 5
In getRecurse and num is 4
In getRecurse and num is 3
In getRecurse and num is 2
120
```

You can see how 5 × 4 × 3 × 2 is 120, the final line of output.

Objects

As you know, Dart is an object-oriented language, which means it has classes and objects.

Let's start with a simple class and an object. So far you have seen variables and functions. Let's think about something that will hold variables and functions. We call it a *class*.

Suppose we have a Car class that has three properties: name, model number, and whether it is turned on. It has also two methods (outside the object-oriented paradigm we call them *functions*) called turnOn(bool) and isTurnedOn(). Consider these the "action" parts of the class Car. When we pass the bool value true to turnOn(), the car starts, and when we pass the bool value false, the car stops.

Now imagine a manufacturer wants to build many cars that have separate names and model numbers but each one has one method called turnOn(bool). In this scenario, each car is an object or instance of the Car class.

Consider the following code:

```
//code 3.4
main(List<String> arguments) {
  var newCar = new Car();
  newCar.carName = "Red Angel";
  newCar.carModel = 256;
  newCar.turnOn(false);

  if(newCar.isTurnedOn()){
    print("${newCar.carName} starts. It has model number
    ${newCar.carModel}");
  } else print("${newCar.carName} stops. It has model number
  ${newCar.carModel}");
}

class Car {
  int carModel = 123;
  String carName = "Blue Angel";
  bool isOn = true;

  bool turnOn(bool turnOn){
    isOn = turnOn;
  }

  bool isTurnedOn() {
    return isOn;
  }
}
```

It gives us this output:

```
//output of code 3.4
Red Angel stops. It has model number 256
```

Look at the Car class. It has three properties or attributes: carName, carModel, and isOn. We treat them as variables, but since they are inside a class, we will call them *properties, members,* or *attributes.* These values can be changed when we create an instance. In fact, we have done this inside the main() function. The default values were 123, Blue Angel, and true. But we have some output where the name changes to Red Angel, the model has been changed to 256, and the car stops. We have created an instance or object of the Car class by simply writing this line:

```
var newCar = new Car();
```

Next , we have defined the name and the model number as follows:

```
newCar.carName = "Red Angel";
newCar.carModel = 256;
```

The next step is vital, because we check that the method isTurnedOn() returns true.

```
if(newCar.isTurnedOn()){
  print("${newCar.carName} starts. It has model number
  ${newCar.carModel}");
} else print("${newCar.carName} stops. It has model number
${newCar.carModel}");
```

Now according to our logic, if this is true, the car should start. But in the output, we have seen that it stops.

Why does this happen?

It happens because in our Car class, we have already set that value as false.

Let's change it to true, as shown here:

```
//code 3.5
main(List<String> arguments) {
  var newCar = new Car();
```

```
  newCar.carName = "Red Angel";
  newCar.carModel = 256;
  newCar.turnOn(true);

  if(newCar.isTurnedOn()){
    print("${newCar.carName} starts. It has model number
    ${newCar.carModel}");
  } else print("${newCar.carName} stops. It has model number
  ${newCar.carModel}");
}

class Car {
  int carModel = 123;
  String carName = "Blue Angel";
  bool isOn = true;

  bool turnOn(bool turnOn){
    isOn = turnOn;
  }

  bool isTurnedOn() {
    return isOn;
  }
}
```

Take a look at the output again:

```
//output of code 3.5
Red Angel starts. It has model number 256
```

From this example, we can conclude one thing: a class is a blueprint of an object. An object or an instance of a class is extremely powerful; it is not like simple variables, holding one reference to a spot in the memory where we can store only a value. Through an app object we can run a large complicated application; moreover, we can make a complex layer of logic behind an object.

Examining Constructors

The foremost task of constructors is to create objects. Whenever we try to create an object and write this line:

```
var fatherBear = Bear();
```

we are actually trying to arrange a spot in the memory for that object. The real work begins when we connect that spot with class properties and methods.

Using a constructor, we can do that job more efficiently because constructors come first when we instantiate. Not only that, Dart allows us to create more than one constructor, which is a great advantage.

Let's write our Bear class in a new way by using a constructor:

```
//code 3.9
class Bear {
  int numberOfFish;
  int hourOfSleep;
  int weightGain;

  Bear(this.numberOfFish, this.hourOfSleep );// Constructor

  int eatFish(int numberOfFish) => numberOfFish;
  int sleepAfterEatingFish(int hourOfSleep) => hourOfSleep;
  int weightGaining(int numberOfFish, int hourOfSleep) =>
  weightGain = numberOfFish * hourOfSleep;
}

main(List<String> arguments){
  var fatherBear = Bear(6, 10);
    print("Father bear eats ${fatherBear.eatFish(fatherBear.
    numberOfFish)} fishes. And he sleeps for ${fatherBear.
    sleepAfterEatingFish(fatherBear.hourOfSleep)} hours.");
```

```
print("Father bear has gained ${fatherBear.weightGaining
(fatherBear.numberOfFish, fatherBear.hourOfSleep)} pounds of
weight.");
}
```

Creating a constructor is extremely easy. Look at this line:

```
Bear(this.numberOfFish, this.hourOfSleep);
```

The same class name works as a method, and we have passed two arguments through that method. Once we get those values, we calculate the third variable for the weight gain. In a later section of this chapter of the book we will talk more about constructors.

Now it gets easier to pass the two values while creating the object. We have used the this keyword. The this keyword represents an implicit object pointing to the current class object.

We could have done the same thing by creating a constructor in this way, which is more traditional:

```
//code 3.10
class Bear {
  int numberOfFish;
  int hourOfSleep;
  int weightGain;

  Bear(int numOfFish, int hourOfSleep ){// constructor
    this  .numberOfFish = numOfFish   ;//using this keyword to
                                        point out the current
                                        class object
    this  .hourOfSleep = hourOfSleep;
  }
  //Bear(this.numberOfFish, this.hourOfSleep);
```

```
  int eatFish(int numberOfFish) => numberOfFish;
  int sleepAfterEatingFish(int hourOfSleep) => hourOfSleep;
  int weightGaining(int numberOfFish, int hourOfSleep) =>
  weightGain = numberOfFish * hourOfSleep;
}

main(List<String> arguments){
  var fatherBear = Bear(6, 10);
  print("Father bear eats ${fatherBear.eatFish(fatherBear.
  numberOfFish)} fishes. And he sleeps for ${fatherBear.
  sleepAfterEatingFish(fatherBear.hourOfSleep)} hours.");
  print("Father bear has gained ${fatherBear.
  weightGaining(fatherBear.numberOfFish, fatherBear.
  hourOfSleep)} pounds of weight.");
}
```

In both cases, the output is the same as before:

```
//output of code 3.10
Father bear eats 6 fishes. And he sleeps for 10 hours.
Father bear has gained 60 pounds of weight.
```

In the previous code, you can even get the object's type very easily. We can change the type of value quite easily. Watch the main() function again:

```
//code 3.11
main(List<String> arguments){
  var fatherBear = Bear(6, 10);
  fatherBear.weightGain = fatherBear.numberOfFish * fatherBear.
  hourOfSleep;
  print("Father bear eats ${fatherBear.eatFish(fatherBear.
  numberOfFish)} fishes. And he sleeps for ${fatherBear.
  sleepAfterEatingFish(fatherBear.hourOfSleep)} hours.");
```

```
print("Father bear has gained ${fatherBear.
weightGaining(fatherBear.weightGain)} pounds of weight.");
print("The type of the object : ${fatherBear.weightGain.
runtimeType}");
String weightGained = fatherBear.weightGain.toString();
print("The type of the same object has changed to :
${weightGained.runtimeType}");
}
```

Here is the output:

```
//code 3.12
main(List<String> arguments){
  var fatherBear = Bear(6, 10);
  print("Father bear eats ${fatherBear.eatFish(fatherBear.
  numberOfFish)} fishes. And he sleeps for ${fatherBear.
  sleepAfterEatingFish(fatherBear.hourOfSleep)} hours.");
  print("Father bear has gained ${fatherBear.
  weightGaining(fatherBear.numberOfFish, fatherBear.
  hourOfSleep)} pounds of weight.");
  print("The type of the object : ${fatherBear.weightGain.
  runtimeType}");
  String weightGained = fatherBear.weightGain.toString();
  print("The type of the same object has changed to :
  ${weightGained.runtimeType}");
}
```

How to Implement Classes

Now you have an idea of how classes and objects work together. A class is a blueprint that has some instance variables and methods. A class might have many tasks, but it is a good practice and one of the major paradigms of object-oriented programming that a single class should have a single task. When many classes work together, they should not be tightly coupled. They should be loosely coupled.

Loosely coupled means when you use many objects from different classes, they should not be glued together. They should not affect other objects when they are affected.

This is a principle that is known as the SOLID design principle. Briefly, it means that one object should not interfere with another object. Consider a Car class, where the Wheel class should not be glued to the Steering class. That is why when we get a flat tire, we can still steer the car to a safe place. When building software applications, you should always try to decouple all classes.

In Dart, we might implement the same principle while creating classes.

Let's create a single class with a single task. We are going to create a class that will check whether a URL is secure or not.

```
//code 3.13
class CheckHTTPS {
  String urlCheck;
  CheckHTTPS(this.urlCheck);

  bool checkURL(String urlCheck){
    if(this.urlCheck.contains("https")){
      return true;
    } else return false;
  }
}
main(List<String> arguments){
  var newURL = CheckHTTPS('http://sanjib.site');
  if(!newURL.checkURL(newURL.urlCheck)) {
    print("The URL ${newURL.urlCheck} is not secured");
  }
}
```

We get this output after checking the URL:

```
//output of code 3.13
The URL http://sanjib.site is not secured
```

So, we have some basic steps to follow. Whenever we want to create a class, we should have a clear vision about what this class will do. What will be its task?

First, we need some variables. Next, we need one or more methods where we can play with these variables.

```
//code 3.14
class MyClass {
  String myVariable; //property or instance variable, initially
                      null
  MyClass(this.myVariable); //constructor

  String myMethod(){ //method declaration
    return "This is my method and this is ${myVariable}";
    //returning value
  }
}

main(List<String> arguments){
  var myObject = MyClass("My String"); //creating new instance
                                        of class MyClass
  print("${myObject.myMethod()}"); //printing the value
}
```

Look at the code: we have declared an instance variable first. It is of the String type. Since we have not initialized the variable, it is initially null. In the next step, we have constructed an object by declaring a constructor where we have passed the instance variable. Our method's type is also String. In the method, we have returned a String object.

In the main() function, we have created an object and declared the type as MyClass; and at the same time, we have passed a string value to the constructor. Finally, we have called the class method and displayed the output.

In the next section, we will write some methods and try to understand how they work. Methods are essential parts of any class because they are the action part.

Lexical Scope in Functions

This concept is extremely important as far as Dart functions are concerned.

Note   Later, when we dig deep into object-oriented programming, we will see how the concepts of access plays a vital role in Dart.

Let's return to functions. First look at the following code and read the comments:

```
//code 3.15
var outsideVariable = "I am an outsider.";

main(List<String> arguments){
  //we can access the outside variable
  print(outsideVariable);
  // we cannot access the insider variable, it gives us error
  //print(insiderVariable);
  // it is an insider function
  String insiderFunction(){
    // I can access the outside variable, no problem
    print("This is from the insider function.");
    print(outsideVariable);
```

```
  String insiderVariable = "I am an insider";
  print(insiderVariable); // it's okay to access this insider
 }
 insiderFunction();
}
```

First, we have declared a variable outside our main() function. It is called outsideVariable. We can access that variable inside the main() function as an object. Remember, everything in Dart is an object.

Second, we have declared an insider function called insiderFunction(). Now inside that insider function, we can safely call the outsider variable. In addition, if we create another insider variable, we can also call it.

So, we get this output:

```
//output of code 3.15
I am an outsider.
This is from the insider function.
I am an outsider.
I am an insider
```

As such, there is no problem regarding the output. However, it will not be the same experience if we try to call the insider variable from outside the scope of our insider function.

```
//code 3.16
var outsideVariable = "I am an outsider.";
main(List<String> arguments){
  //we can access the outside variable
  print(outsideVariable);
  // we cannot access the insider variable, it gives us error
  print(insiderVariable);
  // it is an insider function
```

```
String insiderFunction(){
    // I can access the outisde variable, no problem
    print("This is from the insider function.");
    print(outsideVariable);
    String insiderVariable = "I am an insider";
    print(insiderVariable); // it's okay to access this insider
  }
  insiderFunction();
}
```

Now, look at the output:

```
//output of code 3.16
bin/main.dart:11:9: Error: Getter not found: 'insiderVariable'.
  print(insiderVariable);
        ^^^^^^^^^^^^^^^
```

We should understand this "inside and outside" case.

This is called *lexical scope*. You can call an outside variable inside the main() function. However, if you define an object inside a function, you cannot call it from outside of that function.

A Few Words About Getter and Setter

Let's again return to the topic of object-oriented programming to learn about a key concept called the getter and setter. We can explicitly set a value and get it in this way, using the . notation:

```
//code 3.17
class myClass {
    String name;
    String get getName => name;
    set setName(String aValue) => name = aValue;
}
```

```
main(List<String> arguments){
  var myObject = myClass();
  myObject.setName = "Sanjib";
  print(myObject.getName);
}
```

This gives us the output Sanjib. But how does this happen? In myClass, we have defined the setName() method to accept a parameter called aValue. Later we have called that method through the instance (myObject. setName) of the class myClass. The interesting thing is that the method setName(String aValue) defined inside myClass now works as an attribute.

You may ask why we should use getter and setter when every class has been associated with a default getter and setter?

Actually, we are overriding the default value by explicitly defining the getter and setter.

Different Types of Parameters

Whether in a class method or in a function, sometimes you need to pass values. You can call them *arguments* or *parameters*, whichever you like.

Dart is flexible; it gives ample opportunity to developers to manipulate the parameters. You can use default parameters; in such cases, you need to give a value for the defaults. This is compulsory. But there are three other options available in Dart. You can use positional parameters, named parameters, and optional parameters.

The following code uses default and positional parameters:

```
//code 3.18
//default parameters
String defaultParameters(String name, String address, {int
age = 10}){
  return "$name and $address and age $age";
}
```

```
//optional parameters
String optionalParameters(String name, String address,
[int age] ){
  return "$name and $address and $age";
}

main(){
  print(defaultParameters("John", "Jericho"));
  print(optionalParameters("John", "Form Chikago"));
  // overriding the default age
  print(defaultParameters("JOhn", "Jericho", age : 20));
}
```

Inside the main() function, in our default parameter function, we have passed only two values: name and address. We did not pass the age. We did not have to, because it already was defined in our function: {int age = 10}. Remember to use the curly braces to define the default parameter.

Can we override the default parameter? Yes, we can. Look at this part inside the main() function:

```
// overriding the default age
print(defaultParameters("JOhn", "Jericho", age : 20));
```

We have overridden the default age and made it from 10 to 20.

Next, in the optional parameter function, we have made the age optional by keeping the value inside the square brackets.

```
//optional parameters
String optionalParameters(String name, String address, [int
age] ){
  return "$name and $address and $age";
}
```

Since the parameter age is optional, we can either pass it or ignore it. However, ignoring the optional parameter will set it to null. So, the output of the previous code will look like this:

```
//output of code 3.19
John and Jericho and age 10
John and Form Chikago and null
JOhn and Jericho and age 20
```

In the case of a named parameter, we can swap the values because it, using the named parameter is very flexible. Here sequence does not matter. Let's consider this code:

```
//code 3.20
//named parameter
int findTheVolume(int length, {int height, int breadth}){
  return length * height * breadth;
}

void main(){
  //sequence does not matter
  var  result1 = findTheVolume(10, height: 20, breadth: 30);
  var  result2 = findTheVolume(10, breadth: 30, height: 10);
  print(result1);
  print(result2);
}
```

In the previous code, we have placed height and breadth inside curly braces. So, they are named parameters that we can interchange while passing the values. Interchanging the value will not affect our code.

That is the advantage of named parameters.

More About Constructors

In any class, there are many types of constructors that can be used in any application. As usual, we have a default constructor. We can pass parameters through it. We also have named parameters. Let's look at the following code snippet and try to understand how they work:

```
//code 3.21
class Bear {
  //reference variable
  int collarID;
  //default and parameterized constructor
  Bear(this.collarID);
  //first named constructor
  Bear.firstNamedConstructor(this.collarID);
  //second named constructor
  Bear.secondNamedConstructor(this.collarID);
  void trackingBear() {
    String color; // local varia   print("Tracking the bear
                  with collar ID ${collarID}");
  }
}

main(List<String> arguments){
  // bear1 is reference variable
  // Bear() is object// It should be class no object I suppose
  var bear1 = Bear(1);
  bear1.trackingBear();
  var bear2 = Bear.firstNamedConstructor(2);
  bear2.trackingBear();
  var bear3 = Bear.secondNamedConstructor(3);
  bear3.trackingBear();
}
```

In the previous code, by Dart convention, when we write a class, we might have many things in place. First, we have a reference variable here: int collarID;. The variable called collarID contains a reference to an int object with a value of a Bear object.

Inside the main() function, when we create an instance, we will again have a reference variable.

```
// bear1 is reference variable
// Bear() is object
var bear1 = Bear(1);
```

We have passed the class-level reference variable collarID through the default constructor.

So, while defining a class and afterward creating an instance, we have two types of reference variable: the first is class-level reference variable, and the second one is an object-level or instance-level reference variable. If this does not make any sense, don't worry. We'll cover it in Chapter 7.

In the constructor part, we have one default and parameterized constructor, shown here:

```
//default and parameterized constructor
Bear(this.collarID);
Besides, we have two named constructors.
//first named constructor
Bear.firstNamedConstructor(this.collarID);
//second named constructor
Bear.secondNamedConstructor(this.collarID);
```

Through the named constructors, we have created three bear instances; moreover, each instance has the same functionality. Finally, when you run the code, you cannot distinguish between the behavior of the code that uses the default constructor and the code that uses the named constructors.

```
Tracking the bear with collar ID 1
Tracking the bear with collar ID 2
Tracking the bear with collar ID 3
```

In the next chapter, we will look at another important concept: inheritance.

CHAPTER 4

Inheritance and Mixins in Dart

One of the key features of object-oriented programming is that you can extend your classes. You extend a class to create another class, and the extended class is known as a *subclass*. The subclass inherits reference variables and class methods from the parent class, which is known as a *superclass*.

The properties of the parent class are inherited by the child class; because the properties from the parent class are extended to the child class, the parent class is also called the *base class*. For the same reason, the child class is known as the *derived class*, since it is inheriting the properties of the base class. This capability, known as *inheritance*, works in two ways.

First, you can create new classes from an existing class. That is called *single inheritance*. Dart does not support multiple inheritance (inheriting from more than one class). However, it supports *multilevel inheritance*. Therefore, we can conclude that Dart supports two types of inheritance.

- Single inheritance
- Multilevel inheritance

© Sanjib Sinha 2020
S. Sinha, *Quick Start Guide to Dart Programming*,
https://doi.org/10.1007/978-1-4842-5562-9_4

A First Look at Inheritance

Consider this simple example where we have extended an Animal class to a Cat class. This is an example of single inheritance.

```dart
//code 4.1
class Animal {
  String name = "Animal";
  Animal(){
    print("I am Animal class constructor.");
  }

  Animal.namedConstructor(){
    print("This is parent animal named constructor.");
  }

  void showName(){
    print(this.name);
  }

  void eat(){
    print("Animals eat everything depending on what type it
    is.");
  }
}

class Cat extends Animal {
  //overriding parent constructor
  //although constructors are not inherited
  Cat() : super(){
    print("I am child cat class overriding super Animal
    class.");
  }
```

```dart
Cat.namedCatConstructor() : super.namedConstructor(){
    print("The child cat named constructor overrides the parent
    animal named constructor.");
  }

  @override // method overriding
  void showName(){
    print(this.name);
  }

  @override
  void eat(){
    super.eat();
    print("Cat doesn't eat vegetables..");
  }
}

main(List<String> arguments){
  var cat = Cat();
  cat.name = "Meaow";
  cat.showName();
  cat.eat();
  var anotherCat = Cat.namedCatConstructor();
}
```

Let's first look at the output; after that, we will discuss the features of subclasses and superclasses.

```
//output of code 4.1
I am Animal class constructor.
I am child cat class overriding super Animal class.
Hi from cat.
```

Animals eat everything depending on what type it is.
Cat doesn't eat vegetables..

This is parent animal named constructor. The child cat named
constructor overrides the parent animal named constructor.

The code is quite simple to follow; the superclass or base class Animal
has two constructors: the default and a named constructor. Subclasses
don't inherit constructors from their superclass. The subclass or
derived class Cat overrides both constructors. You have to specify which
constructor you are overriding in the subclass's constructor definition. If
you do not, then your named subclass constructor will override the default
constructor of the parent class.

```
Cat.namedCatConstructor() : super.namedConstructor(){
  print("The child cat named constructor overrides the parent
  animal named constructor.");
}
```

Now, let's change the code a little bit and follow the output. You will
understand the concept of single inheritance better in the second example.

```
//code 4.2
class Animal {
  String name = "Animal";
  Animal(){
    print("I am Animal class constructor.");
  }
  Animal.namedConstructor(){
    print("This is parent animal named constructor.");
  }
  void showName(){
    print(this.name);
    print("Hi from ${this.name}");
  }
```

```dart
  void eat(){
    print("Animals eat everything depending on what type it
    is.");
  }
}

class Cat extends Animal {
  //overriding parent constructor
  //although constructors are not inherited
  Cat() : super(){
    print("I am child cat class overriding super Animal class.");
  }
  Cat.namedCatConstructor() : super.namedConstructor(){
    print("The child cat named constructor overrides the parent
    animal named constructor.");
  }

  @override
  void showName(){
    print("Hi from cat.");
    print(this.name);
  }

  @override
  void eat(){
    super.eat();
    print("Cat doesn't eat vegetables..");
  }
}

class Cow extends Animal {
  //overriding parent constructor
  //although constructors are not inherited
```

```dart
  Cow() : super(){
    print("I am child cow class overriding super Animal
    class.");
  }
  Cow.namedCatConstructor() : super.namedConstructor(){
    print("The child cow named constructor overrides the parent
    animal named constructor.");
  }

  @override
  void showName(){
    print("Hi from cow.");
    print(this.name);
  }

  @override
  void eat(){
    super.eat();
    print("Cow does eat grass..");
  }
}

main(List<String> arguments){
  var cow = Cow();
  cow.name = "Daisy";
  cow.showName();
  var cat = Cat();
  cat.name = "Meaow";
  cat.showName();
  cat.eat();
  var anotherCat = Cat.namedCatConstructor();
}
```

We have added more lines in the parent class, created a new Cow class, and added some lines to both child classes; at the same time, we have added a few lines in our main() function to get the output.

Here is the new output:

```
//output of code 4.2
/home/ss/flutter/bin/cache/dart-sdk/bin/dart --enable-vm-
service:33101 /home/ss/IdeaProjects/bin/main.dart
Observatory listening on http://127.0.0.1:33101/

I am Animal class constructor.
I am child cow class overriding super Animal class.
Hi from cow.
Daisy
I am Animal class constructor.
I am child cat class overriding super Animal class.
Hi from cat.
Meaow
Animals eat everything depending on what type it is.
Cat doesn't eat vegetables..
This is parent animal named constructor.
The child cat named constructor overrides the parent animal
named constructor.

Process finished with exit code 0
```

You can see that more than one class can be based on a superclass.

Multilevel Inheritance

Let's consider the code first, and after looking at the output, we will discuss how multilevel inheritance works.

```
//code 4.3
class Animal {
  String name = "Animal";
  Animal(){
    print("I am Animal class constructor.");
  }
  Animal.namedConstructor(){
    print("This is parent animal named constructor.");
  }
  void showName(){
    print(this.name);
    print("Hi from ${this.name}");
  }
  void eat(){
    print("Animals eat everything depending on what type it
    is.");
  }
}

class Dog extends Animal {
  //overriding parent constructor
  //although constructors are not inherited
  Dog() : super(){
    print("I am child class dog overriding super Animal
    class.");
  }
```

```dart
  Dog.namedDogConstructor() : super.namedConstructor(){
    print("The child dog named constructor overrides the parent
    animal named constructor.");
  }
  Dog.anotherNamedConstructor(){
    print("This is parent Dog named constructor.");
  }
  @override
  void showName(){
    print("Hi from parent dog.");
    print(this.name);
  }
  @override
  void eat(){
    super.eat();
    print("Dog doesn't eat vegetables..");
  }
}

class PuppyDog extends Dog {
  //overriding parent constructor
  //although constructors are not inherited
  PuppyDog() : super(){
    print("I am child class puppy dog overriding my immediate
    parent Dog class.");
  }
  PuppyDog.namedDogConstructor() : super.anotherNamedConstructor(){
    print("The child puppy dog named constructor overrides the
    parent Dog another named constructor.");
  }
```

CHAPTER 4   INHERITANCE AND MIXINS IN DART

```dart
  @override
  void showName(){
    print("Hi from puppy dog.");
    print(this.name);
  }
  @override
  void eat(){
    super.eat();
    print("Puppy Dog eats milk only ...");
  }
}

main(List<String> arguments){
  var animal = Animal();
  animal.name = "Cow";
  animal.showName();
  var dog = Dog();
  dog.name = "Lucky";
  dog.showName();
  dog.eat();
  var anotherDog = Dog.namedDogConstructor();
  var puppy = PuppyDog();
  puppy.name = "I am offspring of Lucky";
  puppy.showName();
  puppy.eat();
  var anotherPuppy = PuppyDog.namedDogConstructor();
}
```

Here is the output:

```
//output of code 4.3
/home/ss/flutter/bin/cache/dart-sdk/bin/dart --enable-vm-
service:40767 /home/ss/IdeaProjects/bin/main.dart
Observatory listening on http://127.0.0.1:40767/
```

```
I am Animal class constructor.
Cow
Hi from Cow
I am Animal class constructor.
I am child class dog overriding super Animal class.
Hi from parent dog.
Lucky
Animals eat everything depending on what type it is.
Dog doesn't eat vegetables..
This is parent animal named constructor.
The child dog named constructor overrides the parent animal
named constructor.
I am Animal class constructor.
I am child class dog overriding super Animal class.
I am child class puppy dog overriding my immediate parent Dog class.
Hi from puppy dog.
I am offspring of Lucky
Animals eat everything depending on what type it is.
Dog doesn't eat vegetables..
Puppy Dog eats milk only ...
I am Animal class constructor.
This is parent Dog named constructor.
The child puppy dog named constructor overrides the parent Dog
another named constructor.

Process finished with exit code 0
```

In the previous code, the parent class is Animal. The Dog class inherits all its properties. After that, the Dog class has its offspring, a PuppyDog class. Now, the PuppyDog class inherits from the Dog class. Here, we have actually two child or base classes: Dog and PuppyDog. However, this is different from single inheritance because with multilevel inheritance, one child class is inherited from another child class.

In this example, the child class PuppyDog inherits from another child class, Dog. You can compare this tree of family lineage to a human's. I have a father, yet my father has a father, who is my grandfather, and on it goes.

Mixins: Adding More Features to a Class

Dart has a lot to offer when classes need to be reused; there is an important concept called a *mixin*. It is a way of reusing any class's code in multiple class hierarchies.

We can rewrite the previous code using mixins. All we need to do is use the keyword with. Suppose we have a class Dog that has a method canRun(). A Cat object can also run, can't it? Let's try the same code in a slightly different way.

```
//code 4.4
class Animal {
  String name = "Animal";
  Animal(){
    print("I am Animal class constructor.");
  }
  Animal.namedConstructor(){
    print("This is parent animal named constructor.");
  }
  void showName(){
    print(this.name);
  }
  void eat(){
    print("Animals eat everything depending on what type it
    is.");
  }
}
```

```dart
class Dog {
  void canRun(){
    print("I can run.");
  }
}

class Cat extends Animal with Dog {//reusing another class
  //overriding parent constructor
  //although constructors are not inherited
  Cat() : super(){
    print("I am child cat class overriding super Animal class.");
  }
  Cat.namedCatConstructor() : super.namedConstructor(){
    print("The child cat named constructor overrides the parent
    animal named constructor.");
  }
  @override
  void showName(){
    print("Hi from cat.");
  }
  @override
  void eat(){
    super.eat();
    print("Cat doesn't eat vegetables..");
  }
}

main(List<String> arguments){
  var cat = Cat();
  cat.name = "Meaow";
  cat.showName();
  cat.eat();
```

```
  var anotherCat = Cat.namedCatConstructor();
  anotherCat.canRun();
}
```

The subclass Cat has been extended, and at the same it has used mixins by reusing the Dog class's code. Look at this line:

```
class Cat extends Animal with Dog {...}
```

In the main() function, the Cat object uses the Dog class's method in this way:

```
anotherCat.canRun();
```

The output has not been changed except the last line, as shown here:

```
//output of code 4.4
I am Animal class constructor.
I am child cat class overriding super Animal class.
Hi from cat.
Animals eat everything depending on what type it is.
Cat doesn't eat vegetables..
This is parent animal named constructor.
The child cat named constructor overrides the parent animal
named constructor.
I can run.
```

Remember, for mixins, you need to use the with keyword followed by one or more mixin names.

Note   Support for mixins was introduced in Dart 2.1. Before that, in such cases, an abstract class was used. In the next chapter, you will learn about abstract classes and methods.

Mixins are a kind of limited multiple inheritance; in the previous code, we extend from one class (`Animal`) and then use a mixin to bring in features from another (`Dog`).

You should notice one characteristic here; at every stage, we use only classes. We can inherit from a class, and we can also use a class as a mixin using the `with` keyword.

In the next chapter, we'll add another feature: interfaces. These build a contract between two classes so we don't have to hard-code a class's functionality into another class. As long as a class conforms to the contract, we can change it without affecting the calling class.

CHAPTER 5

Entity Relationships: Abstract Classes, Interfaces, and Exception Handling

In the previous chapter, you learned that entities do not exist in isolation. You saw some examples of inheritance. You will see more in a minute, although in different forms.

There are a few more types of relationships between classes. A relationship between each class is always defined beforehand so that we don't have to use same code again and again. Like C#, PHP, Python, and Java, in Dart, the classes in a program can be related to each other. Identifying and establishing the relationships between them is an important aspect of object-oriented programming (OOP).

Therefore, the main objective of this chapter is to learn how we can identify relationships between classes, how we can define abstract classes and methods, and how we can use interfaces. We'll also look at exception handling because it's affected by entity relationships, and we use inheritance and interfaces as part of efficient error handling.

© Sanjib Sinha 2020
S. Sinha, *Quick Start Guide to Dart Programming*,
https://doi.org/10.1007/978-1-4842-5562-9_5

Identifying Relationships Between Entities

In general, our challenge is to create an application that is as close as possible to the real world. To do that, in a software application, we relate classes and objects to each other in such a manner that they remain loosely coupled. They act and react with other classes and objects. This dynamism makes them as close as possible to the real world.

In OOP, objects perform actions in response to messages from other objects, defining the receiving object's behavior.

There are similarities and differences among the entities, objects, and classes as a whole. Let's take a look at the following observations:

- A bus is a kind of an automobile.

- A car is a kind of an automobile.

- An engine is a part of an automobile.

- A wheel is a part of an automobile.

- A driver drives a car.

The preceding entities represent different objects and classes; still, they are related to each other. Furthermore, they should be loosely coupled; if one gets affected, that does not have any effect on the other (for example, if the design of a steering wheel on a car changes, the relationship with the driver does not). Now, based on the preceding observations, we can summarize our entity relationships in the following manner:

- Inheritance relationship

- Composition relationship

- Utilization relationship

- Instantiation relationship

In the previous chapter, you saw examples of inheritance. We can say that an automobile is a superclass of a car and bus. On the other hand, car and bus are subclasses. They derive features defined in the base class or superclass automobile. They have a relationship where one object is a type of another object, yet the reverse is not true. Every car is an automobile, but every automobile is not a car. Recall that Dart allows single inheritance and multilevel inheritance. Multiple inheritance in Dart is not allowed, although you can compensate that with the help of mixins, as we saw in Chapter 4.

Let's consider another set of relationships.

- A human is a kind of mammal.

- A cat is a kind of mammal.

- A tiger is a kind of cat.

- A lion is a kind of cat.

Now we can depict this relationship in Figure 5-1.

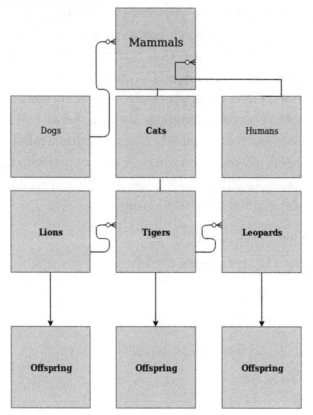

Figure 5-1. *A simple relationship between mammal entities*

In Figure 5-1, there is a set of classes: mammals, dogs, cats, humans, lions, tigers, leopards, and their offspring classes. The superclass mammals have the following set of characteristics:

- They are warm-blooded.

- They are vertebrates.

- They all have external ears.

- They all have internal brains covered by skulls.

We can say that dog, cat, and humans have similarities; they have similar characteristics because they have inherited these attributes from the superclass mammals. However, subclass cat is a superclass of lions, tigers, and leopards; therefore, they will have similarities that they don't share with dogs and humans.

One key feature of object-oriented programming in Dart is it allows us to create an object that includes another object as its part. This mechanism of creating an object is called *composition relationship*. Keeping Figure 5-1 in mind, we can conclude that humans and tigers do not have a composition relationship, whereas cats and tigers have a composition relationship. It is called *composition* because one class has some traits in other classes that are directly related to the previous class. Cat, Tiger, Lion, etc., are examples.

A utilization relationship is different. Consider Figure 5-1. A human can use a dog to hunt, for example. Dart allows a class to make use of another class.

An instantiation relationship is nothing but a relation between a class and its object or instance. John is an object of a human class. When we create a John object, we use the mammal class as an abstract superclass.

In the next section, you will see how we can use abstract classes.

Using Abstract Classes

An abstract class is used to provide a partial class implementation, leaving the unimplemented piece to a subclass. Abstract methods can exist only in abstract classes. In abstract methods, we just leave a semicolon (;) at the end of the method name. We don't define the method body.

An abstract class is also where we can define an interface but leave its implementation up to other classes. As I said at the end of Chapter 4, an interface is a contract between two classes. Any class, abstract or concrete, in Dart can be an interface. It's just much more common to use an abstract class and leave the specifics up to the child class.

These are two key points to remember when you write an abstract class:

- You cannot create an instance of an abstract class.

- You cannot declare an abstract method outside an abstract class.

```
//code 5.1
//we cannot instantiate any abstract class
abstract class volume{
  //we can declare instance variable
  int age;
  void increase();
  void decrease();
  // a normal function
  void anyNormalFunction(int age){
    print("This is a normal function to know the $age.");
  }
}

class soundSystem extends volume{
  void increase(){
    print("Sound is up.");
  }
  void decrease(){
    print("Sound is down.");
  }
  //it is optional to override the normal function
  void anyNormalFunction(int age){
    print("This is a normal function to know how old the sound
    system is: $age.");
  }
}
```

```
main(List<String> arguments){
  var newSystem = soundSystem();
  newSystem.increase();
  newSystem.decrease();
  newSystem.anyNormalFunction(10);
}
```

Here is the output of the previous code:

```
Sound is up.
Sound is down.
This is a normal function to know how old the sound system is: 10.
```

We have used the `abstract` modifier to define an abstract class that cannot be instantiated.

So, we can say that the abstract class and methods summarize the main ideas, and we can extend that idea.

There are a few more things to remember about an abstract class in Dart.

- In an abstract class, we can also use normal properties and methods.

- It is optional to override the method.

- We can also define instance variables in the abstract class.

Consider the following code to understand how abstract classes in Dart are different from other object-oriented programming languages:

```
//code 5.2
abstract class Mammal {
  void run();
  void walk();
```

```dart
  void sound(){
    print("Mammals make sound");
  }
}

class Human implements Mammal {

  void run(){
    print("I am running.");
  }
  void walk(){
    print("I am walking");
  }
  void sound(){
    print("Humans make sound");
  }
}

main(List<String> arguments){
  var John = Human();
  print("John says: ");
  John.run();
  print("John says: ");
  John.walk();
  print("John makes no sound.");
  John.sound();
}
```

Here is the output where we can clearly see how we overrode the
abstract method:

```
//output of code 5.2
/home/ss/flutter/bin/cache/dart-sdk/bin/dart --enable-vm-
service:35727 /home/ss/IdeaProjects/bin/main.dart
Observatory listening on http://127.0.0.1:35727/
```

John says:
I am running.
John says:
I am walking
John makes sound.
Humans make sound

Process finished with exit code 0

Advantages of Interfaces

In some cases, we need to use reference variables and methods of many
classes at the same time. Mixins can help. But there is another good feature
in Dart: we can also use an interface.

An interface defines the syntactical contract that all the derived classes
should follow. You will see in a minute how that works.

Let's see the code first, and then we will discuss it in detail. Remember that
an interface in Dart is written as a class, but we don't extend; we implement it.

```
//code 5.3
// interface in Dart is a class, but we don't extend,
// we implement it
class Vehicle {
  void steerTheVehicle() {
    print("The vehicle is moving.");
  }
}

class Engine {
  //in the interface
  final _name; // final means single assignment and it must
               have an initializer as I use here
  //not in the interface, since it is a constructor
```

```dart
    Engine(this._name);
    String lessOilConsumption(){
      return "It consumes less oil.";
    }
}

class Car implements Vehicle, Engine{
  var _name;

  void steerTheVehicle() {
    print("The car is moving.");
  }

  String lessOilConsumption(){
    print("This model of car consumes less oil.");
  }

  void ridingExperience() => print("This car gives good ride,
  because it is an ${this._name}");
}

main(List<String> arguments){
  var car = Car();
  car._name = "Opel";
  print("Car name: ${car._name}");
  car.steerTheVehicle();
  car.lessOilConsumption();
  car.ridingExperience();
}
```

Here is the output of the previous code:

```
Car name: Opel
The car is moving.
This model of car consumes less oil.
This car gives good ride, because it is an Opel
```

When a class implements an interface, it implicitly defines all the
instance members of the implemented interface. A class implements one
or more interfaces at a time by declaring the implements keyword.

Considering the previous code, we see that class Car supports class
Vehicle and class Engine's API, and for that requirement, the class Car
implements class Vehicle and class Engine's interfaces. You can see the
Car object can call methods specified in Vehicle and Engine, as well as its
own methods.

An interface is used when we need a standard structure of methods; it
is not necessary that you should implement the interface members within
any interface. Consider this code:

```
//code 5.4
class OrderDetails {
  void UpdateCustomers(){
  }
  void TakeOrder(){
  }
}

class ItemDetails implements OrderDetails{
  void UpdateCustomers(){
    //implementing interface members
    print("Updating customers.");
  }
  void TakeOrder(){
    //implementing interface members
    print("Taking orders from customers.");
  }
}
```

```
main(List<String> arguments){
  var book = ItemDetails();
  book.TakeOrder();
  book.UpdateCustomers();
}
```

Now, look at the output, shown here:

```
//output of code 5.4
/home/ss/flutter/bin/cache/dart-sdk/bin/dart --enable-vm-
service:40359 /home/ss/IdeaProjects/bin/main.dart
Observatory listening on http://127.0.0.1:40359/

Taking orders from customers.
Updating customers.

Process finished with exit code 0
```

What happens if we don't follow this standard structure? When we implement an interface, we should implement interface members.

The next code snippet and the output will explain this:

```
//code 5.5
class OrderDetails {
  void UpdateCustomers(){
  }
  void TakeOrder(){
  }
}

class ItemDetails implements OrderDetails{
  void UpdateCustomers(){
    //implementing interface members
    print("Updating customers.");
  }
```

```
  /*
  void TakeOrder(){
    //implementing interface members
    print("Taking orders from customers.");
  }
  */
}

main(List<String> arguments){
  var book = ItemDetails();
  //book.TakeOrder();
  book.UpdateCustomers();
}
```

We didn't implement the interface member TakeOrder(). We have
commented out that part of the preceding code.

In this case, the exceptions raised in Android Studio and the errors
given as output tell us what we should have done. Look at the output:

```
//output of code 5.5
/home/ss/flutter/bin/cache/dart-sdk/bin/dart --enable-vm-
service:34271 /home/ss/IdeaProjects/bin/main.dart
Observatory listening on http://127.0.0.1:34271/

bin/main.dart:40:7: Error: The non-abstract class 'ItemDetails'
is missing implementations for these members:
 - OrderDetails.TakeOrder
Try to either
 - provide an implementation,
 - inherit an implementation from a superclass or mixin,
 - mark the class as abstract, or
 - provide a 'noSuchMethod' implementation.

class ItemDetails implements OrderDetails{
      ^^^^^^^^^^^
```

```
bin/main.dart:36:8: Context: 'OrderDetails.TakeOrder' is
defined here.
  void TakeOrder(){
       ^^^^^^^^^
```

```
Process finished with exit code 254
```

From the previous output, it is clear that Dart clearly notices that we have not implemented a method when we should have. If there is an implementation in an abstract class, we can use it when we extend that class.

Consider this code:

```dart
//code 5.6
class OrderDetails {
  //int age;
  /*
  void anyNormalFunction(int age){
    print("This is a normal function to know the $age.");
  }
  */
  void UpdateCustomers(){
  }
  void TakeOrder(){
  }
}

abstract class CustomerDetails {
  void Customers(){
    print("A list of customers.");
  }
}
class ItemDetails extends CustomerDetails implements
OrderDetails {
```

```dart
  void anyNormalFunction(int age){
    print("This is a normal function to know the age: $age.");
  }
  void UpdateCustomers(){
    //implementing interface members
    print("Updating customers.");
  }

  void TakeOrder(){
  }

}

main(List<String> arguments){
  var book = ItemDetails();
  //book.TakeOrder();
  book.UpdateCustomers();
  book.anyNormalFunction(12);
  book.Customers();
}
```

In the preceding code, we extended the abstract class, and at the same time, we implemented the interface. The output is here:

```
//output of code 5.6
/home/ss/flutter/bin/cache/dart-sdk/bin/dart --enable-vm-
service:39205 /home/ss/IdeaProjects/bin/main.dart
Observatory listening on http://127.0.0.1:39205/

Updating customers.
This is a normal function to know the age: 12.
A list of customers.

Process finished with exit code 0
```

You can see that the abstract class's `Customers()` method is called when we don't implement it ourselves.

There is another major difference between an abstract class and an interface. An abstract class can use normal properties and methods. However, it will give errors if we don't implement any part of an interface, in other words, if we leave the interface to keep its own implementation of a property or method. Look at this code and its output:

```
//code 5.7
class OrderDetails {
  int age;
  void anyNormalFunction(int age){
    print("This is a normal function to know the $age.");
  }

  void UpdateCustomers(){
  }
  void TakeOrder(){
  }
}

abstract class CustomerDetails {
  void Customers(){
  }
}

class ItemDetails extends CustomerDetails implements
OrderDetails {
//trying to implement interface normal functions
  void anyNormalFunction(int age){
    print("This is a normal function to know the age: $age.");
  }
```

```
  void UpdateCustomers(){
    //implementing interface members
    print("Updating customers.");
  }

  void TakeOrder(){
  }

  void Customers(){
  }

}

main(List<String> arguments){
  var book = ItemDetails();
  //book.TakeOrder();
  book.UpdateCustomers();
  book.anyNormalFunction(12);
}
```

Here is the error report:

```
//output of code 5.7
/home/ss/flutter/bin/cache/dart-sdk/bin/dart --enable-vm-
service:38747 /home/ss/IdeaProjects/bin/main.dart
Observatory listening on http://127.0.0.1:38747/

bin/main.dart:50:7: Error: The non-abstract class 'ItemDetails'
is missing implementations for these members:
 - OrderDetails.age
Try to either
 - provide an implementation,
 - inherit an implementation from a superclass or mixin,
 - mark the class as abstract, or
 - provide a 'noSuchMethod' implementation.
```

```
class ItemDetails extends CustomerDetails implements
OrderDetails {
      ^^^^^^^^^^^
```

```
bin/main.dart:34:7: Context: 'OrderDetails.age' is defined here.
  int age;
      ^^^
```

```
Process finished with exit code 254
```

Therefore, here are a few things to remember about interfaces in Dart:

- The biggest advantage of interfaces is that we can implement multiple interfaces. Since multiple inheritance is not allowed in Dart, we can design our application in a way so that we can mimic inheriting multiple classes using interfaces. However, we cannot use any normal properties and behaviors in interfaces.

- Although we cannot inherit multiple classes through inheritance, we can overcome that limitation by combining abstract classes, interfaces, and mixins.

Static Variables and Methods

To implement class-wide variables and methods, we use the static keyword. Static variables are also called *class variables*. Let's first see a code snippet, and after that, we will discuss the advantages and disadvantages of static variables and methods.

```
//code 5.8
// static variables and methods consume less memory
// they are lazily initialized
class Circle{
  static const pi = 3.14;
```

```
static void drawACircle(){
  //from static method you cannot call a normal function
  print(pi);
}

void aNonStaticFunction(){
  //from a normal function or method you can call a static meethod
  Circle.drawACircle();
  print("This is normal function.");
}
}

main(List<String> arguments){
  var circle = Circle();
  circle.aNonStaticFunction();
  Circle.drawACircle();
}
```

Here is the output:

```
3.14
This is normal function.
3.14
```

As you see, static variables are useful for class-wide state and constants. So, in the main() method, we can add this line at the end:

```
main(List<String> arguments){
  var circle = Circle();
  circle.aNonStaticFunction();
  Circle.drawACircle();
  print(Circle.pi);
}
```

We get the value of constant pi again. Here, `Circle.pi` is the class variable, and the class method is `Circle.drawACircle()`. The biggest advantage of using static variables and methods is it consumes less memory. An instance variable, once instantiated, consumes memory whether it is being used or not. The static variables and methods are not initialized until they are used in the program. It consumes memory when they are used. By the way, it is also important to note that constants make maintenance easier and make programs easier to read.

Here are a few things to remember:

- From a normal function, you can call a static method.

- From a static method, you cannot call a normal function.

- In a static method, you cannot use the `this` keyword. This is because the static methods do not operate on an instance and thus do not have access to `this`.

So, in the end, we can conclude that using static variables and methods depends on the context and situations.

Exception Handling

During the execution of any program, some errors can occur that will disrupt the flow of the program automatically. These errors are called *exceptions*. In the exception handling cases, the class `Exception` is the superclass of all exceptions to prevent the application from terminating abruptly. This is why I'm covering exception handling in Chapter 7.

Figure 5-2 illustrates this concept where a computing process has two possible outputs. One could be the processed data we wanted, and another could be an error. We should enable ourselves to catch this error before it gives an ugly exception on the user's interface.

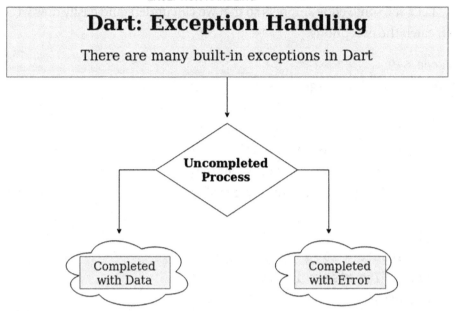

Figure 5-2. *Any uncompleted process could lead us to two possible*
outputs

Suppose you want to divide a number by zero. It is an impossible task
and will disrupt the flow, resulting in some errors. However, you cannot
control a user's behavior, so you need to take every precaution to handle
errors gracefully.

Dart programmers have thought about it, and they have included many
built-in exception classes. One of them is `IntegerDivisionByZeroException`;
it is thrown when a number is divided by zero. Likewise, when a
scheduled timeout happens while waiting for an asynchronous result,
the timeout exception occurs. If deferred libraries fail to load, there is
`DeferredLoadException` that happens.

Suppose a string cannot be parsed because it does not have the proper
format. In that case, `FormatException` occurs. Any input- and output-
related exceptions are captured through the `IOException` class.

133

Let's see some code snippets so that we can understand easily how we can catch the exceptions.

```
//code 5.9
main(List<String> arguments){
  try{
    int result = 10 ~/ 0;
    print("The result is $result");
  } on IntegerDivisionByZeroException{
    print("We cannot divide by zero");
  }
  try{
    int result = 10 ~/ 0;
    print("The result is $result");
  } catch(e){
    print(e);
  }
  try{
    int result = 10 ~/ 0;
    print("The result is $result");
  } catch(e){
    print("The exception is : $e");
  } finally{
    print("This is finally and it always is executed.");
  }
}
```

We have caught these errors before they give some ugly output to the user.

```
//the output of code 5.9
We cannot divide by zero
IntegerDivisionByZeroException
The exception is : IntegerDivisionByZeroException
This is finally and it always is executed.
```

As you can see in the output, there are several methods through which we can catch the exceptions. If we know the type of exception, we can use try/on, as we have used in the following previous code:

```
try{
  int result = 10 ~/ 0;
  print("The result is $result");
} on IntegerDivisionByZeroException{
  print("We cannot divide by zero");
}
```

In this case, we did know what type of exception can be generated. So, we have used try/on. But what happens when we do not know the exception?

In most cases, presumably a beginner will not know all the exception classes that are predefined in Dart libraries. However, it is important to know a few, which I have mentioned previously. Besides, the main reason to wrap our code inside the try/catch block is this: we may have errors in our code. Our code may contain problems. As a programmer, we should not take any risks.

The syntax of handling exception is the following:

```
try{
  int result = 10 ~/ 0;
  print("The result is $result");
} catch(e){
  print(e);
}
```

The catch block is used when the handler needs the exception object.

The try block can be followed by the finally block after the catch block. We used the same thing in the following previous code:

```
try{
  int result = 10 ~/ 0;
  print("The result is $result");
} catch(e){
  print("The exception is : $e");
} finally{
  print("This is finally and it always is executed.");
}
```

The finally block will be executed at the end, whatever the outcome:

```
The exception is : IntegerDivisionByZeroException
This is finally and it always is executed.
```

If an exception occurs in the try block, the control goes to the catch block; and at the end, the finally block gives the output.

We can now wrap this section up with Figure 5-3 that depicts how many types of exception handling are used in Dart with the help of Exception classes.

In Figure 5-3, you will find the term *stack trace*. When a program is run, memory is allocated in two places, the stack and the heap. If there is a problem in our code, before allocating the memory, some events fire, and this can be traced in the stack. Simply put, a stack trace is the list of method calls that the application was in the middle of when an exception was thrown. We will look for the topmost method and know where the errors happen. In Dart, you will have to read the stack trace report; I am sure you will learn many things about how a program is run.

In addition, we can create our custom exception handling class that will catch the error. Why do we need that? You can add more flexibility to your code by building custom exception handling to give more useful

names to exceptions, for example. However, I won't suggest as a beginner
you should get your hands dirty with building custom exception classes
immediately.

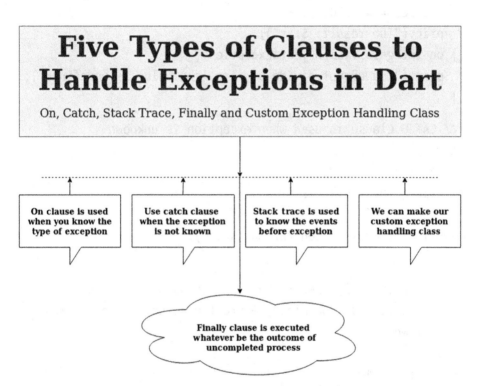

Figure 5-3. *Five types of exception handling in Dart*

We can also finally finish the task completely with a single codebase
where we get through all the clauses of exception handling.

```
//code 5.10
class InputException implements Exception {
  String customException() {
    return "The input of negative number is not valid.";
  }
}
```

```dart
void main() {
  // ON Clause is used when the exception is known
  try {
    var res = 4 ~/ 0;
    print("The result: $res");
  } on IntegerDivisionByZeroException {
    print("You cannot divide by zero, the value is undefined");
  }

  // CATCH Clause is used when exception is unknown
  try {
    var res = 3 ~/ 0;
    print("The result is $res");
  } catch (e) {
    print("The exception thrown is $e");
  }

  // STACK TRACE is used to know the steps of the events
  // these events took place before the actual Exception was
    thrown
  try {
    int res = 10 ~/ 0;
    print("The result is $res");
  } catch (e, s) {
    print("The exception: $e");
    print("Stack trace is \n $s");
  }

  // FINALLY Clause is always Executed
  // whether exception is thrown or not
  try {
    int res = 9 ~/ 0;
    print("The result: $res");
```

```
  } catch (e) {
    print("The exception: $e");
  } finally {
    print("The finally clause is always executed.");
  }

  // we can make our Custom Exception by creating a class
  try {
    inputValue(-14);
  } catch (e) {
    print(e.customException());
  } finally {
    print("The finally clause is always executed");
  }
}

void inputValue(int inputNumber) {
  if (inputNumber < 0) {
    var inputException = InputException();
    throw inputException;
  }
}
```

Note the use of the throw keyword in the inputValue() function. This throws the specified exception and passes control back to the calling code. The try/catch block can then handle this thrown exception. Now we can take a look at the output to see the stack trace:

```
//output of code 5.10
/home/ss/Downloads/flutter/bin/cache/dart-sdk/bin/dart
--enable-asserts --enable-vm-service:42201 /home/ss/
IdeaProjects/my_app/main.dart
Observatory listening on http://127.0.0.1:42201/eUtYODGP6ro=/
```

```
You cannot divide by zero, the value is undefined
The exception thrown is IntegerDivisionByZeroException
The exception: IntegerDivisionByZeroException
Stack trace is
#0      int.~/ (dart:core-patch/integers.dart:18:7)
#1      main (file:///home/ss/IdeaProjects/my_app/main.
        dart:24:18)
#2      _startIsolate.<anonymous closure> (dart:isolate-patch/
        isolate_patch.dart:301:19)
#3      _RawReceivePortImpl._handleMessage (dart:isolate-patch/
        isolate_patch.dart:172:12)

The exception: IntegerDivisionByZeroException
The finally clause is always executed.
The input of negative number is not valid.
The finally clause is always executed

Process finished with exit code 0
```

Now, it entirely depends on the developer how they handle the exception. All we should remember is that the user will not like it if an exception is raised by the code. Therefore, it is mandatory to go through the test before going live, and it is always better to use an exception handling mechanism where needed.

CHAPTER 6

Anonymous Functions

In Dart, most of the functions we have seen so far are named functions, which are similar to functions in languages like C# and Java. Still, the function syntax of Dart has more similarities with JavaScript than in many strongly typed languages like C# or Java.

Because in Dart everything is object, a function is also an object; this means we can store it in a variable and use it anywhere in our application. The advantage of Dart is we that can pass a function like any other type, such as string, integer, etc. These features are greatly enhanced when the functions have no names at all. These nameless functions act the same as named functions; they can have any number of parameters, including zero parameters. The type annotations are optional.

These functions are called *anonymous functions*. Like named functions, we can assign any anonymous function to a function object variable. We can also pass it to another function.

Lambdas, higher-order functions, and lexical closures all are anonymous functions, and they have some similarities. In their namelessness and anonymity, these features of Dart are very interesting. Let's start with lambdas. Then we will discuss higher-order functions and closures. In reality, you will find that lambdas actually implement higher-order functions.

© Sanjib Sinha 2020
S. Sinha, *Quick Start Guide to Dart Programming*,
https://doi.org/10.1007/978-1-4842-5562-9_6

A First Look at Lambdas

Figure 6-1 shows how we can use lambdas, one type of anonymous function.

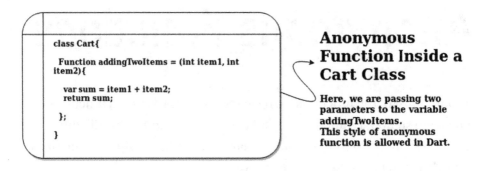

```
class Cart{

  Function addingTwoItems = (int item1, int
  item2){

    var sum = item1 + item2;
    return sum;

  };

}
```

Anonymous Function Inside a Cart Class

Here, we are passing two parameters to the variable addingTwoItems.
This style of anonymous function is allowed in Dart.

In the above Figure, An anonymous function is defined and assigned to a variable named addingTwoItems. The ; is used to terminate the variable assignment.

Figure 6-1. *An anonymous function is assigned to a variable*

In Figure 6-1, the longhand version of the anonymous function needs a terminating semicolon; this is because we assign the value to a variable named addingTwoItems. In addition, the longhand version, we can use the fat arrow notation, as covered in Chapter 5. Figure 6-2 shows the two types of anonymous functions and how we can use them in our application. We will also see the code in a minute.

Returning to the T-Shirt Company Example

Let's consider again the T-shirt company example to clarify why you need a REST API interface. You learned about the different services and apps available from the T-shirt company application. Third-party sellers who are happily using the platform to sell their T-shirts and goods normally have a tracking system for orders and inventory. In most cases, they need the ability to determine the status and order details from the website. They need to keep track of the product sold and the products in the cart to make sure they are stocking products in inventory to meet demand.

You can either build a separate application for the third-party sellers or expose part of the code as a REST API and provide access through the API. There aren't any other demands or unique restrictions placed on the API format. This makes it easier for the third-party sellers to integrate their application with this one.

Each service can serve their REST API interface and they can all be connected through an API gateway. In application architectures using microservices, a REST API is the most commonly used way to provide service-to-service communication. As mentioned, in the case of the T-shirt company, the entire application does not have to be exposed to the third party. You can restrict which services need to be exposed through the API.

This section doesn't get into the details about creating the REST API methods (see Figure 6-1) for the T-Shirt application. It's solely meant for developers who write the application's feature sets. The intention here is to focus on the NSX API part, which can be used to create DFW rules.

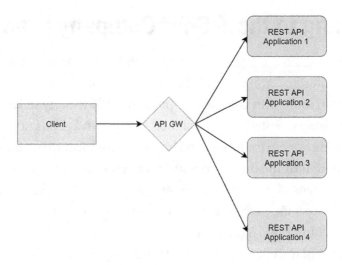

Figure 6-1. *REST API connectivity*

The NSX REST API

The NSX REST API allows you to interact with NSX objects through REST calls. The NSX objects include the following:

- Data centers

- Clusters/hosts

- Resource groups

- Distributed switches

- Port groups

- VMs

These are some of the objects which you can target to your REST calls. Here are the REST API methods for NSX calls:

- GET: Can be used to query the status or information about the NSX objects. This operation won't make any changes related to the objects; it will only display the status in a preferred data format like JSON, XML, or HTTP.

- POST: Used to create a new NSX object like security group, port group, etc. This method adds new resources, which are then visible across all management tools.

- PUT: Used to modify existing NSX objects, like adding new IP sets to existing DFW rules. Its equivalent CRUD operation is UPDATE.

- DELETE: This deletes the existing the NSX object. This is the same as removing the object using the management tool.

You can do all the CRUD operations using these REST API methods. The REST API is a common standard used across the industry. REST API queries should be initiated by a client call. The client can be curl, a wget command from Linux terminal, or even a web browser using the POSTMAN client application (see Figure 6-2).

Figure 6-2. *POSTMAN GUI interface*

In the REST API call, you can see that the connection is done through the HTTPS secure channel. NSX FQDN is used to connect to the NSX Manager. The API version should be specified in the URL. The object information is given in the last section of the REST call.

Figure 6-3. POSTMAN client headers

The Header includes two pieces of information—the content type, which is marked as application/xml, and the authorization, which is selected as basic.

The fields listed in Figure 6-3 are the bare minimum requirements for all API requests. Figure 6-4 shows the POSTMAN REST API GET call syntax for the syslog server.

Figure 6-4. POSTMAN REST API GET call syntax for the syslog server

The output shows that there is no syslog server configured in the NSX Manager.

You can configure this using the NSX Manager GUI. You can also do it using the REST API or using a POST request.

Updating Syslog Server Details Using the REST API

Syslog server details can be added to the NSX Managers, controllers, and ESXi host to forward the logs to a centralized repository. This repository can be VMware Log Insight or any other third-party log management tool. The prerequisites are to add the syslog server IP/FQDN to all the mentioned servers. Adding the syslog server IP manually is a straightforward process. Regarding the benefits of end-to-end automation, there might be use cases where you need to update the syslog servers in multiple setups and this can be done along with another workflow. In such cases, invoking the REST API to achieve this might be beneficial.

Figure 6-5 shows the XML body required to achieve the result. This can be run using the curl command or using the POSTMAN application.

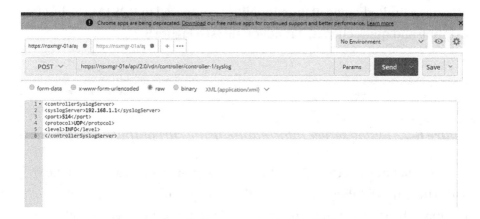

Figure 6-5. *REST API POST for adding syslog server IP addresses*

Syslog server is now configured using the given information in the REST request, as confirmed in Figure 6-6.

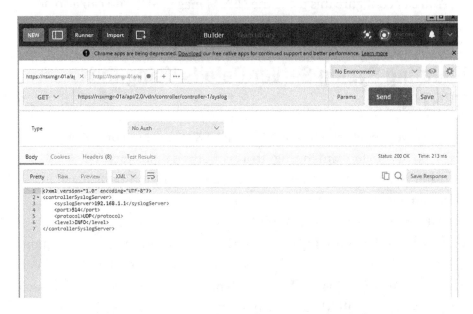

Figure 6-6. *The REST API verifying changes in the syslog server*

The Linux `curl` command can also be used to achieve similar results. Curl has a limited range of functionalities compared to POSTMAN, but for scripting and quick checks, it is adequate (see Figure 6-7).

```
root@linux-01a [ ~ ]# curl -k -u admin:VMware1! https://nsxmgr-01a/api/2.0/vdn/controller/controller-1/syslog
<?xml version="1.0" encoding="UTF-8"?>
<controllerSyslogServer><syslogServer>192.168.1.1</syslogServer><port>514</port><protocol>UDP</protocol><level>INFO</level></
controllerSyslogServer>root@linux-01a [ ~ ]#
```

Figure 6-7. *Syslog server information using curl output*

Note that most of the REST API use cases can be managed from the GUI. These REST API queries and actions are useful when you want to automate the status or functionalities and integrate them with another automation tool or other infrastructure automation workflows. If you can integrate them with other toolsets, the NSX REST API interface provides seamless opportunities for automation. This can be useful for micro-segmentation use cases as well.

NTP Configuration Using the REST API

This section shows you how to use REST API calls to configure the NTP server for the controller cluster. NTP servers are required to keep the time synced across the NSX cluster. There are options to configure up to five NTP servers in the cluster. The IP address or FQDN can be used as a parameter. DNS servers have to be configured when you are using FQDN.

For versions before NSX 6.4, the NTP for the control cluster can only be changed using the API. VMware added this functionality in version 6.4.

Request Body

```
<ControllerClusterNtpServers>
<ntpServers>
<string>192.168.110.10</string>
<string>192.168.110.11</string>
</ntpServers>
</ControllerClusterNtpServers
```

Figure 6-8 shows the REST API call using curl.

```
root@linux-01a [ ~ ]# curl -k -u admin:VMware1! https://nsxmgr-01a/api/2.0/vdn/controller/cluster/ntp
<?xml version="1.0" encoding="UTF-8"?>
<ControllerClusterNtpServers><ntpServers><string></string></ntpServers></ControllerClusterNtpServers>root@linux-01a [ ~ ]#
```

Figure 6-8. *REST API call using curl*

GET Request

```
curl -k -u admin:VMware1!  https://nsxmgr-01a/api/2.0/vdn/
controller/cluster/ntp
```

Using POSTMAN

Figure 6-9 shows the REST API GET call in a POSTMAN client for NTP information.

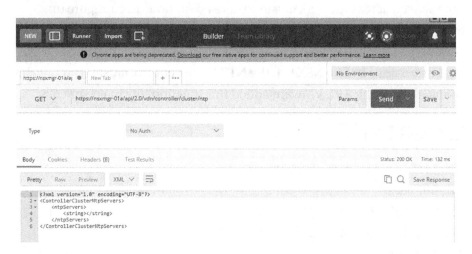

Figure 6-9. *REST API GET call in a POSTMAN client for NTP information*

You can see that the NTP is not configured for now. You used the GET method to query the status of the NTP servers in the controller cluster. You should be able to update the NSX controller cluster with NTP details using PUT. The PUT method is used to modify an existing NSX object. In this case, you already have an NSX controller cluster, so the requirement here is to modify the cluster information with the new NTP server IP.

The header information remains the same as in the GET request in the XML template. In the body of the PUT request, you have to mention the IP address of the NTP server. If the NTP server is reachable by a FQDN, it can also be mentioned (see Figures 6-10 and 6-11).

```
root@linux-01a [ ~ ]# curl -k -u admin:VMware1! https://nsxmgr-01a/api/2.0/vdn/controller/cluster/ntp
<?xml version="1.0" encoding="UTF-8"?>
<ControllerClusterNtpServers><ntpServers><string>192.168.110.10</string><string>192.168.110.11</string></ntpServers></Control
lerClusterNtpServers>root@linux-01a [ ~ ]# ▉
```

Figure 6-10. *REST API call using the curl command*

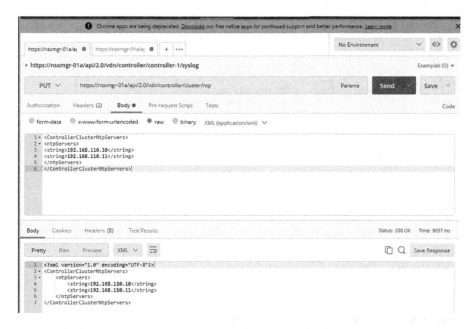

Figure 6-11. *REST API POST call changing the NTP server information*

Python Code Snippet

This is one of the most useful features of POSTMAN. You can convert any REST method into code in your favorite programming language. There are multiple language options available in the POSTMAN client (see Figure 6-12).

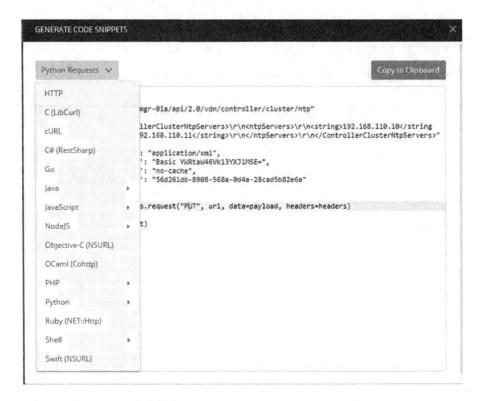

Figure 6-12. *Available languages to export*

Figure 6-13 shows the example Python code snippet of the REST query that you just ran. POSTMAN can use either request modules or HTTPS modules to achieve this same result.

There are multiple programing languages available to import the code. Each will use language-specific module. In Python, the most popular HTTPS and requests modules are given as options for generating the code.

```
GENERATE CODE SNIPPETS                                                    ✕

Python Requests ∨                                            Copy to Clipboard

1   import requests
2
3   url = "https://nsxmgr-01a/api/2.0/vdn/controller/cluster/ntp"
4
5   payload = "<ControllerClusterNtpServers>\r\n<ntpServers>\r\n<string>192.168.110.10</string
        >\r\n<string>192.168.110.11</string>\r\n</ntpServers>\r\n</ControllerClusterNtpServers>"
6 ▾ headers = {
7       'content-type': "application/xml",
8       'authorization': "Basic YWRtaW46Vk13YXJlMSE=",
9       'cache-control': "no-cache",
10      'postman-token': "56d261db-8908-568a-0d4a-28cad5b82e6a"
11      }
12
13  response = requests.request("PUT", url, data=payload, headers=headers)
14
15  print(response.text)
```

Figure 6-13. *Code in Python using Python requests*

Creating Firewall Rules in DFW Using the REST API

This section briefly goes through the steps you need to follow to achieve a similar configuration using API calls (see Figure 6-14).

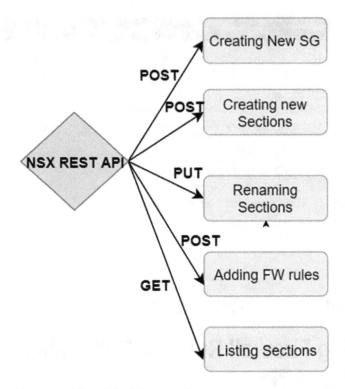

Figure 6-14. *NSX REST API flows*

Creating New Security Groups Using the REST API

You already read about how to create security groups using the VMware web client. As you learned, there can be use cases where the customer wants to integrate it into a VM deployment workflow, where the security group is created in a scripted manner along with the application.

```
<securitygroup>
<name></name>
<extendedAttributes>
<extendedAttribute>
<name>localMembersOnly</name>
```

```
<value>true</value>
</extendedAttribute>
</extendedAttributes>
NSX API Guide Version: 6.4 Page 118
</securitygroup>
```

Using Curl

```
curl -k -u admin:VMware1!
https://nsxmgr-01a/api/2.0/services/securitygroup/globalroot-0
```

Using POSTMAN

See Figures 6-15 and 6-16.

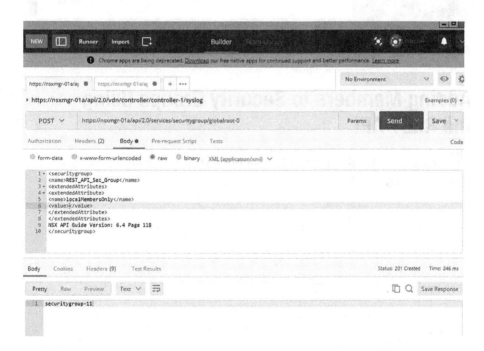

Figure 6-15. *Creating a SG using a POST call*

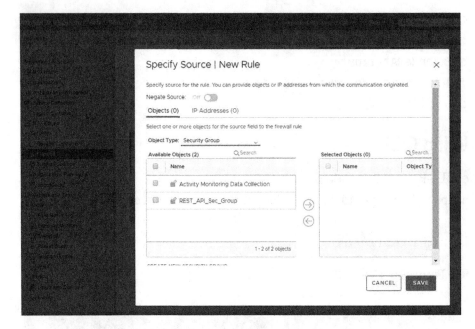

Figure 6-16. *Verifying in the GUI after creation*

Adding Members to Security Groups Using the REST API

You can get information about the security groups you created in the previous steps (see Figure 6-17).

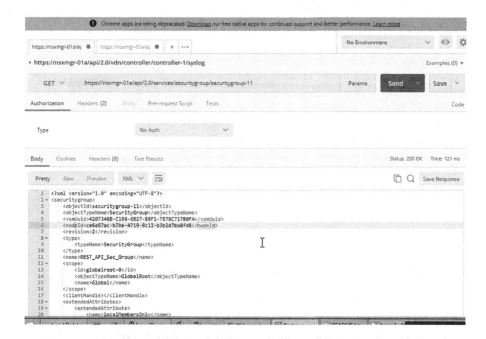

Figure 6-17. *GET call giving the SG information*

Creating a New Firewall Section Using the REST API

You can create new firewall sections using the REST API call (see Figure 6-18).

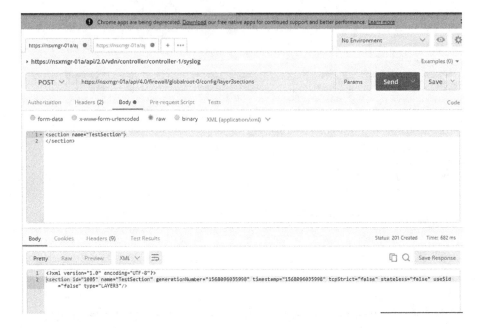

Figure 6-18. *Adding a new section using the REST API*

The previously mentioned REST call will create a new section, as shown in Figure 6-19.

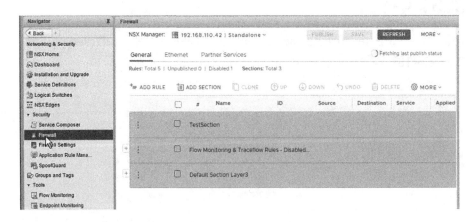

Figure 6-19. *Verifying sections in the NSX GUI*

Renaming a Firewall Section

You can even rename and edit objects via slight modifications to the API call. As mentioned, changes to an existing object are done using the PUT method (see Figure 6-20).

Figure 6-20. *Renaming sections using the REST API*

Once the API call is done, the new section will be available in the GUI (see Figure 6-21).

Figure 6-21. *Verifying the modification in the NSX GUI*

137

Creating Firewall Rules in the Section

To add a rule to an existing section, you include the Section ID and ETAG details in the REST API call. An extra header needs to be placed to make sure you are hitting the API call and the correct target. The ETAG can be found from the POSTMAN response headers (see Figure 6-22).

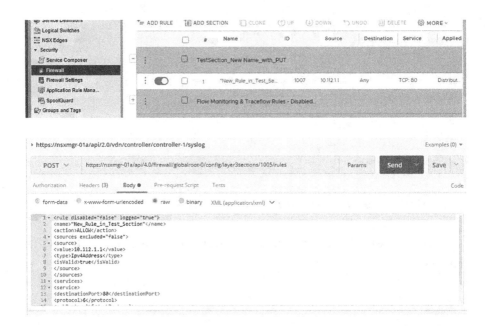

Figure 6-22. *Creating a firewall rule using the REST API*

This section demonstrated the process of creating security sections and firewall rules using only the NSX REST API. It is also possible to create all the actions you have done using NSX GUI. In comparison, in the NSX REST API, there are minor cases like NTP update that can be tagged as REST API only. But VMware normally ensures that most features are in sync with the API.

Note that you can even do the entire deployment and configuration using the REST API interface. This includes configuring DFW and adding the vCenter details.

Some actions that can be performed for reference include the following:

- Distributed vSwitch CRUD operations

- Segment ID pools and multicast ranges CRUD operation

- Service group CRUD operations

- Security tag CRUD operations

- NSX manager registration

- NSX user management

- Security groups

- Firewall rule creation

- NSX appliance manager

- CrossVC NSX setup

- Network fabric configuration

- Activity monitoring

- NSX edge

- Service composer

These are a few of the NSX features that can be configured and modified using REST API calls. In-depth details about the request body and header tags are included in the NSX REST API documentation. Always make sure you are validating against the latest or the most relevant API documentation according to the installed NSX version.

Creating a REST API call can get tricky, as the header and body size can soon become complicated if you want to do complex operations using the REST API.

139

Using PowerNSX

If you are a heavy vSphere user, you might have come across PowerCLI. PowerCLI is a command-line tool that can automate all the features of VMware. This automation tool is hugely popular and is a big help to all the sysadmins out there. vSphere is based on the SOAP API. API interfaces, in most cases, are advantageous to developers as they need to combine different feature sets in an API-based interaction. For sysadmins, automating using the SOAP or REST API is possible but requires extra effort. Having a quick automation tool with all the feature sets and that can be scripted in no time can increase a sysadmin's productivity.

That is the where PowerCLI shines and is hugely popular among sysadmins. If you want to script any kind of operation against a vSphere suite, PowerCLI will come handy. In a period where the time to go live is getting shorter, you need automation to do those repetitive tasks in less time.

Even with vSphere, with hundreds of machines, you can easily imagine several use cases where you need to update a certain feature in all the VMs, either by changing the VLAN tag or adding a vNIC. You need to use tools like PowerCLI for these repetitive tasks.

PowerNSX is open source and is not supported officially by VMware. This means there are no licensing requirements or costs involved. At the same time, not all use cases have been implemented in the PowerNSX. There is a thriving ecosystem around PowerShell, so VMware engineers decided to use the PowerNSX module to integrate NSX.

Even with NSX, you can easily imagine many of the actions you perform in NSX being linked to vSphere as well. In the process of creating a new edge VM, for example, you need to specify the datastore, computer, and data center you need to deploy the machine. Integrating with PowerShell will give you the ability to combine the use case of PowerCLI and PowerNSX.

PowerNSX can be installed on Linux, Windows, or Mac systems. It has to be connected to NSX for it to execute the instructions.

You can use the Get-Help option, shown in Figure 6-23, to find the correct syntax for PowerNSX.

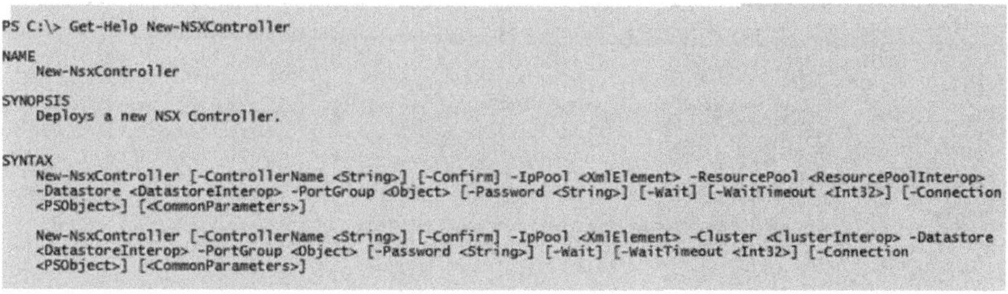

```
PS C:\> Get-Help New-NSXController

NAME
    New-NsxController

SYNOPSIS
    Deploys a new NSX Controller.


SYNTAX
    New-NsxController [-ControllerName <String>] [-Confirm] -IpPool <XmlElement> -ResourcePool <ResourcePoolInterop>
    -Datastore <DatastoreInterop> -PortGroup <Object> [-Password <String>] [-Wait] [-WaitTimeout <Int32>] [-Connection
    <PSObject>] [<CommonParameters>]

    New-NsxController [-ControllerName <String>] [-Confirm] -IpPool <XmlElement> -Cluster <ClusterInterop> -Datastore
    <DatastoreInterop> -PortGroup <Object> [-Password <String>] [-Wait] [-WaitTimeout <Int32>] [-Connection
    <PSObject>] [<CommonParameters>]
```

Figure 6-23. *PowerNSX help options*

In the help example shown in Figure 6-23, you can see the options available for creating a new controller cluster.

To run PowerShell scripts in the NSX, PowerNSX has to be connected to vCenter and to the NSX Manager. It is possible to connect PowerNSX only with the NSX Manager as well (see Figure 6-24).

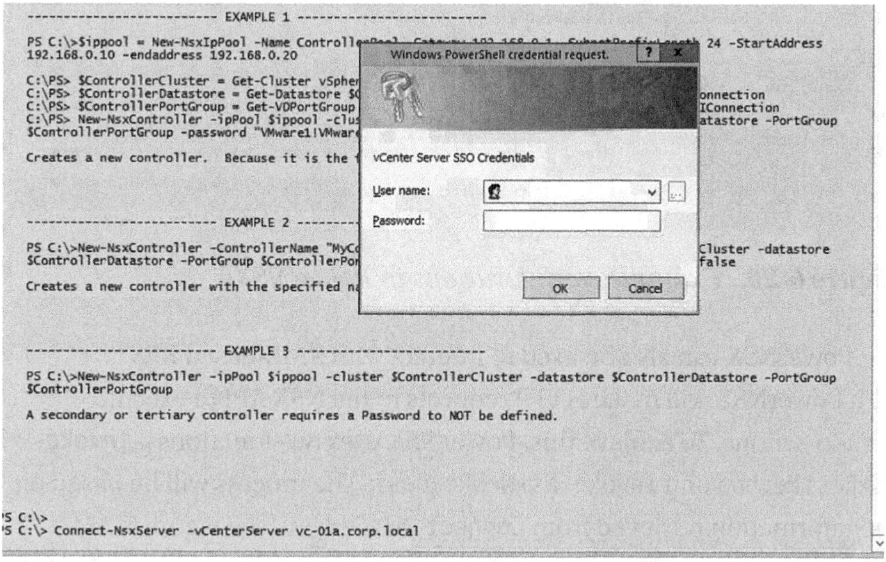

Figure 6-24. *Connecting to vCenter from PowerNSX*

Once the connection is complete, information regarding the version and server IP is displayed (see Figure 6-25).

```
PS C:\> Connect-NsxServer -vCenterServer vcsa-01a.corp.local

Version              : 6.4.1
BuildNumber          : 8599035
Credential           : System.Management.Automation.PSCredential
Server               : 192.168.110.42
Port                 : 443
Protocol             : https
UriPrefix            :
ValidateCertificate  : False
VIConnection         : vcsa-01a.corp.local
DebugLogging         : False
DebugLogFile         : C:\Temp\1\PowerNSXLog-administrator@corp.local@-2019_09_10_02_00_36.log
```

Figure 6-25. *Output from PowerNSX after a vCenter connection*

The -examples argument can be used to determine the example script configurations to run. It can be used with most PowerNSX commands (see Figure 6-26).

```
PS C:\>
PS C:\> Get-Help New-NSXController -examples

NAME
    New-NsxController

SYNOPSIS
    Deploys a new NSX Controller.

    -------------------------- EXAMPLE 1 --------------------------

    PS C:\>$ippool = New-NsxIpPool -Name ControllerPool -Gateway 192.168.0.1 -SubnetPrefixLength 24 -StartAddress
    192.168.0.10 -endaddress 192.168.0.20

    C:\PS> $ControllerCluster = Get-Cluster vSphereCluster
    C:\PS> $ControllerDatastore = Get-Datastore $ControllerDatastoreName -server $Connection.VIConnection
    C:\PS> $ControllerPortGroup = Get-VDPortGroup $ControllerPortGroupName -server $Connection.VIConnection
    C:\PS> New-NsxController -ipPool $ippool -cluster $ControllerCluster -datastore $ControllerDatastore -PortGroup
    $ControllerPortGroup -password "VMware1!VMware1!"

    Creates a new controller.  Because it is the first controller, a password must be specified.
```

Figure 6-26. *Example configurations in PowerNSX*

PowerNSX can also be used to interact with XML-based REST API. PowerNSX will make HTTP requests to the NSX API to execute certain actions. To achieve this, PowerNSX uses two functions—Invoke-NsxRestMethod and Invoke-NsxWebRequest. The process will be based on the information retrieved from Connect-NsxServer (see Figure 6-27).

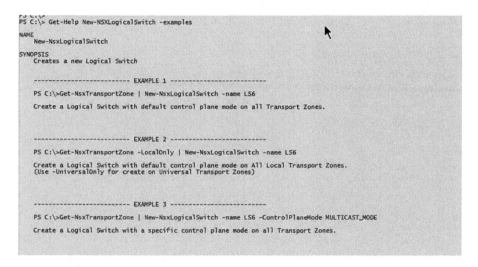

Figure 6-27. *PowerNSX examples related to logical switch*

Summary

This chapter discussed the automation options available in VMware NSX. These options are vast and most are very well documented in the NSX REST API user guide. To use any REST call efficiently, it is important to keep in sync with the API documentation. There are often changes concerning different NSX versions. So be sure to update according to the current NSX versions. PowerNSX, as mentioned, is a useful tool for any sysadmin. Scripting is necessary in enterprise setups and PowerNSX is the tool that does it right.

The coming chapter discusses the tools—like Log Insight and Network Insight—that help you analyze your network flows.

CHAPTER 7

NSX Log Insight and Network Insight

Previous chapters discussed how to create firewall policies and architectures through APIs and Graphical User Interfaces (GUIs). Creating and deploying only addresses half of the problem; the other half is all about how you manage and plan changes in the network.

VMware Log Insight is the central log management tool available with the VMware SDDC stack. Recall that logging is crucial to identifying risk and sometimes avoiding it. You need to keep logs for security audits to follow standard security practices. The traditional way of doing this is through a syslog server. All the logs are forwarded from individual systems to a syslog server. This works fine if the purpose is to store the log somewhere outside of the application systems and to save the storage resource demands of the production server.

Introduction

One serious drawback to such a design is when analyzing the logs for troubleshooting or optimization purposes. It's a laborious process. Raw logs are hard to search. Without an easy-to-use search engine, the majority of the logs can end up being useless. In modern systems,

© Sreejith Keeriyattil 2019
S. Keeriyattil, *Zero Trust Networks with VMware NSX*,
https://doi.org/10.1007/978-1-4842-5431-8_7

the need for a log management solution is becoming more and more prominent. Productivity can be vastly improved by using a centralized log management solution.

Network Insight is a powerful tool for micro-segmentation preparation and analysis. VMware delivers Network Insight and it aids the customer in planning and easily accessing the network internals. Network Insight can be utilized to see the overall traffic flow. It can also suggest new distributed firewall policies and routing optimization changes. A Network Insight database can be queried to give much better insight into the East-West traffic flow. In a traditional network, this will require a bunch of third-party toolsets to achieve a similar outcome.

This chapter doesn't explain the installation steps, as this information is freely available in the VMware documentation. Following a similar trend, this chapter focuses on the use cases of these two solutions. The REST API is also available with these management tools and that makes it easier to integrate with other automation toolsets. Log Insight uses its REST API interface to search and analyze log data.

Why Central Log Management?

Log Sources

Every application and infrastructure component can act as a log source. This can be front webserver logs, application server logs, or database logs. Logs have to be transferred from the computer's host, like ESXi for infrastructure troubleshooting. Over time, the log source will increase the storage space requirements. Saving all logs in their respective original locations may seem easy at first, but will soon become cumbersome to manage. You need to have a log rotation policy or storing policy per server to make sure the drives are not full and the retention is kept to the required level.

A centralized log server can prevent a lot of these issues. Most new-generation log management tools provide intelligent log search and queries through the CLI command set. Anyone who has searched through logs to troubleshoot a certain issue with a Linux terminal CLI interface knows the daunting task ahead of them. Even the filter command options like `grep` and `find` only help you to a certain extent. In a log management tool, if you want to search for a log at a particular time from a specific server and a specific service, you can formulate log queries and run them in the log management server and get the result. This is beneficial when your infrastructure is too big and all the servers in the infrastructure are connected to centralized log management.

Another advantage to using a log management tool is that you can get a nice customized dashboard where you can get a quick overview of the generated logs and their log sources. This can be used from a quick monitoring perspective. As discussed, as the number of microservice increases so do the log sources. You can even use some custom tags to identify and prioritize logs from different sources.

Another advantage is the API available for the log management server. Regarding storage, most of server hardware uses SAS disks or SSD based on the application needs. Storing logs in these drives may not be economically better, as there are security and audit requirements if your organization wants to keep in line with security ISO standards. In such cases, creating a centralized log management server with cheap disks like SATA in the backend is beneficial. This would reduce the overall cost with respect to storage disks.

VMware Log Insight

VMware Log Insight can ingest data using the syslog protocol and TCP or UDP on port 514. Log Insight deployment is appliance based. This is the easy-to-deploy, straightforward approach used with any OVA deployment. You have to select the data center and cluster options.

Log Insight deployment won't take a significant amount of time. In most cases, it will be up and running within minutes. This section doesn't go through the OVA deployment steps, as they are straightforward and can be completed without much trouble if the download file is intact and error-free. Make sure you apply all the relevant features and configurations as you do for a production VM, like thick/thin configuration, sizing details, etc.

Once the deployment is complete and the Log Insight VM is running on the cluster, you can access the web interface by logging into `https://<Log Insight IP address or FQDN>`.

You are then greeted with a login screen where you have two options:

- Join an existing deployment

- Create a new one

If you don't have any other Log Insight deployments, you can safely choose to create a new one. Enter the details like the username/password and licensing information. For the licensing information, it is always advisable to visit the VMware website for further information, as there might be changes concerning the release.

VM Log Insight was part of the VMware SDDC suite and it is available for free, up to 25 OSI. This means you can configure up to 25 data sources for free. If you want to try it out, you can use this free version. The minimum requirements for an OVA are shown in Figure 7-1.

Resources	Minimum Requirement
Memory	8 GB
vCPU	4
Storage Space	530 GB

Figure 7-1. *Minimum requirements for an OVA*

Sizing Requirements

In most non-production environments, a single Log Insight appliance might suffice, but if you have to integrate Log Insight into a full-scale production setup, you have to go with a cluster setup. For a Log Insight cluster, the minimum cluster size is three nodes. Now, this is where the sizing of the Log Insight cluster is important. You have to design the cluster size and storage requirements as per the events per second. Or you have to know the data ingested per second and convert it to EPS (events per second) to size the Log Insight cluster.

Once you start integrating all the data sources into Log Insight, the cluster will need to scale out as per the storage and bandwidth requirements. This sizing and design aspect of Log Insight has to be done carefully if you are going to deploy it in a production setup.

The first requirement you will come across is to convert events per second to gigabytes so you have a sizing based on how many gigabits are required. VMware provides a Log Insight calculator available for free. Excel is based on formulas required to convert EPS to GB and vice versa. (See Figure 7-2).

Average event size (bytes)	220	vSphere hosts	52
Events per second	10,000	Network/Firewall devices	10
Calculate per	Day	Non-Windows/API devices	10
Total events	1,506,301,117	Windows/API devices	10
Average storage utilization per day (GB)	200		

Figure 7-2. *Log Insight sizing*

In the previous section, based on input such as the average event size, events per second, estimate, and total events, you will get the respective storage requirements. Based on this, you can design the required Log Insight cluster nodes. (See Figure 7-3).

Events per second -> Storage utilization (GB)	230
Total events -> Storage utilization (GB)	401
Storage utilization (GB) -> Events per second	8691

Figure 7-3. *Log Insight storage sizing*

You now need to determine the minimum nodes required and the Log Insight node size preference. The VM's node can be small, medium, or large. Each of these nodes has a different set of CPU/RAM size requirements (see Figure 7-4).

Log Insight version	4.8
Log Insight node size preference	Medium
Average event size (bytes)	220
Events per second (EPS)	10000

Figure 7-4. *Log Insight node size with respect to EPS*

For an infrastructure setup with an EPS of 10,000, you need the recommended number of nodes set to 3, with an average utilization of 186GB per day (see Figure 7-5).

Average storage utilization per day (GB)	186
Recommended number of nodes (production)	3
Minimum number of nodes (non-production)	3
Recommended network bandwidth per ILB node (Mb/s)	17
Recommended storage per node (GB)	900

Figure 7-5. *Log Insight sizing recommendations*

Design and sizing have to be done based on current and future needs, as this will directly affect the capital investment you make in terms of hardware. This dimensioning has to be done as a prerequisite for using this kind of solution. The decision to use or not use a log management solution has to be weighed against the benefits you get from the provided tool.

There are cases where you'll have several toolsets and administrators and developers still follow the old method of troubleshooting without using LI. Well-intended training across the IT team is required so that everyone is aware of the tool and uses it properly.

You can scale out per computer node and the storage requirement per computer node has to be analyzed and decided upon based on the ingestion rate. The current statistics of EPS and storage utilization can be found in the LI dashboard. This can be used to find the percentage of storage used when you need to plan for a scale-out of the storage.

Another point to mention here is that log sources can be from any system that generates the logs, including a third-party firewall. The network port requirements are listed in Figure 7-6 for the LI deployment.

Port	Protocol
22/TCP	SSH
80/TCP	HTTP
443/TCP	HTTPS
514/UDP, 514/TCP	Syslog
1514/TCP	Syslog ingestion via SSL only
9000/TCP	vRealize Log Insight Ingestion API
9543/TCP	vRealize Log Insight Ingestion API (SSL)

Figure 7-6. *Required ports to be opened*

VMware Log Insight Dashboard

The Log insight dashboard shown in Figure 7-7 provides an intuitive GUI experience where you will be able to glance at the statistics and see any problems or issues from the log sources.

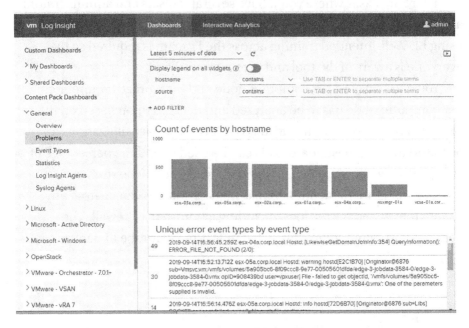

Figure 7-7. *Log Insight Problems dashboard*

From the General tab, you get the information about event types, statistics of the connections, and syslog agent status. Another useful feature is in the Problem section. If you want to know all the events associated with esx-03a, you can right-click and go directly to the Interactive Analytics tab for a more granular view, according to a certain period. (See Figure 7-8).

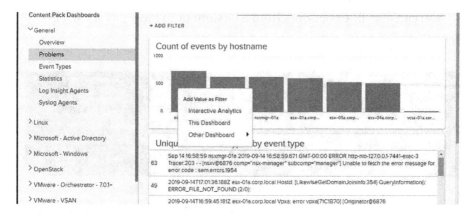

Figure 7-8. *Selecting interactive analytics from the dashboard*

You can see that the filter has automatically been applied and the
result only has the events from esx03-a (see Figure 7-9).

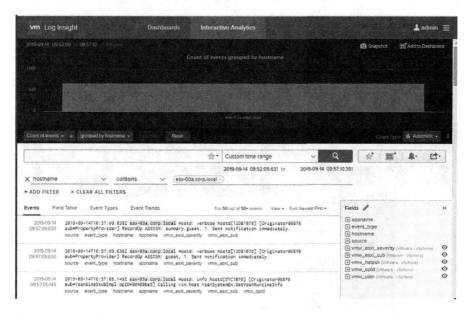

Figure 7-9. *Interactive analytics dashboard*

You can also filter out data from a custom time range, as shown in Figure 7-10.

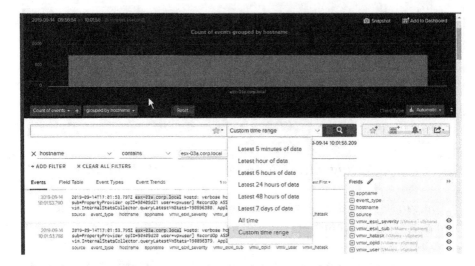

Figure 7-10. *Selecting time range for interactive analytics*

You can also apply other filters to the output to further drill down to specific information (see Figure 7-11).

Figure 7-11. *Filtering logs by different options*

You might imagine how useful this can be in the event of a troubleshooting session. Going through all this information using syslog can be a tedious task and filtering out useful data requires a great level of experience and possibly some luck.

Administration and Statistics

As discussed, it is equally important to know about resource usage in a log management solution. As you add data sources, your need for storage will grow and you could quickly end up exhausting the allocated storage and CPU resources. Sometimes it is important to add CPU or upgrade to the large size node when the resource demand increases. Log Insight provides a glimpse at these requirements in the Administration window, as shown in Figure 7-12.

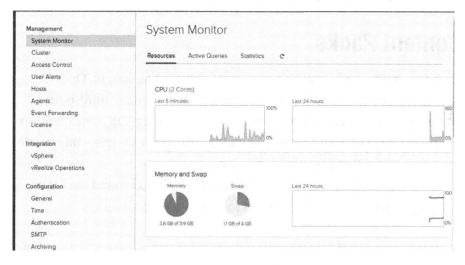

Figure 7-12. *System monitoring in Log Insight*

Free storage space and read/write operations can be seen in Figure 7-13.

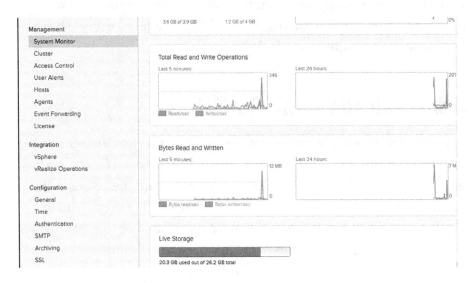

Figure 7-13. *Storage statistics in Log Insight*

Content Packs

There are many useful content packs available for Log Insight. Once you install a content pack, you can directly integrate many third-party components with Log Insight. You can integrate MongoDB, Linux, and so on, as a content pack in Log Insight. In the following example, you can see the installed content pack in the infrastructure,

Take a look at the dashboard in Figure 7-14. If you expand the Linux option, you will get multiple options for logs in Linux servers.

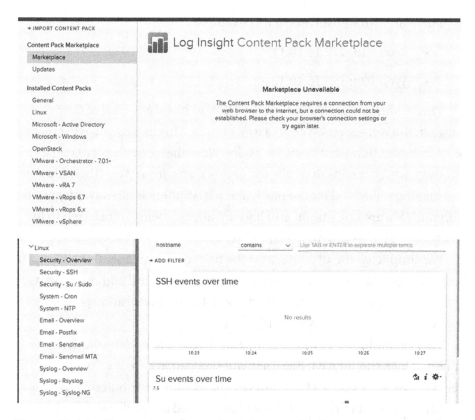

Figure 7-14. *Content packs and options in the Linux content pack*

Using VMware Log Insight for Firewall Security Log Analysis

Enabling the logging firewall rule is a must if you need to analyze or track your traffic flow. This section includes an example to illustrate how easy it is to identify that a certain action has been taken by the VMware NSX DFW. Once you integrate vSphere with NSX, you query these logs for details regarding a particular traffic flow.

There are two webservers in this example:

- Web-01a: 172.16.10.11

- Web-02a: 172.16.10.12

This example creates a rule in the DFW to block any kind of traffic between the webservers Web-01a to Web-02a. This means you will create a block rule and publish it to all the nodes. Note that the rule is created as a one-way, which means that only the egress traffic from Web-01a is blocked and logging is enabled for the particular log. vSphere is already integrated with the VMware Log Insight and logs are already being transferred to the centralized Log Insight management servers.

For simplicity, the IP address for the two servers are mentioned, as you have already learned about creating security groups and adding the server to a security group in the previous chapter. For demonstration purposes, you will add the servers by their IP address.

This example blocks all the ports from Web-01a to Web-02a. The intended logs should have these activities logged in case there is traffic between these servers and the flows are hitting the distributed firewall.

Another point to note is that there is no need to log all the flows in the DFW. This can be done for troubleshooting or auditing purposes. It is recommended that you log the flows of frontend and critical servers, in the event of a security threat. The other less critical server and flows between management and operation servers can be ignored from logging, as this will end up filling up the Log Insight storage. (See Figure 7-15).

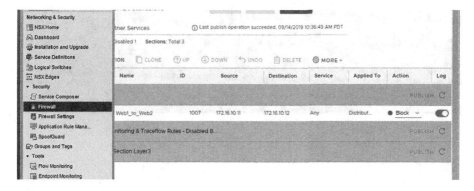

Figure 7-15. *Creating DFW policies*

You can see the ping happening between the two servers; it's blocked once you apply the DFW rule, as shown in Figure 7-16.

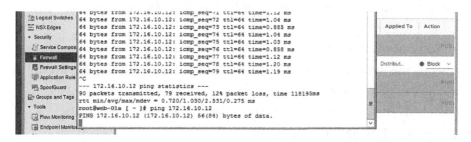

Figure 7-16. *ICMP blocked after adding the block rule*

The block rule will work as expected, which means the packet hits the DFW and is dropped after the DFW checks it against the configured firewall ruleset.

The log for the firewall flow can now be checked in the Log Insight Interactive Analytics tab. If you simply search using the IP address of Web-01a (172.16.10.11), Log Insight will analyze the logs for the keyword and present you with the statistics (see Figure 7-17).

Figure 7-17. *Logs visible from the Log Insight dashboard*

You can see in Figure 7-18 the ICMP drop message that was generated between the two servers. This can be further filtered out using the firewall ID. You can also test that only the egress from Web-01a 172.16.10.11 is blocked. The other traffic from Web-02a 172.16.10.12 to Web-01a 172.16.10.11 is working as expected.

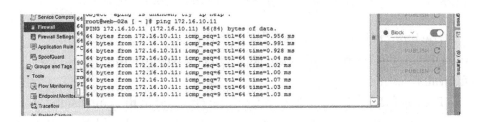

Figure 7-18. *Ping happening to Webserver-1*

The search can be further fine-tuned to only `dfwpktlogs` in order to filter out only DFW rule logs (see Figure 7-19).

Figure 7-19. *Filtering logs using dfwpktlogs*

You can try multiple combinations of these results to determine how to filter out the traffic from the DFW logs. One of the use cases is when you want to add a DENY rule to the bottom of the DFW ruleset.

In that case, you need a way to determine that no valid flows are hitting this DENY rule; only the packets that are not supposed to enter the data path are getting blocked. To achieve this, you can add an ALLOW ALL section to the end and monitor this flow for any valid traffic. Once you are sure that no valid packets are hitting this rule, you can change the action item for this rule from ALLOW to DENY to drop unwanted traffic. In such cases, Log Insight is highly useful in the analysis of log data.

For an infrastructure based on Zero Trust policies and micro-segmentation rules with centralized logging, this mechanism is not good to have but a must. Once you start the journey toward full-fledged implementation and automation of the firewall ruleset, the old way of checking logs manually might not suffice. Thus, a well-planned implementation and integration of Log Insight in the beginning phase may help on the operations side of things.

VMware Network Insight

Network Insight is a VMware-specific tool that you can use to plan and visualize the networking architecture and flows in a VMware based software-defined networking environment. You have learned about the complexities of software-defined networking solutions and the benefits they offer, as well as the importance of automation in the mix. When the infrastructure is in production and is growing, automation becomes a key difference.

Along with automation in a software-defined networking setup, visibility of the entire networking stack is also important. When you combine VXLAN, DLR, DFW, edge devices, VPN, and load balancer, the setup will soon become more complicated, and it is easy to get lost in the architecture. This applies to traditional networking as well. But with a traditional perimeter firewall, there are normally firewall admins who take care of this, and it works in an isolated administrative domain compared to VMware. The same with router and switches, which are controlled by the network team.

VMware SDDC stacks break down this architecture, as this model combines most of the network services into a virtualized form. NSX can provide a wide range of virtualized network services. As you can see here, this can also act as an advantage, as VMware knows and controls the end-to-end packet flow. This enables tools like VMware Network Insight to get a detailed and graphical view of the connectivity inside the NSX and recommend the security flows required in the existing setup.

As with using VMware Log Insight, utilizing Network Insight requires additional knowledge and a skillset for that particular tool. If the IT team managing the SDDC stack does not have enough knowledge about how to utilize this tool, it may soon end up another unused network tool taking up unnecessary bandwidth.

Recall that every resource you deploy inside the vSphere cluster should have a business benefit. Resources like CPU/RAM cost money. This is more evident when you are using a public cloud, as each VM will be billed and you need to be sure that the application hosted in the VM is providing a business benefit.

VMware Network Insight Deployment

Deployment with Log Insight is straightforward, especially with an OVA template. In the case of Network Insight, you have two virtual applications. One is the Network Insight Platform VM, which provides analysis and management for NI. The other VM is a collector, which will act as a collector from various supported data sources like VMware NSX, vSphere, etc. (See Figure 7-20).

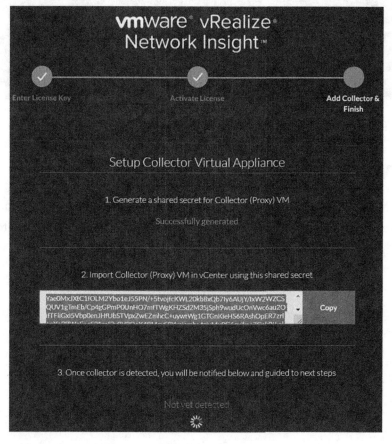

Figure 7-20. *Network Insight installation progress*

Once the platform VM is deployed, you need to add the collector appliance to complete the deployment steps. The generated shared secret is used for collector VM deployments.

Once you deploy the collector, the platform VM will detect the collector and will complete the deployment steps, as shown in Figure 7-21.

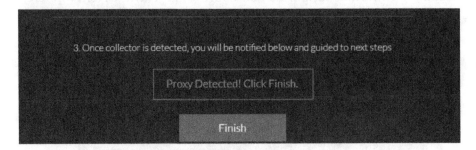

Figure 7-21. *Proxy detected after installation*

Network Insight GUI Overview

This chapter does not cover all the features of Network Insight. In-depth feature set configuration is detailed on the VMware documentation site (see Figure 7-22).

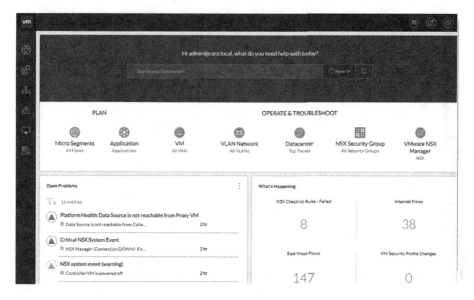

Figure 7-22. *Network Insight dashboard*

In the login dashboard (see Figure 7-22), you can view the E-W flows and the flows toward the Internet. Some of the open problems related to the SDN are listed in the frontend view of the dashboard. All the information presented here is collected from the data source using the virtual machine's collector. Analyzing this data and displaying meaningful results is the job of the virtual machine's platform.

Let's dig into the details of the flows of the Web-01a 172.16.10.11. If you want to see the connectivity of Web-01a 172.16.10.11 to the Internet and the NSX VXLAN connectivity, you can do this with a few clicks instead of having to traverse through multiple GUI windows.

Search in the NI searchbar for the virtual machine with FQDN. This will take you directly to the particular VM options and you can see the details listed for that VM. Information like flows, applied firewall rules, and recent problems concerning SDN can all be analyzed from the window (see Figure 7-23).

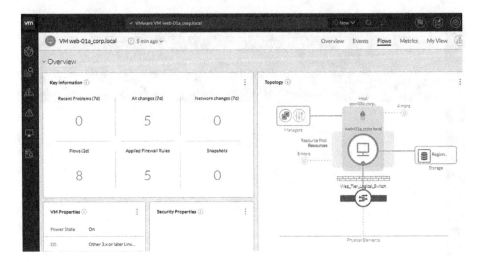

Figure 7-23. *Webserver 01a connectivity in Network Insight*

This window will also give you the topology of this virtual machine. From Figure 7-23, you can identify that the VM is connected to the Web_ Tier_Logical_Switch VXLAN segments, the ESXi host where it is located, and the storage details.

If you want to get information about the path this virtual machine will take to the Internet, this can be seen from the Figure 7-24 as well.

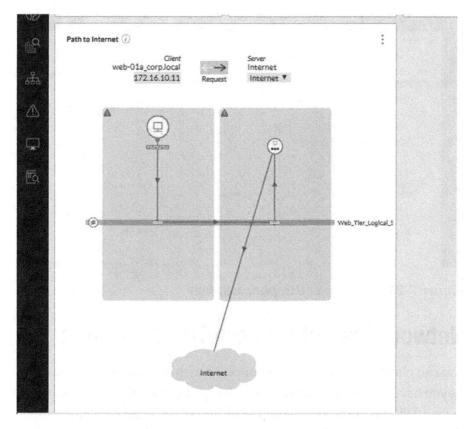

Figure 7-24. *Webserver 01a Internet connection flow*

If you are managing a small or medium environment with a minimum
number of ESXi hosts, this might not make a big difference. But you
can imagine the difference this level of visibility can provide to a large
enterprise deployment that has thousands of VMs running and where you
want to quickly see the SDN details of a particular virtual machine.

Another way to use this is to query the traffic between two virtual
machines. The same query can run in the NI window and you can get
a graphical view of the topology and the path details (see Figure 7-25).
This level of visibility into the network has been a dream for network
administrators. Now, with Network Insight, the possibilities are unlimited.

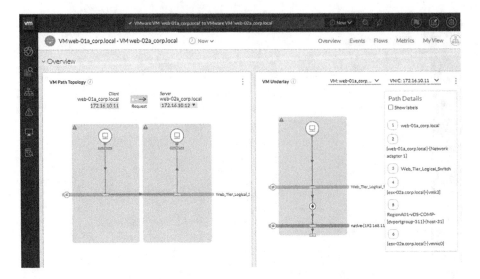

Figure 7-25. *Webserver 01a path topology*

Network Insight for Zero Trust Planning

You can plan for a Zero Trust network even without Network Insight. As you have seen in the examples in this chapter, you can filter down to the VM level, the security group level, and so on, to plan the micro-segmentation firewall rule.

Once VMware NI has enough information about the configured security group, application, and flows, NI can suggest the required micro-segmentation rules. This feature can be used alongside the application rule manager to create distributed firewall rules.

Listing all the features of Network Insight is beyond the scope of this book; the intention here is to introduce the toolsets that help you build a Zero Trust network.

In Figure 7-26, you can see the virtual machine in the particular VXLAN segment and the connectivity.

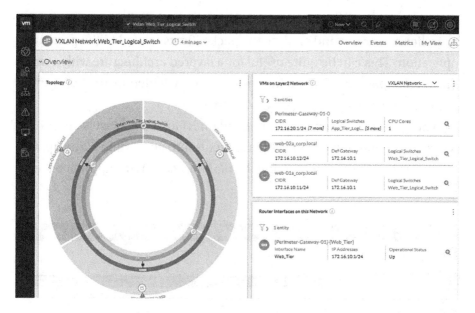

Figure 7-26. *Logical Switch information for Web_Tier*

The NI query to identify the flow that has to go DFW is shown in
Figure 7-27.

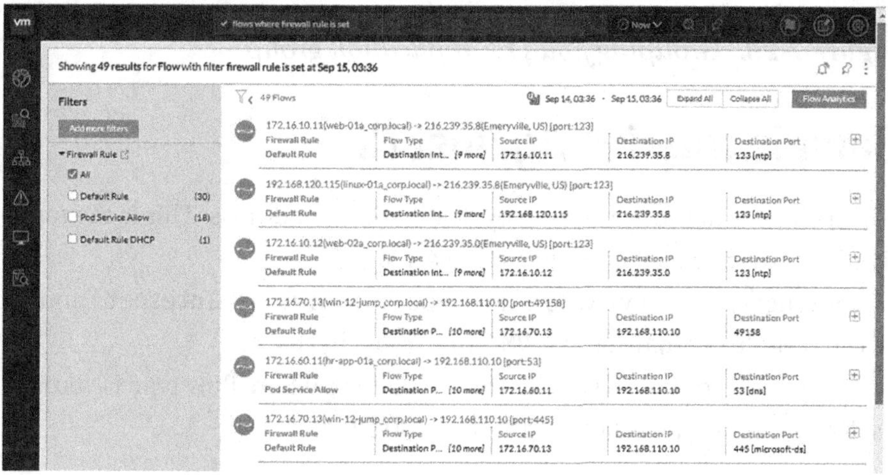

Figure 7-27. *DFW flows*

The use cases for VMware Network insight are broad. You can create an application group and analyze the packet flows related to the particular application. This can be quite useful for a layered architecture with a web/app and database application framework. This will identify the flows and even make micro-segmentation flow suggestions.

Whether you can completely depend on NI for Zero Trust is doubtful. As discussed, you need to take different tools into account to come up with the best strategy for implementing the planned Zero Trust approach (see Figure 7-28).

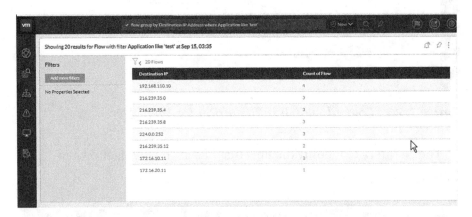

Figure 7-28. *Grouping flows by application group*

Sample Queries Against NI

Flow rules count the flow group by destination IP address. This is the top five flow order by packets flow group by VM.

Internet traffic flows, where flow type is `'Source is Internet'` and flow type is `"Destination is VM"` `order by bytes`.

Total VTEP traffic is the sum (bytes) of flows where flow type is `source is VTEP` or flow type is `Destination is VTEP`.

There are also:

- Flows protected by the NSX firewall

- Flows where a firewall rule is set

- Flows not protected by the NSX firewall

- FLows where the firewall rule is not set

- Flow metrics

- Average TCP RTT

- Bytes

- Bytes rate

- Destination bytes

- Maximum TCP RTT

- Packets

- Session count

- Source bytes

- TCP RTT norm dev

Filters include the following:

```
=,!=,like,not like
            in,notin
                is set is not set
                    >,<,AND,OR
            SUM(),MAX(),MIN(),AVG(),LIST(),COUNT(),GROUP
            BY,ORDER BY
```

Summary

The final note about this chapter is that there is no single tool that can be used to achieve the final Zero Trust framework you need in order to combine different toolsets to plan and achieve military-grade security for your infrastructure. Choosing your tools should be done carefully, as each tool has its benefits and is at the same time costly. Before adding a tool, have a plan as to how to utilize it in your micro-segmentation project.

The next chapter discusses how you can extend the security policies and architecture to mobile platforms as well, thereby expanding the Zero Trust policies to all other parts of the enterprise network.

CHAPTER 8

VMware NSX/AirWatch and Conclusion

AirWatch is a VMware offering in the enterprise mobility management (EMM) software product arena. AirWatch can be used to secure and manage mobile devices and applications. The need to extend access to corporate applications beyond the office network has been always a challenge and a security threat. Considering the security issues and concerns, most organizations enable this very cautiously. Exposing their core business applications across the Internet has advantages and disadvantages.

AirWatch mainly deals with mobile device management. When you have different applications installed on your mobile device, even in your corporate mobile device or own device, there is a need to connect to the corporate VPN. In AirWatch terms, it will create a VPN tunnel from the mobile device to the application.

As a final chapter and parting note, I want to stress the *management* part of the Zero Trust network, as this is as important as the implementation component.

© Sreejith Keeriyattil 2019
S. Keeriyattil, *Zero Trust Networks with VMware NSX*,
https://doi.org/10.1007/978-1-4842-5431-8_8

AirWatch Scenario

AirWatch, in normal cases, creates a VPN tunnel from the mobile device to the application. Normally this access will span across an entire subnet. This means there is less possibility of segregating application access within the subnets. For example, in a healthcare IT system, a doctor and nursing assistant can have the same application installed on each of their mobile devices and both will have access to the healthcare application. But the level of access that a doctor requires would be different than other users. Another factor to consider is when you have another corporate application installed in the same mobile device. It shouldn't be able to access that particular application. AirWatch helps segregate application-specific access by creating a specific VPN tunnel for each application.

T-Shirt Application

This example scenario will use the T-shirt application. Let's assume that you have allowed the mobile devices to connect per application through VPN and have already integrated the VMware AirWatch with VMware NSX (see Figure 8-1).

The integration part of AirWatch and NSX is outside the scope of this chapter. It simply provides an overview of how Zero Trust policies and the micro-segmentation approach relate to mobile VPN access scenarios such as the following.

- Email

- Skype

- Catalog inventory app

- Corporate accounting software

- Real-time analytics applications

- Third-party sellers inventory application

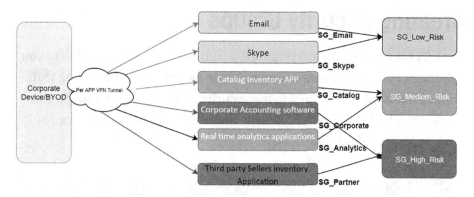

Figure 8-1. *Per application VPN tunnel for the t-shirt company*

In a traditional setup, once the VPN connection is established, the application would be able to access the entire subnet. In this case, you are further segmenting the application traffic based on risk and are filtering out the application traffic based on the access levels. A normal user shouldn't be able to connect to the corporate accounting software even if he is using the same application as the auditor. Likewise, an auditor should be able to access the corporate accounting software, but not the third-party inventory catalog.

In a similar way, you can split the entire subnet into multiple micro-segments and then allow only required traffic. All other traffic can be blocked by default.

The concept of Zero Trust can be applied to any toolset; the idea here remains the same. The purpose here is to rethink the way security infrastructure is designed. Instead of allowing access to the whole subnet, you can further segment the network into smaller chunks.

Like you do with AirWatch, you can apply similar segmenting strategies across other products as well. Previous chapters briefly discussed how the same strategy can be applied to the VMware horizon, a VMware product for the virtual desktop infrastructure.

Creating Security Groups

Security groups, as shown in Figure 8-2, can be created inside NSX, as you saw in the t-shirt company example. All virtual machines belonging to the application have to be added to the security group, either by using tags or manually. The firewall rules can be logged into a Log Insight and can be analyzed further for traffic flows.

Application Security Groups	User Security Groups
SG_Email	SG_Low_Risk
SG_Skype	SG_Medium_Risk
SG_Catalog	SG_High_Risk
SG_Corporate	
SG_Analytics	
SG_Partner	

Figure 8-2. *Application and user security groups*

The same design can be validated and planned with Network Insight tools as well. With Network Insight, you can use custom queries to analyze the flow; proper DFW rules can then be formed.

You can even filter out traffic using specific ports and services. As you already learned, the overall idea behind this can be expanded according to the environment. Figure 8-3 displays the NSX DFW ruleset.

#	Name	ID	Source	Destination	Service	Applied To	Action
	AirWatch_Group						PUBLIS
1	AppGroup_3	1009	SG_Hi...	SG_Corporate SG_Partner	Any	Distribut...	Allow
2	AppGroup_2	1008	SG_Me...	SG_Catalog SG_Analytics	Any	Distribut...	Allow
3	AppGroup_1	1007	SG_Lo...	SG_Email SG_Skype	Any	Distribut...	Allow

Figure 8-3. *DFW ruleset*

Managing a Zero Trust Network

Once you have the setup ready and running, you can concentrate on maintaining and creating a workflow so that the changes and effort required to scale out the design are minimal. I have mentioned many times before that it's not wise to design a security infrastructure with a short-term solution mindset. This kind of approach will always end in a larger capital investment. The solution you design should be flexible enough so that the scaleout process is reliable and fast. In terms of Zero Trust policies, if you set up security groups and automation frameworks, you will be on your way to setting up a scalable, elastic security network.

Summary

This book covered all the requirements, deployment processes, and toolsets needed to implement Zero Trust networks. This book was not intended to cover all the details related to NSX configuration and toolsets. The idea is to give you an introduction to setting up a Zero Trust network in an enterprise network. As with any other technology, there is no one right way of doing things. There will always be a better way and a better tool available at some time. Your job as a solution architect or integrator is to learn these tools and use the most appropriate tool available to do the design and integration.

I hope this book increases your understanding of micro-segmentation and Zero Trust policies. Together, we can all strive toward a secure and reliable IT infrastructure.

VMware NSX in itself is vast, and VMware is adding new feature sets aggressively. In the latest release, there are advanced DFW features, such as universal firewall rules and cross-VC NSX setup, not covered in this book. Universal DFW synchronization and how it helps with multi-data center setup is one area I suggest you look into in order to gain a better understanding of the VMware NSX security features.

Index

© Sreejith Keeriyattil 2019
S. Keeriyattil, *Zero Trust Networks with VMware NSX*,
https://doi.org/10.1007/978-1-4842-5431-8

Printed in the United States
By Bookmasters

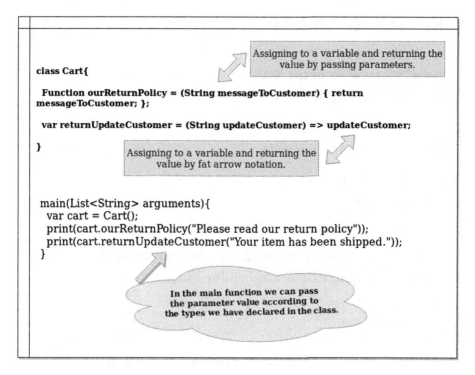

Figure 6-2. *Two types of declaring anonymous functions*

In Figure 6-2, we mentioned the type of parameters. In case we didn't mention it, Dart dynamically allocates them.

Let's look at the code of Figure 6-1 and see the output also to understand this concept.

```
//code 6.1
class Cart{

  Function addingTwoItems = (int item1, int item2){

    var sum = item1 + item2;
    return sum;

  };

}
```

```
main(List<String> arguments){

  var cart = Cart();
  print("Your total price is:");
  print(cart.addingTwoItems(120, 458));
}
```

Here is the output of this code:

```
//output of code 6.1
Your total price is:
578
```

The code used in Figure 6-2 is shown next. We used two methods to declare anonymous functions: longhand and shorthand.

```
//code 6.2
class Cart{

  Function ourReturnPolicy = (String messageToCustomer) {
    return messageToCustomer;
};

  var returnUpdateCustomer = (String updateCustomer) =>
  updateCustomer;

}

main(List<String> arguments){
  var cart = Cart();
  print(cart.ourReturnPolicy("Please read our return policy"));
  print(cart.returnUpdateCustomer("Your item has been
  shipped."));
}
```

The output is quite straightforward. We passed one parameter with each function and get this string output:

```
//output of code 6.2
Please read our return policy
Your item has been shipped.
```

Here we summarize the key features of anonymous functions:

- We can declare any anonymous function without a function name.

- We can assign it to a variable.

- The anonymous function can be passed into another function, as we'll see later.

- In the longhand version, we need to use a semicolon to terminate the statement because we assign it to a variable.

- The only disadvantage of an anonymous function is we cannot use it recursively as it has no name.

Exploring Higher-Order Functions

The specialty of higher-order functions is that they can accept a function as a parameter. That is why they are called higher-order functions. They not only can accept a function as a parameter; they can also return it.

Let's look at the following simple code snippet to get accustomed to the idea:

```
//code 6.3
//returning a function
Function DividingByFour(){
  Function LetUsDivide = (int x) => x ~/ 4;
  return LetUsDivide;
}
```

```
main(List<String> arguments){
  var result = DividingByFour();
  print(result(56));
}
```

The output is 14.

So, we return the LetUsDivide() function quite easily through a higher-order function called Function DividingByFour().

Let's see some more examples to understand how anonymous functions work. Look at this line in the previous code:

```
Function LetUsDivide = (int x) => x ~/ 4;
```

The function LetUsDivide() is assigned to an anonymous function called (int x). Then we used fat arrow notation to return a value.

The main advantage is that we can store functions in a variable or reference them by the name of the variable. Having a variable containing a function object gives us freedom to pass it around the application like any other variable. Furthermore, we can return a function object stored in a variable, or we can pass it into another function where we can call it as any declared function.

In the next section, we will see how the concept of closures changes according to the situation.

A Closure Is a Special Function

We can define closure in two ways.

- We can say that a closure is the only function that has access to the parent scope, even after the scope is closed.

- The term *closure* is derived from the term *close-over*. Since it wraps any nonlocal variable that was valid at the time of declaration, it actually closes over that variable.

When one function is returned by another function, we can say that closures are *formed*; the same thing happens in higher-order functions.

The next example will explain this concept. To understand this definition, let's look at the following short code snippet where an anonymous function closure is overriding the parent scope:

```
//code 6.4
//a closure can modify the parent scope
String message = "Any Parent String";
Function overridingParentScope = (){
  String message = "Overriding the parent scope";
  print(message);
};

main(List<String> arguments){
  print(message);
  overridingParentScope();
}
```

The output is as follows:

```
Any Parent String
Overriding the parent scope
```

In the second definition, we can say that a closure is a function object that has access to the variables in its lexical scope, even when the function is used outside of its original scope.

```
//code 6.5
//declaring an anonymous function without any parameter
Function show = (){
  Function gettingImage(){
    String path = "This is a new path to image.";
```

```
    print(path);
  }
  return gettingImage;
};
main(List<String> arguments){
  String path = "This is an old path.";
  var showing = show();
  showing();
}
```

Here is the output:

```
This is a new path to image.
```

This code actually returns a function object called gettingImage that has accessed the variable in its lexical scope. Dart is a lexically scoped language that means the innermost scope is searched first.

So, at the end of this section, we can summarize a few points about closures.

- In several other languages, including Python and PHP, you are not allowed to modify the parent variable.

- However, within a closure, you can mutate or modify the values of variables present in the parent scope.

Figure 6-3 shows a little more detail about closures (specifically their underlying types when they are created).

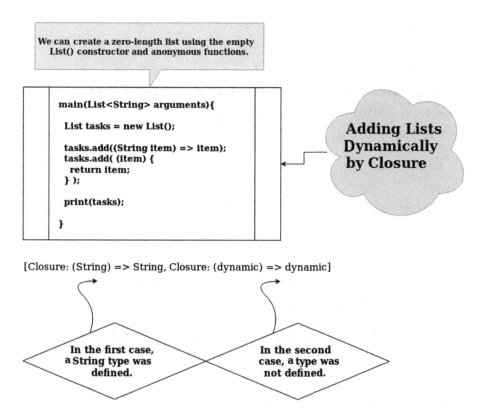

Figure 6-3. *In the output, Dart recognizes this anonymous function as a closure*

Bringing It All Together

Now we will conclude our journey of studying the nameless or anonymous functions in a single codebase, and we will also look at the output. In the following code snippet, we have tried to give you a feel of all the types of anonymous functions. Read the comments in the code to see what types of anonymous functions we are using here.

```
//code 6.6
//Lambda is an anonymous function
class AboutLambdas{
  //first way of expressing Lambda or anonymous function
  Function addingNumbers = (int a, int b){
    var sum = a + b;

    return sum;
  };
  Function multiplyWithEight = (int num){
    return num * 8;
  };

  //second way of expressing Lambda by Fat Arrow
  Function showName = (String name) => name;

  //higher order functions pass function as parameter
  int higherOrderFunction(Function myFunction){
    int a = 10;
    int b = 20;
    print(myFunction(a, b));
  }

  //returning a function
  Function returningAFunction(){
    Function showAge = (int age) => age;
    return showAge;
  }

  //a closure can modify the parent scope
  String anyString = "Any Parent String";
  Function overridingParentScope = (){
    String message = "Overriding the parent scope";
    print(message);
  };
```

```
  Function show = (){
    // the anonymous function will return this originally
    Function gettingImage(){ // anonymous function returns a
                             function
      String path = "This is a new path to image.";
      print(path);
    }
    return gettingImage;
  };
}

main(List<String> arguments){
  var add = AboutLambdas();
  var addition = add.addingNumbers(5, 10);
  print(addition);
  var mul = AboutLambdas();
  var result = mul.multiplyWithEight(4);
  print(result);
  var name = AboutLambdas();
  var myName = name.showName("Sanjib");
  print(myName);
  var higher = AboutLambdas();
  var higherOrder = higher.higherOrderFunction(add.addingNumbers);
  higherOrder;
  var showAge = AboutLambdas();
  var showingAge = showAge.returningAFunction();
  print(showingAge(25));
  var sayMessage = AboutLambdas();
  sayMessage.overridingParentScope();
  var image = AboutLambdas();
  String path = "This is an old path.";
```

```
  var imagePath = image.show();
  imagePath();
}
```

The output shows how the nameless functions work.

```
//output of code 8.6
15
32
Sanjib
30
25
Overriding the parent scope
```

```
This is a new path to image.
```

CHAPTER 7

Data Structures and Collections

Understanding the concepts of data structures and collections, as a whole, plays a crucial role in your future Dart programming. You will learn in a minute that there are four types of data structures in Dart.

- List

- Set

- Map

- Queue

In my opinion, Lists and Maps will cover almost everything, so you hardly need the other two types in your programming life, except on a few occasions. However, my suggestion is to not ignore learning about Set and Queue; on a few occasions, they have incalculable worth. We will discuss them in this chapter in detail.

Figure 7-1 shows what type of collections we are going to use.

© Sanjib Sinha 2020
S. Sinha, *Quick Start Guide to Dart Programming*,
https://doi.org/10.1007/978-1-4842-5562-9_7

Core Interfaces of Collections in Dart

There are four types of data structure of which Lists and Maps are mostly used in building applications.

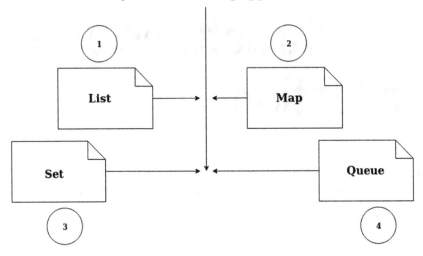

Figure 7-1. *All types of collections in Dart*

You will learn about these data structures in this chapter. We will cover all the concepts of Dart collections in detail. Moving/processing collections of data in a type-safe manner is always our priority in software development. To do that, first we need to have a basic understanding of how to organize a large chunk of data for later retrieval.

In a nutshell, data structures help you to organize information for storage and later retrieval.

Using the built-in collection classes in Dart is a big advantage to us. List and Map both fall into this category. They allow us to manipulate lists of data, and they allow us to access the collections of data in a type-safe manner; furthermore, we can benefit from the additional validations done by the type checker provided by Dart. Not only that, the built-in utilities provided by Dart help us to access elements directly in Lists and Maps; you will also learn how to build Maps and Lists from preexisting values.

So, let's start with Lists.

Lists: An Ordered Collection

A list is a simple ordered group of objects. Creating a List seems easy because the Dart core libraries have the necessary support and a List class. There are two types of Lists.

- Fixed-length list

- Growable list

In a fixed-length list, the length of the list cannot change at runtime; however, in the second type, a growable list, the length can change at runtime.

Figure 7-2 describes how these Lists works.

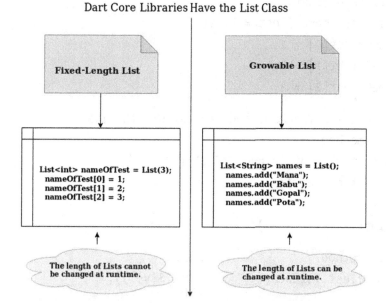

Figure 7-2. *Two types of Lists are available in Dart*

In the next examples, we will look at the two types of List separately. We will also see how they work. First simply create a List, as shown here:

```
void main() {
    var lst = new List();
    lst.add(3);
    lst.add(4);
    print(lst);
}
```

```
//output
[3, 4]
```

Now here's our first example:

```
//code 7.1
int listFunction(){
  List<int> nameOfTest = List(3);
  nameOfTest[0] = 1;
  nameOfTest[1] = 2;
  nameOfTest[2] = 3;

  //there are three methods to capture the list
  //1. method
  for(int element in nameOfTest){
    print(element);
  }
  print("-----------");

  //2. method
  nameOfTest.forEach((v) => print('${v}'));
  print("-----------");
```

The separator line used in between the output helps show how the other default methods of the List class work.

We have used several default methods such as toList(), contains(), skip(), etc.

We can take any number of elements from the List class. We can eliminate the first two numbers and print other values.

There are also other List methods that are extremely flexible to add some special keywords to a List. Consider this small example first:

```
//code 7.4
main(){
  var names = ["John", "Robert", "Smith", "Peter"];
  names.forEach((name) => print(name));
}
```

It will give us some nice output of names.

```
//output of code 7.4
John
Robert
Smith
Peter
```

Can we add some extra functionality into this List of names so that they might have something in common? Suppose every name we have listed is absconding. We need to prepend each name with Absconding. The map() function gives us an opportunity to produce a new List by transforming each element at one go. Now the preceding code changes to this:

```
//code 7.5
main(){
  var names = ["John", "Robert", "Smith", "Peter"];
  names.forEach((name) => print(name));
```

```
var mappedNames = names.map((name) => "Absconding $name").
toList();
print(mappedNames);
}
```

The output changes to this:

```
//output of code 7.5
John
Robert
Smith
Peter
[Absconding John, Absconding Robert, Absconding Smith,
Absconding Peter]
```

We have successfully mapped each element and transformed it, putting the results in a new list.

For further reading about the List class, you can go to the Dart language repositories on Lists:

```
https://api.dartlang.org/dev/2.0.0-dev.65.0/dart-core/List-
class.html
```

Set: An Unordered Collections of Unique Items

The heading says everything. A Set represents a collection of objects in which each object can occur only once. In the Dart core library, there is a Set class with this functionality.

Since Set is an unordered collection of unique items, you cannot get elements by index. There is a concept called a HashSet that actually implements the unordered Set, and it is based on a hashtable-based Set implementation. We will look into those features in a minute.

We can create sets in two ways.

```
Set <type> set name = {};
var setname = <Type> {};
```

```
//code 7.6
void setFunction(){
  //set is an unordered collections of unique items
  //cannot get elements by INDEX since the items are unordered
  //1. method of creating Set
  Set<String> countries = Set.from(['India', 'England', 'US']);
  Set<int> numbers = Set.from([1, 45, 58]);
  Set<int> moreNumbers = Set();
  moreNumbers.add(178);
  moreNumbers.add(568);
  moreNumbers.add(569);

  //1. method
  for(int element in numbers){
    print(element);
  }
  print("-----------");

  //2. method
  countries.forEach((v) => print('${v}'));

  print("-----------");
  for(int element in moreNumbers){
    if(moreNumbers.lookup(element) == 178){
      print(element);
      break;
    }
  }
}
```

```
//set
var fruitCollection = {'Mango', 'Apple', 'Jack fruit'};
print(fruitCollection.lookup('Something Else'));
//it gives null
//lists
List fruitCollections = ['Mango', 'Apple', 'Jack fruit'];
var myIntegers = [1, 2, 3, 'non-integer object'];
print(myIntegers[3]);
print(fruitCollections[0]);
}

main(List<String> arguments){
  setFunction();
}
```

Let's look at the output first; then we will be able to understand what happens.

```
//output of code 7.6
1
45
58
- - - - - - - - - - -
India
England
US
- - - - - - - - - - -
178
null
non-integer object
Mango
```

We have created a Set of `countries`, `numbers`, and `morenumbers`; finally, we created a List at the end to distinguish between the characters of Lists and Sets.

These three methods have created Sets:

```
Set<String> countries = Set.from(['India', 'England', 'US']);
Set<int> numbers = Set.from([1, 45, 58]);
Set<int> moreNumbers = Set();
```

We get the output of the first one we have using this method:

```
countries.forEach((v) => print('${v}'));
```

The second List has been retrieved by this method:

```
for(int element in numbers){
  print(element);
}
```

We have captured the values of the third Set using this method:

```
for(int element in moreNumbers){
    if(moreNumbers.lookup(element) == 178){
      print(moreNumbers);
      break;
    }
}
```

We used the `lookup()` method with each element of the List as the argument. When we match 178, we print the whole list.

To manipulate a Set, there are lots of methods available in the Dart core libraries. You can use `moreNumbers.contains(value)`, `moreNumbers.remove(value)`, `moreNumbers.isEmpty()`, etc.

In the following code snippet, the return value of lookup() is null, since there is no such value present in the Set:

```
//set
  var fruitCollection = {'Mango', 'Apple', 'Jack fruit'};
  print(fruitCollection.lookup('Something Else'));
```

We need to remember one thing. When the Set type is an integer, it is easier to use a for loop to loop over the elements. Otherwise, it is wise to use foreach as we have used in the previous code.

```
countries.forEach((v) => print('${v}'));
```

In the next section, we will see how Map in Dart works.

Maps: The Key-Value Pair

An unordered collection of key-value pairs is known as a Map in Dart. The main advantage of a Map is that the key-value pair can be of any type. The flexibility of extending and shrinking these unordered collections is another great advantage when managing a big chunk of data.

Figure 7-3 summarizes how Maps in Dart work.

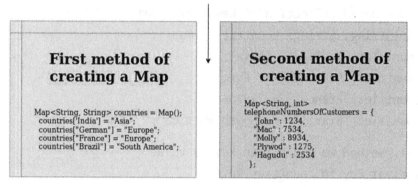

Figure 7-3. *Key-value pair of unordered collections in Dart*

To begin with, let's start with a few key features of Map that we should remember while we work with Map.

- Each key in a Map should be unique.

- The value can be repeated.

- The Map can commonly be called a hash or a dictionary.

- The size of a Map is not fixed; it can either increase or decrease as per the number of elements. In other words, Maps can grow or shrink at runtime.

- A HashMap is an implementation of a Map, and it is based on a hashtable.

Let's look at the following code snippet to understand how a Map works in Dart:

```
//code 7.7
void mapFunction(){
  //unordered collection of key=>value pair
  Map<String, String> countries = Map();
  countries['India'] = "Asia";
  countries["Germany"] = "Europe";
  countries["France"] = "Europe";
  countries["Brazil"] = "South America";

  //1. method we can obtain key or value
  for(var key in countries.keys){
    print("Country's name: $key");
  }
  print("-----------");
  for(String value in countries.values){
    print("Continent's name: $value");
  }

  //2. method
  countries.forEach((key, value) => print("Country: $key and
  Continent: $value"));
  //we can update any map very easily
  if(countries.containsKey("Germany")){
    countries.update("Germany", (value) => "European Union");
    print("Updated country Germany.");
    countries.forEach((key, value) => print("Country: $key and
    Continent: $value"));
  }
```

```
//we can remove any country
countries.remove("Brazil");
countries.forEach((key, value) => print("Country: $key and
Continent: $value"));
print("Barzil has been removed successfully.");
print("-----------");

//3. method of creating a map
Map<String, int> telephoneNumbersOfCustomers = {
  "John" : 1234,
  "Mac" : 7534,
  "Molly" : 8934,
  "Plywod" : 1275,
  "Hagudu" : 2534
};

telephoneNumbersOfCustomers.forEach((key, value) =>
print("Customer: $key and Contact Number: $value"));
}

main(List<String> arguments){
  mapFunction();
}
```

Here is the output of the previous code:

```
Country's name: India
Country's name: Germany
Country's name: France
Country's name: Brazil
-----------
Continent's name: Asia
Continent's name: Europe
Continent's name: Europe
```

```
Continent's name: South America
Country: India and Continent: Asia
Country: Germany and Continent: Europe
Country: France and Continent: Europe
Country: Brazil and Continent: South America
Updated country Germany.
Country: India and Continent: Asia
Country: Germany and Continent: European Union
Country: France and Continent: Europe
Country: Brazil and Continent: South America
Country: India and Continent: Asia
Country: Germany and Continent: European Union
Country: France and Continent: Europe
Barzil has been removed successfully.
-----------
Customer: John and Contact NUmber: 1234
Customer: Mac and Contact NUmber: 7534
Customer: Molly and Contact NUmber: 8934
Customer: Plywod and Contact NUmber: 1275
Customer: Hagudu and Contact NUmber: 2534
```

There are three methods that we can use to retrieve the values of a Map.

```
//1. method we can obtain key or value
for(var key in countries.keys){
 print("Country's name: $key");
}
print("-----------");

//2. Method
for(String value in countries.values){
 print("Continent's name: $value");
}
```

```
//3. method
countries.forEach((key, value) => print("Country: $key and
Continent: $value"));
```

In addition, there are several methods to add, update, or remove the elements in a Map.

Using Collections Together

We can combine Lists and Maps and test the validations. There is a lot of flexibility involved in Dart when we want to confirm that each element passes a particular test. Suppose we want to check that every user's age is over 18.

```
//code 7.8
main(){
  var name;
  var age;
  List<Map<String, dynamic>> users = [
    { name: "Peter", age: 18 },
    { name: "Mira", age: 20 },
    { name: "Jason", age: 22 },
  ];
  var is18AndOver = users.every((user) => user[age] >= 18);
  print(is18AndOver);

}
```

The output will be true. All users in our combined Lists and Maps are either 18 or older. We can also check whether every user's name starts with *A* or not. We use the same every() method in a different way. The following code snippet is interesting because here we have used an anonymous function:

```
//code 7.9
main(){
  var name;
  var age;
  List<Map<String, dynamic>> users = [
    { name: "Peter", age: 18 },
    { name: "Mira", age: 20 },
    { name: "Jason", age: 22 },
  ];
  var isEighteenAndOver = users.every((user) => user[age] >= 18);
  print(isEighteenAndOver);

  var hasNamesWithLetterA = users.every((user) => user.
  toString().startsWith("A"));
  print(hasNamesWithLetterA);

}
```

Let's look at the output in the editor's console this time:

```
//output of code 7.9
/home/ss/Downloads/flutter/bin/cache/dart-sdk/bin/dart
--enable-asserts --enable-vm-service:45239 /home/ss/
IdeaProjects/my_app/main.dart
Observatory listening on http://127.0.0.1:45239/o1AwiUzW7MQ=/

true
false

Process finished with exit code 0
```

172

The first test passes; however, the second test fails because every user's name does not start with the letter *A*.

Let's make this code more interesting with more options for testing. This time we have added more names to this list, mapping their age records to find how many users are older than 21.

```
//code 7.10
main(){
  var name;
  var age;
  List<Map<String, dynamic>> users = [
    { name: "Peter", age: 18 },
    { name: "Mira", age: 20 },
    { name: "Jason", age: 22 },
    { name: "Morgan", age: 32 },
    { name: "Mary", age: 50 },
    { name: "Will", age: 86 },
    { name: "Bruce", age: 96 },
  ];
  var isEighteenAndOver = users.every((user) => user[age] >= 18);
  print(isEighteenAndOver);

  var hasNamesWithLetterA = users.every((user) => user.
  toString().startsWith("A"));
  print(hasNamesWithLetterA);

  var overTwentyOne = users.where((user) => user[age] > 21);
  print(overTwentyOne.length);

}
```

Look at the output this time:

```
//output of code 7.10
true
false
5
```

There are five users altogether who have their ages older than 21. Next, we can make this test complete with the method singleWhere() to confirm that there are no users whose age is younger than 18.

```
//code 7.11
main(){
  var name;
  var age;
  List<Map<String, dynamic>> users = [
    { name: "Peter", age: 18 },
    { name: "Mira", age: 20 },
    { name: "Jason", age: 22 },
    { name: "Morgan", age: 32 },
    { name: "Mary", age: 50 },
    { name: "Will", age: 86 },
    { name: "Bruce", age: 96 },
  ];
  var isEighteenAndOver = users.every((user) => user[age] >= 18);
  print(isEighteenAndOver);

  var hasNamesWithLetterA = users.every((user) => user.
  toString().startsWith("A"));
  print(hasNamesWithLetterA);

  var overTwentyOne = users.where((user) => user[age] > 21);
  print(overTwentyOne.length);
```

```
var underEighteen = users.singleWhere((user) => user[age]
< 18, orElse: () => null);
print(underEighteen);
```

```
}
```

Let's first see the output in our console, as shown here:

```
//output of code 7.11
/home/ss/Downloads/flutter/bin/cache/dart-sdk/bin/dart
--enable-asserts --enable-vm-service:36063 /home/ss/
IdeaProjects/my_app/main.dart
Observatory listening on http://127.0.0.1:36063/vr10kScPAEw=/

true
false
5
null

Process finished with exit code 0
```

The last line of output tells us that there is no user who has an age younger than 18. We want you to look at the last bit of code here:

```
var underEighteen = users.singleWhere((user) => user[age] < 18,
orElse: () => null);
  print(underEighteen);
```

In the orElse conditional, we have used the anonymous function ()
=> null; this anonymous function returns null only when the condition is true.

Lastly, we will see another collection feature in Dart, which is called a Queue.

Queue Is Open-Ended

The queue is useful when you try to build a collection that can be added from one end and can be deleted from another end. The values are removed or read using an index based on the order of their insertion.

Consider this code:

```
//code 7.12
import 'dart:collection';  // we are about to import some extra
                            methods from collection library
main(List<String> arguments){
  Queue myQueue = new Queue();
  print("Default implementation ${myQueue.runtimeType}");

  myQueue.add("Sanjib");
  myQueue.add(54);
  myQueue.add("Howrah");
  myQueue.add("sanjib12sinha@gmail.com");
  for(var allTheValues in myQueue){
    print(allTheValues);
  }
  print("----------");

  print("We are removing the first element ${myQueue.
  elementAt(0)}.");
  myQueue.removeFirst();
  for(var allTheValues in myQueue){
    print(allTheValues);
  }
  print("----------");

  print("We are removing the last element ${myQueue.
  elementAt(2 )}.");
  myQueue.removeLast();
```

```
for(var allTheValues in myQueue){
    print(allTheValues);
  }
}
```

The output gives us the full lists of what we have added in the Queue. After that, we have removed the first and last elements.

```
//output of code 7.12
Default implementation ListQueue<dynamic>
Sanjib
54
Howrah
sanjib12sinha@gmail.com
----------
We are removing the first element Sanjib.
54
Howrah
sanjib12sinha@gmail.com
----------
We are removing the last element sanjib12sinha@gmail.com.
54
Howrah
```

In most cases, as I said at the beginning of the chapter, we can handle this with Lists and Maps. So, Queue is an option that you may need sometimes, but not very often.

CHAPTER 8

Multithreaded Programming Using Future and Callable Classes

As you know, everything is an object in Dart. A class is an object. A function is also an object. Because of this object-oriented approach, objects should contain some methods to allow them to behave like functions. In this chapter, you will see how we can make them behave like functions. We will allow an instance of any class to behave like a function. Now Dart allows objects with call methods to be called and, at the same time, to be assigned to variables of a function type. In this chapter, we will look into one of the most important aspects of Dart programming, multithreaded programming using future and callable classes.

Callable Classes

Internally, Dart implicitly changes the `call()` method (like, `someVariable.call()`) to a closure. When an object is assigned with a call method to a function type, it adopts the features of an anonymous function.

© Sanjib Sinha 2020
S. Sinha, *Quick Start Guide to Dart Programming*,
https://doi.org/10.1007/978-1-4842-5562-9_8

Calling a class like a function is an interesting feature in Dart. All we need to do is just implement the call() method. Consider Figure 8-1, before we test some example code.

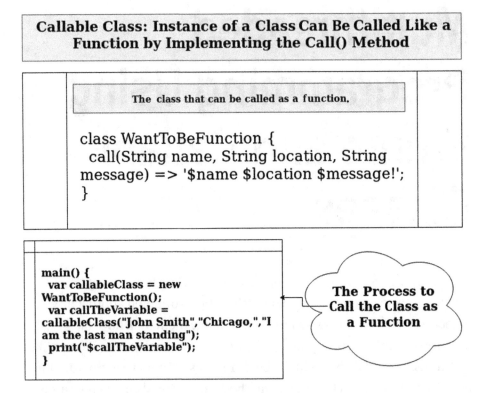

Callable Class: Instance of a Class Can Be Called Like a Function by Implementing the Call() Method

The class that can be called as a function.

```
class WantToBeFunction {
  call(String name, String location, String
message) => '$name $location $message!';
}
```

```
main() {
  var callableClass = new
WantToBeFunction();
  var callTheVariable =
callableClass("John Smith","Chicago,","I
am the last man standing");
  print("$callTheVariable");
}
```

The Process to Call the Class as a Function

Figure 8-1. *Instance of a class implementing the call method*

Let's test some code and see the output.

```
//code 8.1
class CallableClassWithoutArgument {
  String output = "Callable class";
  void call() {
    print(output);
  }
}
```

180

```
class CallableClassWithArgument {
  call(String name) => "$name";
}

main(){
  var withoutArgument = CallableClassWithoutArgument();
  var withArgument = CallableClassWithArgument();
  withoutArgument(); // it is equivalent to withoutArgument.
                     call()
  print(withArgument("John Smith")); //OK.
  // withArgument(); //it'll give error
  print(withArgument.call("Calling John Smith"));
}
```

Here is the output of the preceding code:

```
//output of code 8.1
Callable class
John Smith
Calling John Smith
```

We can also use a callable class so that it can take an optional parameter. In the following code, the [name] parameter is optional in a callable class called Person:

```
//code 8.2
//when dart class is callable like a function, use call() function
class Person{
  String name;
  String call(String message, [name]){
    return "This message: '$message', has been passed to the
    person $name.";
  }
}
```

```
main(List<String> arguments){
  var John = Person();
  John.name = "John Smith";
  String name = John.name;
  String msgAndName = John("Hi John how are you?", name);
  print(msgAndName);
}
```

Here is the output:

```
This message: 'Hi John how are you?', has been passed to the
person John Smith.
```

Here, John is the variable, and Person() is the class. The class Person is called like a function because we have implemented the call() function, through which we have passed two parameters: String message and the optional parameter name. Finally, we have passed both and captured the value through msgAndName.

Future, Async, Await, and Asynchronous Programming

Because Dart is a single-threaded language, it is wrong to assume that we cannot use multithreaded, asynchronous programming in Dart. Before delving deep into asynchronous programming and how Dart manages to do it, you need to understand the basic mechanism of any Android application.

Whenever we switch on any Android device, the default process starts. It runs on the main UI thread. This main UI thread handles all core activities, such as button clicking, all types of touchscreen activities, etc. Still, these are not the only things we can expect from an Android device. We should be able to do some heavy operations such as checking mails, downloading files, watching movies, playing games, etc.

To do these heavy operations, Android allows parallel processing, which is multithreaded programming. It opens an application thread, and all the heavy operations are managed there.

When the heavy operations are going on in the background, we need our UI to be responsive; and for that reason, Android allows parallel processing.

This is the normal procedure of how asynchronous programming occurs.

Since Dart is a single-threaded programming language, it manages this asynchronous programming by using a feature called Future. In Dart SDK version 1.9, the Dart language has added asynchrony support. Now it is easier to write and read asynchronous Dart code. We will see that in a minute.

Let's first try to understand the whole concept, as shown in Figure 8-2.

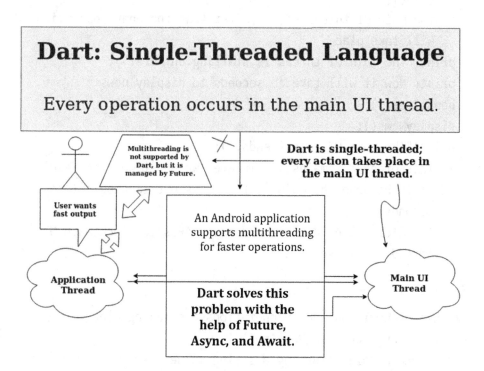

Figure 8-2. How Dart manages asynchronous programming

Before the features async and await were brought into Dart SDK version 1.9, Dart depended mainly on Future and then. We will look at some sample code to see how Dart Future manages the application thread parallel to the main UI thread. Consider the following code where we need to import the async libraries; we import predefined classes from the Dart libraries to add special features in our program:

```
//code 8.3
import 'dart:async';

// our all operations will use the main UI thread
//since dart and flutter are single threaded we need to use
  Future, Async amd Await APIs

void main(){
    // the main UI thread starts after that the heavy operations
      will take place
    print("The main UI thread is starting on here.");
    print("Now it will take 10 seconds to display news
    headlines.");
    displayNews();
    print("The main UI thread ends.");
    // this program remains incomplete, we don't get the result
    // it is because the main UI thread is overlapping before 10
      seconds
    // therefore we need await and async APIs to block main UI
      thread for 10 seconds

}

// this is where our heavy operations are taking place
Future<String> checkingNewsApp() {
    // since we are returning a string value
    // by delaying the main UI thread for 10 seconds
```

```dart
Future<String> delayingTenSeconds =  Future.
delayed(Duration(seconds: 10), (){
  return "The latest headlines are displayed here after
  10 seconds.";
});
// after 10 seconds the news headlines will be displayed
return delayingTenSeconds;
}

void displayNews() {
  // here we will primarily display the news headline
  Future<String> displayingNewsHeadlines = checkingNewsApp();
  // inside then we need an anonymous function like lambda or
    anonymous function
  displayingNewsHeadlines.then((displayString){
    // it will give the future object
    print("Displaying news headlines here:
    $displayingNewsHeadlines");
  });

}
```

In the output, we have gotten the value as a Future object.

```
//output of code 8.3
/home/ss/Downloads/flutter/bin/cache/dart-sdk/bin/dart
--enable-asserts --enable-vm-service:42565 /home/ss/
IdeaProjects/my_app/main.dart
Observatory listening on http://127.0.0.1:42565/vR6Xhf8qofo=/

The main UI thread is starting on here.
Now it will take 10 seconds to display news headlines.
The main UI thread ends.
Displaying news headlines here: Instance of 'Future<String>'

Process finished with exit code 0
```

If you read the comments in the program, you will understand how we got the Future object. However, our objective was different; we wanted to display news headlines instead of a Future object. A mistake was made in this line:

```
// it will give the future object
  print("Displaying news headlines here:
  $displayingNewsHeadlines");
});
```

In the Future method, we passed an anonymous function where we have used a parameter. We need to check that line again. Let's write the code in this manner (changes appear in bold):

```
//code 8.4
import 'dart:async';

// our all operations will use the main UI thread
//since dart and flutter are single threaded we need to use
  Future, Async amd Await APIs

void main(){
  // the main UI thread starts after that the heavy operations
    will take place
  print("The main UI thread is starting on here.");
  print("Now it will take 10 seconds to display news headlines.");
  displayNews();
  print("The main UI thread ends.");
  // this program remains incomplete, we don't get the result
  // it is because the main UI thread is overlapping before
    10 seconds
  // therefore we need the Future API to block main UI thread
    for 10 seconds

}
```

```dart
// this is where our heavy operations are taking place
Future<String> checkingNewsApp() {
  // since we are returning a string value
  // by delaying the main UI thread for 10 seconds
  Future<String> delayingTenSeconds =  Future.
  delayed(Duration(seconds: 10), (){
    return "The latest headlines are displayed here after
    10 seconds.";
  });
  // after 10 seconds the news headlines will be displayed
  return delayingTenSeconds;
}

void displayNews() {
  // here we will primarily display the news headline
  Future<String> displayingNewsHeadlines = checkingNewsApp();
  // inside then we need an anonymous function like lambda or
    anonymous function
  displayingNewsHeadlines.then((displayString){
    print("Displaying news headlines here: $displayString");
  });

}
```

Now the output has been changed. Here is the news headlines we had
initially wanted:

```
//output of code 8.4
/home/ss/Downloads/flutter/bin/cache/dart-sdk/bin/dart
--enable-asserts --enable-vm-service:42565 /home/ss/
IdeaProjects/my_app/main.dart
Observatory listening on http://127.0.0.1:42565/vR6Xhf8qofo=/
```

```
The main UI thread is starting on here.
Now it will take 10 seconds to display news headlines.
The main UI thread ends.
Displaying news headlines here: The latest headlines are
displayed here after 10 seconds.

Process finished with exit code 0
```

Now with the advent of the modern Dart versions, we have async and await. They help us write clean asynchronous code. Yet, you need to know how to use these features properly. They help us write asynchronous code that looks like synchronous code, while still using the Future API. In Dart 2, instead of suspending, it uses the await and async functions to execute synchronously.

Consider the following code where we have not used these features properly. Notice the long exception.

```
//code 8.5
import 'dart:async';

void main(){
  Future checkVersion() async {
    var version = await checkVersion();
    // Do something with version
    try {
      return version;
    } catch (e) {
      // React to inability to look up the version
      return e;
    }
  }
  print(checkVersion());
}
```

In the preceding code, we tried to print the version of the Dart SDK. We got this output:

```
//output of code 8.5
/home/ss/Downloads/flutter/bin/cache/dart-sdk/bin/dart
--enable-asserts --enable-vm-service:34325 /home/ss/
IdeaProjects/my_app/main.dart
Observatory listening on http://127.0.0.1:34325/pJXWzoNT9FO=/

Instance of 'Future<dynamic>'
Unhandled exception:
Stack Overflow
#0      _FutureListener.stateThenOnerror (dart:async/future_
        impl.dart:66:20)
#1      Future._thenNoZoneRegistration (dart:async/future_impl.
        dart:256:22)
#2      _awaitHelper (dart:async-patch/async_patch.dart:110:17)
#3      main.checkVersion (file:///home/ss/IdeaProjects/my_app/
        main.dart:5:19)
#4      _AsyncAwaitCompleter.start (dart:async-patch/async_
        patch.dart:49:6)
#5      main.checkVersion (file:///home/ss/IdeaProjects/my_app/
        main.dart:4:22)
#6      main.checkVersion (file:///home/ss/IdeaProjects/my_app/
        main.dart:5:37)
#7      _AsyncAwaitCompleter.start (dart:async-patch/async_
        patch.dart:49:6)
#8      main.checkVersion (file:///home/ss/IdeaProjects/my_app/
        main.dart:4:22)
#9      main.checkVersion (file:///home/ss/IdeaProjects/my_app/
        main.dart:5:37)
#10     _AsyncAwaitCompleter.start (dart:async-patch/async_
        patch.dart:49:6)
```

```
#11      main.checkVersion (file:///home/ss/IdeaProjects/my_app/
         main.dart:4:22)
#12      main.checkVersion (file:///home/ss/IdeaProjects/my_app/
         main.dart:5:37)
#13      _AsyncAwaitCompleter.start (dart:async-patch/async_
         patch.dart:49:6)
#14      main.checkVersion (file:///home/ss/IdeaProjects/my_app/
         main.dart:4:22)
#15      main.checkVersion (file:///home/ss/IdeaProjects/my_app/
         main.dart:5:37)
#16      _AsyncAwaitCompleter.start (dart:async-patch/async_
         patch.dart:49:6)
....
#11119   _AsyncAwaitCompleter.start (dart:async-patch/async_
         patch.dart:49:6)
#11120   main.checkVersion (file:///home/ss/IdeaProjects/my_app/
         main.dart:4:22)
#11121   main (file:///home/ss/IdeaProjects/my_app/main.
         dart:15:21)
#11122   _startIsolate.<anonymous closure> (dart:isolate-patch/
         isolate_patch.dart:301:19)
#11123   _RawReceivePortImpl._handleMessage (dart:isolate-patch/
         isolate_patch.dart:172:12)

Process finished with exit code 255
```

I have cut the output short for brevity. It was a long exception raised because of our mistake. If we had used the print statement, our problem would not have been solved. Then what will be the right form of writing async and await?

Consider the same code here:

```
//code 8.6
import 'dart:async';
void main(){

  print("The main UI thread is starting on here.");
  print("Now it will take 3 seconds to display the version of
  Dart.");
  checkVersion();
  print("The main UI thread ends.");
}

Future<String> checkingVersion() {
  // since we are returning a string value
  // by delaying the main UI thread for 3 seconds
  Future<String> delayingTenSeconds =  Future.
  delayed(Duration(seconds: 3), (){
    return "The version 2.1 is displayed here after 3 seconds.";
  });
  // after 3 seconds the version will be displayed
  return delayingTenSeconds;
}

void checkVersion() async {
  String version = await checkingVersion();
  // Do something with version
  try {
    print("Displaying version here: $version");
  } catch (e) {
    // React to inability to look up the version
    return e;
  }
}
```

In the preceding code, these lines are important:

```
Future<String> checkingVersion() {
    // since we are returning a string value
    // by delaying the main UI thread for 3 seconds
    Future<String> delayingTenSeconds =  Future.
    delayed(Duration(seconds: 3), (){
....
void checkVersion() async {
    String version = await checkingVersion();
```

What kind of Future method are we using? String. Therefore, the async and await methods should follow that. Now our output is cleaner than before, as shown here:

```
//output of code 8.6
/home/ss/Downloads/flutter/bin/cache/dart-sdk/bin/dart
--enable-asserts --enable-vm-service:41595 /home/ss/
IdeaProjects/my_app/main.dart
Observatory listening on http://127.0.0.1:41595/hMelJx-vdlw=/

The main UI thread is starting on here.
Now it will take 10 seconds to display news headlines.
The main UI thread ends.
Displaying version here: The version 2.1 is displayed here
after 3 seconds.

Process finished with exit code 0
```

Now we can use more async and await to understand how they actually work with Future. We can head back to the news application. This time, we will use async and await instead of Future then.

Consider the following code where we have not used async and await. The main UI thread has finished, and after ten seconds we get the Future object!

```dart
//code 8.7
import 'dart:async';

// our all operations will use the main UI thread
//since dart and flutter are single threaded we need to use
  Future, Async amd Await APIs
//however, we have not used it here and got the future object
  instead of headlines

void main(){
  // the main UI thread starts after that the heavy operations
    will take place
  print("The main UI thread is starting on here.");
  print("Now it will take 10 seconds to display news headlines.");
  displayNews();
  print("The main UI thread ends.");
  // this program remains incomplete, we don't get the result
  // it is because the main UI thread is overlapping before
    10 seconds
  // therefore we need await and async APIs to block main UI
    thread for 10 seconds

}


// this is where our heavy operations are taking place
Future<String> checkingNewsApp(){
  // since we are returning a string value
  // by delaying the main UI thread for 10 seconds
  Future<String> delayingTenSeconds =  Future.
  delayed(Duration(seconds: 10), (){
    return "The latest headlines are displayed here after
    10 seconds.";
  });
```

```
    // after 10 seconds the news headlines will be displayed
    return delayingTenSeconds;
}

void displayNews(){
    // here we will primarily display the news headline
    Future<String> displayingNewsHeadlines = checkingNewsApp();
    print("Displaying news headlines here:
    $displayingNewsHeadlines");
}
```

Our objective was to display the news headlines. Instead, we have gotten the Future object.

```
//output of code 8.7
/home/ss/Downloads/flutter/bin/cache/dart-sdk/bin/dart
--enable-asserts --enable-vm-service:35735 /home/ss/
IdeaProjects/my_app/main.dart
Observatory listening on http://127.0.0.1:35735/q812ySn2w1s=/

The main UI thread is starting on here.
Now it will take 10 seconds to display news headlines.
Displaying news headlines here: Instance of 'Future<String>'
The main UI thread ends.

Process finished with exit code 0
```

Now, we are going to use the async and await features properly to get the news headlines we wanted on the screen.

```
//code 8.8
import 'dart:async';

// our all operations will use the main UI thread
//since dart and flutter are single threaded we need to use
    Future, Async amd Await APIs
```

```
void main(){
  // the main UI thread starts after that the heavy operations
    will take place
  print("The main UI thread is starting on here.");
  print("Now it will take 10 seconds to display news
  headlines.");
  displayNews();
  print("The main UI thread ends.");
  // this program remains incomplete, we don't get the result
  // it is because the main UI thread is overlapping before
    10 seconds
  // therefore we need await and async APIs to block main UI
    thread for 10 seconds

}

// this is where our heavy operations are taking place
Future<String> checkingNewsApp() {
  // since we are returning a string value
  // by delaying the main UI thread for 10 seconds
  Future<String> delayingTenSeconds =  Future.
  delayed(Duration(seconds: 10), (){
    return "The latest headlines are displayed here after
    10 seconds.";
  });
  // after 10 seconds the news headlines will be displayed
  return delayingTenSeconds;
}
```

```dart
void displayNews() async {
  // here we will primarily display the news headline
  String displayingNewsHeadlines = await checkingNewsApp();
  print("Displaying news headlines here:
  $displayingNewsHeadlines");
}
```

This time we find the output has changed, and after the main UI thread has finished, it has displayed the news headlines after ten seconds.

```
//output of code 8.8
/home/ss/Downloads/flutter/bin/cache/dart-sdk/bin/dart
--enable-asserts --enable-vm-service:33305 /home/ss/
IdeaProjects/my_app/main.dart
Observatory listening on http://127.0.0.1:33305/FpBVOpOM2qc=/

The main UI thread is starting on here.
Now it will take 10 seconds to display news headlines.
The main UI thread ends.
Displaying news headlines here: The latest headlines are
displayed here after 10 seconds.

Process finished with exit code 0
```

In the next chapter, you will learn about Dart libraries and packages; furthermore, you need to know that Dart libraries have a lot of functions that return Future objects. These functions are all asynchronous. They handle time-consuming heavy operations (such as I/O). To do that, these functions use the async and await keywords; this lets us write the asynchronous code that looks like synchronous code.

Therefore, to handle Future properly and get the complete Future output, we need to use async and await; in addition, we can use the Future API's old methods like then(), catchError(), and whenComplete().

More on the Future API

Let's look at some more examples to understand how the Future API works. Consider the following code, where we use the Future delayed() method, and then using the then() method, we pass a lambda function to print the value.

```
//code 8.9
import 'dart:async';

void main(){
  Future<int>.delayed(
      Duration(seconds: 6),
      () { return 200; },
  ).then((value) { print(value); });
  print('Waiting for a value for 6 seconds...');
}
```

We have delayed the whole process for six seconds; then we return the value.

```
//output of code 8.9
/home/ss/Downloads/flutter/bin/cache/dart-sdk/bin/dart
--enable-asserts --enable-vm-service:35393 /home/ss/
IdeaProjects/my_app/main.dart
Observatory listening on http://127.0.0.1:35393/ushFPI8yST4=/

Waiting for a value for 6 seconds...
200

Process finished with exit code 0
```

As you see, according to the output of the value we are about to print, we need to mention what type of Future object we are going to use. In the preceding code, this line is important:

```
Future<int>.delayed()//
```

We need to declare the type of Future object. Here it is an integer because we are returning an integer.

In the next code snippet, instead of returning a concrete value, we are going to throw an exception:

```
//code 8.10
import 'dart:async';

void main(){
  Future<int>.delayed(
      Duration(seconds: 6),
      () => throw 'We are throwing some error here.',
  ).then((value) {
    print(value);
  });
  print('Waiting for a value');
}
```

Quite naturally, we get an error in the output.

```
//output of code 8.10
/home/ss/Downloads/flutter/bin/cache/dart-sdk/bin/dart
--enable-asserts --enable-vm-service:43091 /home/ss/
IdeaProjects/my_app/main.dart
Observatory listening on http://127.0.0.1:43091/8Zr4UnbBJMA=/

Waiting for a value_
Unhandled exception:
We are throwing some error here.
```

```
#0      main.<anonymous closure> (file:///home/ss/IdeaProjects/
        my_app/main.dart:6:13)
#1      new Future.delayed.<anonymous closure> (dart:async/
        future.dart:316:39)
#2      Timer._createTimer.<anonymous closure> (dart:async-
        patch/timer_patch.dart:21:15)
#3      _Timer._runTimers (dart:isolate-patch/timer_impl.
        dart:382:19)
#4      _Timer._handleMessage (dart:isolate-patch/timer_impl.
        dart:416:5)
#5      _RawReceivePortImpl._handleMessage (dart:isolate-patch/
        isolate_patch.dart:172:12)

Process finished with exit code 255
```

Finally, we would like to see how some old Future methods, such as catchError() and whenComplete(), work, as shown in the following code:

```
//code 8.11
import 'dart:async';

void main(){
  Future<int>.delayed(
      Duration(seconds: 6),
      () { return 100; },
  ).then((value) {
    print(value);
  }).catchError(
      (err) {
        print('Caught $err');
      },
```

```
    test: (err) => err.runtimeType == String,
  ).whenComplete(() { print("Process completed."); });
  print('The main UI thread is waiting');
}
```

As you can see, the main UI thread waits for six seconds and then produces the output.

```
//output of code 8.11
/home/ss/Downloads/flutter/bin/cache/dart-sdk/bin/dart
--enable-asserts --enable-vm-service:36707 /home/ss/
IdeaProjects/my_app/main.dart
Observatory listening on http://127.0.0.1:36707/AIbh2kXqMxM=/

The main UI thread is waiting
100
Process completed.

Process finished with exit code 0
```

Basically, the Future delays a thread for a few seconds, as mentioned earlier; then it produces either completed data or an error!

CHAPTER 9

Dart Packages and Libraries

Dart programming relies heavily on libraries, which contain critical sets of built-in functionality. Several common libraries are provided for you; in addition, you can do modular programming with the help of libraries. We have already seen many examples, such as predefined collection methods, many mathematical functions, etc.

Several common libraries serve many purposes for building Dart applications. So far, you have seen many built-in functions that we have used in our many user-defined functions. For example, the `dart:core` libraries provide assistance for numbers, string-specific operations, and collections. With the help of `dart:math`, we can do many types of mathematical operations quite easily.

We can also build our own libraries. In fact, as you progress, you will feel the necessity to create your own libraries. In addition, you can get additional libraries by importing them from packages.

Through packages, we can share software such as libraries and tools.

Basically, we can get help from both types of libraries (built-in and custom). Figure 9-1 shows you how we can use libraries and packages in Dart.

© Sanjib Sinha 2020
S. Sinha, *Quick Start Guide to Dart Programming*,
https://doi.org/10.1007/978-1-4842-5562-9_9

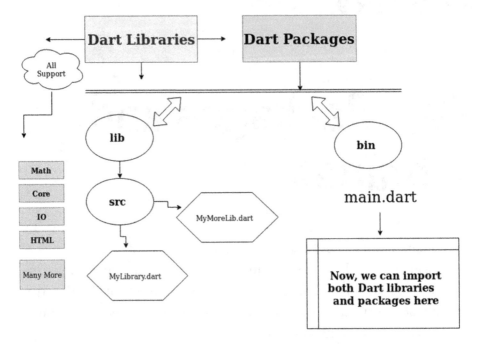

Figure 9-1. Usages of Dart libraries and packages

You should also know why we need libraries. To create a modular and shareable code base, the codebase needs to be well organized. In fact, this is an essential part of object-oriented programming. Libraries not only provide support for modular, object-oriented programming, but they also give you a kind of privacy in your own code.

Identifiers, starting with the underscore (_), are visible only in your libraries. A prepending underscore means this function is private to the library. That means you cannot use that function in other libraries. This is a typical Dart feature. Dart handles visibility with this prepending underscore.

Libraries also help you avoid name conflicts, which is an essential part of coding. Let's look at an example to clarify these points.

Importing Packages

First, let's create a RelationalOperators.dart file inside the lib folder.

```
//code 9.1
//lib/ RelationalOperators.dart
class TrueOrFalse{
  int firstNum = 40;
  int secondNum = 40;
  int thirdNum = 74;
  int fourthNum = 56;
  void BetweenTrueOrFalse(){
    if (firstNum == secondNum || thirdNum == fourthNum){
      print("If choice between 'true' or 'false', in this case
      the 'TRUE' gets the precedence. $firstNum is equal to
      $secondNum");
    } else print("Nothing happens.");
  }
  void BetweenTrueAndFalse(){
    if (firstNum == secondNum && thirdNum == fourthNum){
      print("It will go to else clause");
    } else print("If choice between 'true' and 'false', in
    this case the 'FALSE' gets the precedence. $thirdNum is
    not equal to $fourthNum");
  }
}
```

Next, create a file called PowProject.dart inside the lib folder.

```
//code 9.2
//lib/PowProject.dart
class PowProject{
  void MultiplyByAGivenNumber(int fixedNumber, int givenNumber){
```

203

```
    int result = fixedNumber * givenNumber;
    print(result);
  }
  void pow(int x, int y){
    int addition = x + y;
    print(addition);
  }
}
```

Now take a look at the main() function body, shown here:

```
//code 9.3
import 'dart:math' as math;
import 'package:IdeaProjects/PowProject.dart';
import 'package:IdeaProjects/RelationalOperators.dart' as
relation;

main(List<String> arguments){
  print("Printing 2 to the power 5 using Dart's built-in
  'dart:math' library.");
  var int = math.pow(2, 5);
  print(int);
  print("Now we are going to use another 'pow()' function from
  our own library.");
  var anotherPowObject = PowProject();
  anotherPowObject.MultiplyByAGivenNumber(4, 3);
  anotherPowObject.pow(2, 12);
  print("Now we are going to use another library to test the
  relational operators.");
  var trueOrFalse = relation.TrueOrFalse();
  trueOrFalse.BetweenTrueOrFalse();
  trueOrFalse.BetweenTrueAndFalse();
}
```

In the lib (or libraries) folder, we have created two classes. One of them has a function called pow(). But the built-in dart:math library has a function with the same name: pow(). We cannot use both of these same-name functions in the same code. It would give us errors. So, to avoid the name conflict, we have to create our own library and define it inside the class. Quite naturally, for the book's sake, our created pow() function is doing something different than calculating the power of a number.

Look at the top of the main() function, shown here:

```
import 'dart:math' as math;
import 'package:IdeaProjects/PowProject.dart';
import 'package:IdeaProjects/RelationalOperators.dart' as
Relation;
```

We have used the keyword import to specify how our libraries, besides the core libraries, can be used. Our project directory is IdeaProjects, and PowProject.dart is inside the lib directory. The path after the project directory comes from inside the lib directory. After import, we need to pass an argument, which is nothing but a uniform resource identifier (URI) specifying the libraries. For any built-in libraries, the URI has the special dart:... scheme. For other libraries, you can use the file system path or the package:... scheme.

When we directly use the libraries, we use a normal line like this:

```
import 'package:IdeaProjects/PowProject.dart';
```

In that case, we can directly create the class object that belongs to that particular library, as follows:

```
var anotherPowObject = PowProject();
```

However, there is another good method; we can call any library by using a name, like this:

```
import 'package:IdeaProjects/RelationalOperators.dart' as
relation;
```

The advantage to this is that now we can create any class object belonging to that library using the new name, as follows:

```dart
var trueOrFalse = relation.TrueOrFalse();
```

These prefixes are used to avoid name conflicts and to simplify long package names. You can write same-name classes in libraries, and you can use them by giving them a name.

Using Built-in Dart Libraries

A few good built-in libraries come with Dart; you do not need to write them again. Here are some of them:

- `dart:core`: This gives us many core functionalities. It is automatically imported into every Dart program.

- `dart:math`: You have seen how we have used the core mathematical library in our program. We can do many types of mathematical operations using this library, such as generate random numbers.

- `dart:convert`: Converting between different data representations is made easy through this library; this conversion includes JSON and UTF-8.

Writing a Server Using Dart

By using the default Dart libraries, we can easily build a local server, request an HTML page, and get the response. In the first half of this section, we will see how to include an HTML file in our program and get a response in the client browser. For the server-client relationship, which is the foundation of any kind of web application, our Dart program will play the role of the server, and the client will be the browser that we will use.

Showing Some Simple Text

Let's write some simple Dart back-end server code that will output a string response.

```
//code 9.4
import 'dart:io';
import 'dart:async';

Future main() async {
  var myServer = await HttpServer.bind(
    '127.0.0.1',
    8080,
  );
  print("The server is alive on the above mentioned port and
  it's listening "
      "on ${myServer.port}/");

  myServer.listen((HttpRequest myRequest){
    myRequest.response
      ..write("Bonjour mademoiselle, comment appelez vous?")
      ..close();
  });
}
```

The main() function starts with Future and async, and later we use await. We discussed these concepts in the previous chapter. Then, we use the HttpServer.bind() method to create an HttpServer object. In the bind() method, we pass two parameters: the host (127.0.0.1) and the port (8080). Here, we use a simple print statement to give some simple output to show we are listening to the previously mentioned port.

Now, according to the server-client relationship structure, our new server object should listen for a new HttpRequest object (here myRequest). And, after receiving a request, the server object should respond. The response object calls a write() method that gives us some simple output like this:

```
"Bonjour mademoiselle, comment appelez vous?"
```

This is a French sentence that means, "Good day, Miss, what are you called?"

Now, after running this program, we should type http://127.0.0.1:8080 in any browser. It will give this output. We can run this program using two methods. You can just run it on Android Studio or IntelliJ Community, and in the console you will get the message that the server is listening. After that, we can open the browser to see the output. In another method, we can use our terminal. Open the project folder's bin directory and type the following:

```
//code 9.5
dart main.dart
```

This will also run the program (Figure 9-2).

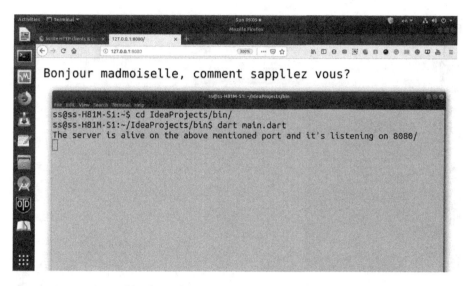

Figure 9-2. *Dart back-end server-client program*

Here is a caveat. You should not run two programs listening to the same port in parallel to each other. If the port is already in use, the connection will automatically be refused. You can use any port number from 1024 and higher.

If you run the same program on Android Studio, you will get the "server listening" message in the console (Figure 9-3).

Figure 9-3. *Running the same program through Android Studio*

To stop the program in the terminal, you can press Control+C, and in any IDE console, you click the red button on the left side. You will see it in the top-right corner also.

Once the program is stopped, it gives us output like this:

```
//code 9.6
```

```
/home/ss/flutter/bin/cache/dart-sdk/bin/dart --enable-vm-
service:40505 /home/ss/IdeaProjects/bin/main.dart
Observatory listening on http://127.0.0.1:40505/
```

```
The server is alive on the above mentioned port and it's
listening on 8080/
```

```
Process finished with exit code 137 (interrupted by signal 9:
SIGKILL)
```

Up to now, we were able to give a simple response as output through our back-end server-client program. Furthermore, we can make our back-end server display an HTML page.

Showing an HTML Page

The process is not very complicated. All we need is an HTML file first. Let's create a simple HTML5 file called index.html in our root directory.

```
//code 9.7

<!doctype html>

<html lang="en">
<head>
    <meta charset="utf-8">

    <title>A Dart WEB Example on Local Server</title>
    <meta name="description" content="The HTML5 Herald">
    <meta name="author" content="SitePoint">

</head>

<body>
<h1>A Dart WEB Example on Local Server</h1>
<a href="https://sanjibsinha.fun" about="It's my unofficial
site" onclick="Click Me!">
    Here is my unofficial site!
</a>
</body>
</html>
```

Let's see the file in Android Studio first (Figure 9-4).

Figure 9-4. *The index.html file in the Android Studio root directory*

Now we can call this `index.html` file to get its contents in the browser. As you saw earlier, the Dart libraries have all the tools to build any kind of web application. Here we need to use our response object to return the contents of our HTML file, setting its `Content-Type` header to HTML:

```
//code 9.8
import 'dart:io';
import 'dart:async';

final File myFile = File("index.html");

Future main() async {
  var myServer = await HttpServer.bind(
    '127.0.0.1',
    8080,
  );
```

```
print("The server is alive on the above mentioned port and
it's listening "
    "on ${myServer.port}/");

// we are going to use the await from dart async library
await for (HttpRequest myRequest in myServer) {

  if(await myFile.exists()){
    print("We're going to serve ${myFile.path}");
    myRequest.response.headers.contentType = ContentType.html;

    await myFile.openRead().pipe(myRequest.response);

  }

 }

}
```

After reading the file, we have used the pipe() method to put the contents of the file into the response, which will give us the response (Figure 9-5).

Figure 9-5. *The response of an HTML file using the Dart back-end server technique*

Now, we can even check the source to see that the HTML file was used for this purpose (Figure 9-6).

Figure 9-6. *The view source of the HTML file displayed in the browser*

You have seen how we can use Dart libraries for many types of complicated application development. We can also easily build our own packages using these libraries to reuse this code in other applications.

What's Next

There's no doubt that Dart will be even more popular in the future. Not only is it popular in the iOS and Android worlds, but it is being used in web applications. This book served as a short introduction to Dart. Good luck in the future.

Index

A, B

Abstract classes
  definition, 117
  key points, 118
  object-oriented programming
    languages, 119–121
  source code, 118
Anonymous function
  closure, 146–149
  definition, 141
  higher-order functions, 145
  lambdas
    key features of, 145
    longhand version, 142, 143
    parameters, 143
    shorthand code, 144
    type of, 142
    variable, 142
  types of, 149–152
Asynchronous programming, 182

C

Callable classes, 179
  call() method, 179, 180
  Person() method, 181
  source code, 180, 181
Closure, 146–149

Collections
  data structures (*see* Data
    structures and collections)
  lists (ordered group), 155
    default methods, 159, 160
    map() function, 161, 162
    source code, 156, 157
    types of, 155
  maps, 166–171
  queue, 176–177
  set (unordered collections),
    162–166
  unique items, 162
  validations (lists and maps),
    171–175
Constructors, 81–84
  default and a named
    constructor, 100–102

D

Dart language, 1
  arrays, 27, 28
  assignment operators, 39, 40
  built-in types, 17–19
  code editors, 2
  features, 2, 4
  get, set, go, 29–33

© Sanjib Sinha 2020
S. Sinha, *Quick Start Guide to Dart Programming*,
https://doi.org/10.1007/978-1-4842-5562-9

Printed in the United States
By Bookmasters